1987

Evaluating Faculty
for Promotion
and Tenure

Richard I. Miller

Evaluating Faculty for Promotion and Tenure

 Jossey-Bass Publishers

San Francisco • London • 1987

EVALUATING FACULTY FOR PROMOTION AND TENURE
by Richard I. Miller

Copyright © 1987 by: Jossey-Bass Inc., Publishers
433 California Street
San Francisco, California 94104
&
Jossey-Bass Limited
28 Banner Street
London EC1Y 8QE

Library of Congress Cataloging-in-Publication Data

Miller, Richard I.
    Evaluating faculty for promotion and tenure.

    (The Jossey-Bass higher education series)
    Bibliography: p.
    Includes index.
    1. College teachers—United States—Rating of.
2. College teachers—United States—Promotions.
3. College teachers—Tenure—United States.
I. Title. II. Series.
LB2333.M468   1987   371.1'44'071173   87-45499
ISBN 1-55542-069-9 (alk. paper)

Manufactured in the United States of America

The paper in this book meets the guidelines for
permanence and durability of the Committee on
Production Guidelines for Book Longevity of the
Council on Library Resources.

JACKET DESIGN BY WILLI BAUM

FIRST EDITION

Code 8740

The Jossey-Bass
Higher Education Series

Contents

Preface

The purpose of this book is to provide assistance to people who are involved in the most important academic personnel decisions that are made by colleges and universities—those involving promotion and tenure. Promotion and tenure decisions are discussed here in the context of faculty evaluation because I believe that the quality of the promotion and tenure system depends on excellent faculty evaluation. In fact, the components of the faculty evaluation system constitute the foundation on which credible and effective promotion and tenure systems are built. The book will also assist the reader in understanding the nature and processes involved in yearly evaluations of faculty performance for purposes other than promotion and tenure, including posttenure evaluations.

Administrators and members of faculty promotion and tenure committees are the primary audiences for whom this book is intended. They will find it a useful guide in reviewing their present systems and planning for revisions. The material will also be useful as a general reference for students of higher education in professional courses that include academic personnel matters. Last, but far from least, college teachers who are personally involved in the promotion and tenure processes will find this book helpful in that their personal success in earning academic advancement is related directly to their knowledge and understanding of these processes.

This book is designed for readers to "adapt, not adopt" its contents to their situations. With more than 3,000 postsecondary institutions in the United States, a case can be made for developing at least four different books on specific systems. The generic approach that this book offers, however, can be applied by readers in many different settings who adapt its message to their specific needs.

Overview of the Contents

Chapter One sets the tone for the book by describing general characteristics of today's promotion and tenure systems. This overview analyzes a number of weaknesses in the procedures that many postsecondary institutions use to make crucial staffing decisions. The bulk of the chapter focuses on characteristics of effective promotion and tenure systems. Gleaned from experience and from available research evidence, this synthesis brought home to me the dearth of research data that are available on this topic.

Chapter Two moves from a view from the tower to the ground floor—to the definitions of evaluation and the purposes of faculty evaluation. The section on changes in faculty evaluation practices over the past decade provides a context for better understanding the present and the future. Readers who are fairly new to the area of faculty evaluation can develop a richer and fuller understanding through studying past developments as well as some classic studies that continue to provide insights. A final section suggests "a conceptual framework for developing and/or evaluating faculty evaluation systems" that can provide yardsticks for judging components and criteria that either are in place or are being planned at an institution.

How students can evaluate their classroom teachers effectively is the topic of Chapter Three. While this chapter concentrates on only one of nine criteria that can be used for evaluating classroom teaching, it is generally acknowledged as the most important one.

Scholarship and service, treated in Chapter Four, complete the trilogy of criteria that form the bases for evaluating faculty performance in most colleges and universities. Scholarship includes research, publications, and presentations; and service includes both professional and public service.

Chapter Five discusses advising, classroom visitation, faculty service and relations, professional growth, self-evaluation, and teaching materials and procedures as further criteria for faculty evaluation. It is very unlikely that any department or college would use all six components on a regular basis. The key is selecting criteria appropriate to each situation.

A number of fundamental issues surrounding promotion and tenure are the focus of Chapter Six. The purposes of promotion and tenure, promotion criteria, tenure criteria, advantages and disadvantages of tenure, and some alternatives to tenure are among the topics covered. A discussion of detenuring is also included. This chapter gives the reader a foundation for understanding the next one.

Chapter Seven, on examining promotion and tenure decision making, provides several approaches for analyzing a promotion and tenure system. These include the use of peer review processes, weightings of various criteria and inputs, individualizing faculty workloads, and the procedural flow for promotion and tenure decision making.

Chapter Eight considers various legal questions and court rulings that are pertinent to faculty evaluation and to promotion and tenure decisions.

The roles of administrators in promotion and tenure decision making are explored in Chapter Nine. It examines the distinct roles of the chief executive officer, the chief academic officer, college deans, and departmental chairs. An annual academic performance review is discussed also.

In Chapter Ten, ten future directions are suggested for promotion and tenure developments. The planning process as it relates to promotion and tenure is also considered.

Appendix A contains forms for evaluating each of the nine components that are mentioned in Chapters Three, Four, and Five. These forms are updated and revised versions of those that were published in my earlier book, *Evaluating Faculty Performance* (1972). They have been in widespread use, so I have had the benefit of feedback from users as well as current research findings in revising them.

Appendix B, which provides detailed information about student rating instruments, updates a useful appendix that appeared in John Centra's *Determining Faculty Effectiveness* (1979).

An annotated bibliography that covers academic promotion and tenure and industrial performance appraisal is included. The bibliography consists of works selected from an extensive search of the literature on topics related to this book's subject. I include literature on industrial performance appraisal because I believe that the business sector has a number of things to offer education.

Acknowledgments

I owe much to many people who in one way or another have been integral parts of this complicated and challenging endeavor. My graduate students have not only contributed pieces of content but have been, and continue to be, sources of challenge and satisfaction. In particular, I would like to acknowledge Thor Gunnarsson, Larry Scheiderer, and John Gerdy, who have served as graduate associates. The annotated bibliography benefits from graduate student works by Jane Dixon McDowell, Frederick Law, Mei Hau Zhai, and Erwin Zitlow.

I am appreciative of the responses from several colleges and universities to three announcements in *The Chronicle of Higher Education* soliciting operational models for faculty evaluation and promotion and tenure systems. Some excellent materials were sent to me, which have been helpful in bettering my understanding of field programs in these areas. Owing to space limitations, I have made only minimal use of those materials in these pages.

The chapter on legal considerations presented some special challenges in view of its complexity. I am indebted to Arthur Vorhies for the initial draft, to David Figuli, J.D., for his helpful comments, and to John Burns, J.D., for subsequent editing and suggestions.

Lawrence Aleamoni provided helpful suggestions on common questions about student ratings, discussed in Chapter Four.

Typing by Hope Socci was fast, accurate, thoughtful, and appreciated.

Financial assistance by the College of Education was most appreciated.

This is the first book that I have written without having our three daughters at home, which always presented a special challenge as well as a source of satisfaction. My wife, Peggy, as she has been through the agonies involved in other books, remains a great source of support and understanding.

Many individuals have been most helpful in the long and lonely vigil that is the plight of any book author. Their assistance is sincerely appreciated, but of course I take full responsibility for what is said—somewhat in the spirit of Sir Thomas More, who said to his executioner, "Help me up. On the way down I will shift for myself."

Athens, Ohio   Richard I. Miller
August 1987

To Peggy

The Author

Richard I. Miller teaches and advises graduate students in the Higher Education Program at Ohio University. He has also taught or served as graduate adviser at the University of Illinois at Urbana, the University of Kentucky, Cornell University, as a visiting scholar, and Southwest Texas State University.

Miller has served in a number of senior academic administrative roles, including academic vice-presidencies at Southwest Texas State University, the State University of New York at Brockport, and Baldwin-Wallace College. His administrative duties have also included serving as a senior academic program officer with the Illinois Board of Higher Education; executive secretary for a national committee appointed by President Johnson on experimentation and innovation in the public schools; and director of a program on educational change at the University of Kentucky.

He is editor of *Institutional Assessment for Self-Improvement* (1981) and author of *The Assessment of College Performance* (1979), *Developing Programs for Faculty Evaluation* (1974), and *Evaluating Faculty Performance* (1972), along with seven other books, a dozen chapters in books, and several dozen articles.

Miller has spoken, conducted workshops, and consulted on program, administration, faculty, and institutional evaluation as well as academic organization, management, and planning at well over 100 campuses in every section of the United States as well as in other countries. He has participated in national associations and studies, has held a number of national offices, and has received several awards and honors. He is also a member of the Cosmos Club, Washington, D.C.

Evaluating Faculty
for Promotion
and Tenure

One

The Need to Strengthen
Promotion and Tenure Systems

Every postsecondary institution has some way of making academic promotion and tenure decisions. At an earlier time the
matter was often a judgment made by the chief academic officer or the chief executive officer or both and was usually based
on a variety of impressions and contacts. No doubt administrators a hundred years ago suffered the same tensions and anguish
that afflict those who make such decisions today, but the scope
and scale of decision making have changed dramatically in view
of our vastly larger and more complex academic enterprises.

Systems for making academic promotion and tenure decisions generally share a number of characteristics. (In the context of this book, the word *systems* refers to an aggregation of
parts that has some unifying and controlling elements.) One
characteristic is the somewhat haphazard manner in which these
systems have evolved. In most systems, changes are not so much
planned efforts as series of procedural adjustments. Institutions
do not often undertake comprehensive studies of their academic
promotion and tenure systems, probably because their current
systems seem to be functioning acceptably, because the complexity and sensitivity of these systems are formidable, and because of the fear that changes might well result in a system that
is less effective than the one currently in place.

A second characteristic is that such systems tend to be
sources of dissatisfaction and objects of suspicion among faculty members. A number of studies (discussed later in this chapter) indicate that faculty members are frequently dissatisfied
with their current promotion, tenure, and merit policies and

1

procedures. Such findings may lead one to question the credibility of one's own system.

The third characteristic, which somewhat counterbalances the second, is that the importance and sensitivity of tenure and promotion decisions may simply render it unrealistic to expect a high degree of satisfaction with any system for handling them. Further, the degree of dissatisfaction may vary not only with the quality of a particular system but probably also with the type of institution. In two-year colleges, where evaluative criteria usually are spelled out quite specifically, satisfaction seems to be relatively high. In comprehensive state universities, where ambivalence about role and mission is often a problem, satisfaction levels seem to be significantly lower. Fluctuations also relate to the economic health of the institution; tenure and promotion denials that result from financial insecurity inevitably reflect negatively on whatever system is in place.

Research universities seem to have the least trouble with their promotion and tenure systems, probably because their research/publications mission is reasonably clear-cut and relatively stable. It is not uncommon for these institutions to provide special incentives for neophyte faculty members. For example, some departments provide lighter teaching and committee loads during the first one or two years of employment to allow new instructors' research interests to take root. And as one experienced dean said, "If we do not elect to keep them, they can never say that they did not have time to do research."

A fourth characteristic is legal vulnerability, which functions negatively as a criterion for success. If a department has not been "taken to court," it must have a good system.

Weaknesses in Making Academic Promotion and Tenure Decisions

A number of weaknesses in academic promotion and tenure systems and in their use can be identified from the literature as well as from the experience of administrators. One simple yet important weakness is inadequately developed faculty applications for promotion. What would you do, as provost, with a disorganized and incomplete faculty file coming from an instructor who you knew was a solid but not an outstanding faculty member? This question may suggest real-life dramas that have faced any number of chief academic officers, yet it describes a situation that can be avoided quite simply. For example, a faculty mentor, a respected senior professor, could be called on to strengthen the file. Another remedy might be to prepare clearly written and detailed procedural suggestions for developing the files. A casual approach toward promotion and tenure policies and procedures at the departmental level may contribute to weak files. Generally, there is much to be said in favor of informal and relaxed departmental operations, but not where promotion and tenure policies are concerned.

Outdated personnel policies and procedures are another weakness found in some institutions. If messages and directions from the president or chief academic office about new academic programs are not translated into policies at the department level, new institutional directions and priorities may not be reflected in the applicants' files nor in departmental procedures.

Individual members of departmental promotion and tenure committees may give inadequate attention to the process of making decisions about applicants' files. Committee members may think, "We all know Jane, and there is no doubt about her getting tenure." Such an approach would not be uncommon in a department where colleagues daily brush shoulders. Yet can one be sure that other committee members share one's opinion of Jane until that final committee vote is taken on her candidacy? To help ensure that any file is given full and objective consideration before it is reviewed, the committee needs to have one meeting that focuses on such matters as definitions and departmental expectations. For example, how do committee members perceive the terms *outstanding, superior, excellent, very good,* and *average?* The committee also may want to review matters such as the relative weight of the various categories, the subsequent steps after the committee's decision, and when the candidate should be informed of the committee's decisions.

The decision-making processes may be complicated if all

department members sit on the promotion and tenure committee, as may be the case in small departments. However, if promotion and tenure policies, procedures, and practices are spelled
out in detail, unproductive or disruptive decision-making sessions may be minimized. Practice sessions may be useful in
these circumstances.

Characteristics of Effective Promotion
and Tenure Systems

A number of characteristics of effective promotion and
tenure systems can be identified, not so much from the sparse
research evidence on this important matter as from academic
administrators' experiences.

1. *The academic promotion and tenure policies and procedures reflect the history and nature of the institution.* Some
colleges and universities have long traditions that affect promotion and tenure decisions, sometimes in ways not known even
to senior professors who often believe, and not without reason,
that they are the conscience and heart of the institution. One
example is a liberal arts college, with a 140-year history, that
survived the Great Depression by using "mirrors and baling
wire," as one faculty member put it. In later years, senior professors would relate with some pride how as junior faculty
members they also worked as carpenters, plumbers, and land-
scape workers in order that both they and the college might survive. The camaraderie engendered by this experience was evident later, and it significantly affected promotion and tenure
decisions in that loyalty and dedication to the institution were
regarded as major, albeit unwritten, criteria in promotion and
tenure.

A second example is a research-oriented university whose
enrollment dropped from 18,000 students in 1968 to 12,000 in
1976. Today a healthy and dynamic university of 15,000, the
"hard times of the early seventies" formed bonds of loyalty
among senior professors that resulted in conservatism, reliance
on personal compatibility, and emphasis on research and scholarship in promotion and tenure decisions, perhaps as a reaction

to the losses in research productivity as well as in institutional prestige in the seventies.

Institutional traditions may change rapidly as a result of external influences, such as a change in leadership; usually change is slow, as Hefferlin (1969, p. 24) noted: "During normal times . . . the major process of academic change is that of accretion and attrition: the slow addition and subtraction of functions to existing structures." In any case, one ignores or treats lightly institutional history and traditions at the risk of making fundamental errors in the sensitive and critical process of making and modifying academic promotion and tenure policies and procedures.

Developing promotion and tenure criteria appropriate to the institution is much easier said than done, yet conscious efforts to do so reduce the chances of an awkward mismatch. The research dimension of scholarship, for example, means something fundamentally different to community colleges and smaller liberal arts colleges and to research-oriented universities. When comprehensive state universities with Ph.D. programs make research as important for academic advancement as it is at land-grant institutions—perhaps from a desire to emulate the flagship institutions—they may pay less attention to regional service needs and to teaching. Furthermore, younger faculty members at comprehensive state universities know that they must do research and publish in order to be considered for appointments at larger research universities in the future.

2. *The system is compatible with current institutional goals and objectives.* Goals are the larger purposes and long-range plans of the institution as a whole. They are barely measurable but nonetheless provide important direction. Objectives are short-range targets, usually to be achieved in one to five years. As a rule of thumb, many institutions plan "hard" for five years and "soft" for ten years.

In most institutions, it is important for senior institutional management to have overall control of the nature and direction of promotion and tenure decisions. For example, professors in a field of study that is growing and in the mainstream of the institution's development might be more likely to receive promotion and tenure than professors in a field that is shrink-ing. This marketplace concept continues to receive strong criti-cism, particularly from professors and administrators in the hu-manities and the fine arts. A professor of English has every reason to believe that his chosen life's work is at least as im-portant as computer science; indeed, some colleges and universi-ties have developed academic reward systems based on this equity. On the other hand, in a technologically oriented nation striving to be internationally competitive, chief executive and chief academic officers on large land-grant or research-oriented campuses (sometimes under pressure from the governing board) must vie with other institutions for talented professionals in technological fields. This dilemma is likely to become more pro-nounced in the nineties when professorial shortages are ex-pected to exacerbate the competition. Predicted shortages are discussed further in Chapter Ten.

Promotion and tenure policies and procedures at the insti-tutional, college, and departmental levels also should be consis-tent. Some new presidents have found that 80 percent of the in-stitution's faculty members were tenured; in some departments, the figure was 100 percent. This creates difficulties for chief executive officers who are personally motivated or instructed by governing boards to increase academic program flexibility or to reduce costs by reducing tenure percentages. For further dis-cussion, see Chapter Nine.

3. *The system balances reasonably well the institution's academic needs and the individual's professional interests.* This challenge is an eternal one, and the balance changes from time to time with changing external conditions and institutional priori-ties. Braskamp, Brandenburg, and Ory (1984, p. 20) pose the question thus: "How can evaluation be designed so that the in-stitution can fulfill its accountability to its constituencies and still allow faculty sufficient autonomy and freedom to experi-ment and to 'profess'?"

This question was discussed by Getzels and Guba (1954); Scriven (1978, p. 1) wrote about the "value" and "merit" di-mensions of evaluation. Lincoln (1983, p. 222) said that the worth of the individual to the institution is primarily an institutional-level decision, whereas the merit of the individual is primarily a professional judgment based on his or her academic credentials and performance and should therefore be determined primarily by professional colleagues. Lincoln contends that a tilt toward merit should be evident in promotion decisions; worth should carry more weight in tenure decisions. In practice, something of this differentiation does take place, although the worth and the merit dimensions are not usually separated as clearly as in Lincoln's description.

4. *The system encompasses both institutional and departmental expectations.* The institutional perspective encompasses administrative, legal, and humane considerations. Administrative considerations include the official faculty handbook's statements about promotion and tenure as well as statements issued by the chief academic officer. The relevant parts of these institutional positions should be compatible with departmental criteria, and the institution-wide statements should be appended to departmental statements. Sometimes even little differences among the various statements can be significant. For example, a department in a research-oriented university asked applicants for promotion or tenure to list all professional activities for only the previous five years, while the procedures issued by the chief academic office asked tenure applicants to provide curricula vitae that listed all professional activities in their entire careers. Unless the department incorporated the instructions from the chief academic office, an applicant's case might have been weakened by the omission of a complete curriculum vitae.

Another problem can arise when the various levels of an institution fail to coordinate their respective expectations. Most departments and colleges want to see documentation, such as articles, books, raw teaching evaluations, and unpublished documents of significance. The institution's academic office, however, often prefers to see only a covering summary notebook. A box or two of documentation in the institution's academic office, when written instructions do not require or positively discourage it, will not be well received and may in fact slightly injure an applicant's chances. Too often institutions have little or no written communication of expectations between the various levels.

5. *The promotion and tenure policies and procedures are clearly articulated in written documents.* In their survey of sixty chairpersons of health education departments, Newell and Price (1983, p. 12) found that 48 percent of the respondents had a written policy concerning promotion, tenure, and merit; 37 percent had a written policy concerning only promotion and tenure; and 13 percent had no written policy concerning any of the three areas. The extensive and important College and University Personnel Association (CUPA) study (1980b, p. 20) reported that 16 percent of colleges and universities surveyed expressed their tenure policy both in writing and in established procedures; 70 percent communicated tenure policy only in written form; and 23 percent conveyed tenure policy only in established practices. One concludes from these data that most colleges and universities have written policy statements but far fewer also have established procedures.

The American Association of University Professors (AAUP) has had a consistent policy on fair procedures in dismissal cases since its first statement in 1915. As stated by its Committee on Academic Freedom and Academic Tenure (1915, pp. 41–42), the policy includes the right of "every university or college teacher . . . before dismissal or demotion, to have the charges against him stated in writing in specific terms and to have a fair trial on those charges before a special or permanent committee chosen by the faculty senate or council, or by the faculty at large." The AAUP issued similar statements in 1925, 1940, 1958, 1970, and 1982. Considering these, and the general oral support in academe for written policies and procedures for judging promotion and tenure, one wonders why detailed procedural statements are not available in a much higher percentage of institutions of higher education.

One reason may be the poor academic personnel management policies and procedures evident in many institutions. Only two short books by Bouchard and by Woodburne, a longer one by Fortunato and Waddell, and a booklet edited by Fuller have been published on academic personnel management in higher education; in contrast, a number of detailed books on business and industrial personnel management are available. A second reason may be the quiet preference of some governing boards and senior administrators for very general policies and procedures for academic promotion and tenure. Such vague policies give them a greater degree of freedom in making these decisions —an observation also made by Stark and Miller (1976).

6. *The policies and procedures are applied consistently and fairly.* Little research has focused on the satisfactions and dissatisfactions of faculties, administrators, and governing boards with the processes of administering and evaluating promotion and tenure cases. The survey of sixty health education chairpersons by Newell and Price (1983) found 65 percent were "dissatisfied" or "very dissatisfied" with their criteria for promotion; 27 percent were "very satisfied" or "satisfied"; and 22 percent were neutral. Responses about tenure were less negative; 36 percent were "dissatisfied" or "very dissatisfied"; 41 percent were "very satisfied" or "satisfied"; and 22 percent were neutral (pp. 13-14). Jolson's study (1974, p. 153) of 350 faculty members listed in the directory of the American Assembly of Collegiate Schools of Business found that "clearly many AACSB faculty members are at odds with perceived administrative criteria for promotion and tenure." If faculty members see "an aura of mystery" about the promotion and tenure processes, as Saaty and Ramanujam (1983, p. 312) suggest, then is it not logical that that they may conclude that these policies and procedures are not applied consistently or fairly? The significant number of court cases on these matters should also be weighed.

Some dimensions of fairness are suggested by Lincoln (1983, p. 223): "Fairness involves equitable treatment. Criteria must be open. Processes must be consistent, clearly stated, and applied equally to all faculty members." In addition, one should ask whether the standards for promotion and tenure in a department are appropriate to the quality and expectations of the department as well as those of the institution. Harvard University and other prestigious universities and colleges go for the "stars"; their subsequent academic personnel appraisals reflect this. It is sometimes difficult for institutions to blend realism with optimism when meshing their appraisal criteria with market realities and institutional aspirations.

7. *The overall system for making promotion and tenure*

recommendations is manageable. Manageability describes the amount of time and effort that the system requires to accomplish its tasks. In written policies and procedures, it is preferable to err on the side of clarity and completeness, yet this virtue can become a fault if the policies and procedures become so complex and detailed that they are difficult to manage. An excessive number of reviews can make committee decisions more difficult but not necessarily more equitable. One might ask, do the review procedures contain redundant layers of reviews? This question may not have an easy answer; sometimes a new president or academic vice-president develops an extra review stage to improve quality control of promotion and tenure processes. One new president at a land-grant university found that the deans almost automatically passed on nominations for promotion and tenure to the academic vice-president. To send a message to the deans (who were all rotated out of their positions within three years), he established four area review committees, in the social sciences, the sciences, liberal arts, and the humanities. These committees were designed to help recognize deserving faculty members who may have been unfairly evaluated by one dean or another and to develop stiffer reviews. This extra layer served its purpose. The following president kept the area committee system in place until he realized that its purpose had been served, then he eliminated it. In academe there is a tendency for academic committees, once established, to endure forever—whether or not they continue to be valuable.

Committees of the whole, where an entire department or unit sits in judgment of a colleague, can also detract from manageability. These committees seem like the quintessence of participatory government, yet in some cases the decisions have been made quietly and privately beforehand and the meetings are, in essence, a facade. Committees of the whole can also get out of hand without adroit leadership by the chairperson; public airings of personal conflicts can leave deep scars that may impede future collegial relationships.

Institutions may want to review the deadlines for completing various phases of the promotion and tenure process. Is sufficient time available to complete the process adequately? Excessive time can encourage indifference and a last-minute scramble to meet half-forgotten deadlines. Scrupulous adherence to deadlines may seem trivial, yet overlooking such details has caused some major management and, in some cases, legal problems.

The management process for making academic personnel decisions should be designed to include essential processes and rights, not to meet every eventuality. All eventualities probably cannot be covered, although some professorially designed systems have tried. Just as public laws are designed to cover the majority of typical cases, so effective academic promotion policies and procedures focus on the most important matters.

8. *An academic grievance procedure allows recourse.* A few grievance procedures have been carefully crafted to provide the form rather than the substance of recourse. The large majority of grievance procedures, however, have sought to provide an authentic avenue for redress. To take an industrial example, IBM has developed a "bypass" policy whereby an employee who believes that he or she has been unfairly evaluated by an immediate superior can bypass that person and appeal to an official on the next level. One IBM official tells of an incident that cemented his lifelong loyalty to the company. When his immediate superior had given him a negative evaluation, he used the bypass policy to appeal to the next highest level. The immediate superior subsequently bypassed *his* superior, taking the case to yet a higher organizational level. In the end, the official was vindicated.

In general, useful and equitable academic grievance procedures are based on common sense and sound legal opinion, meshed with the institution's nature and experiences.

9. *The academic personnel decision-making system and its components are legally defensible.* Writing in 1971 (p. 44) on the role of the academic vice-president in the future, I felt that "most academic deans will need sooner or later, and probably sooner, to enter the world of lawyers, legalism, and court cases." The future was here several years ago. The use of legal assistance has doubled since 1972, according to a 1984 survey (pp. 3-4)

conducted by the National Association of College and University Attorneys. In terms of the workload of house counsels, the area of "faculty non-reappointment layoffs and dismissals" was found to have had the greatest increase among the twenty listed areas of activity. See Chapter Eight for further discussion of legal considerations.

10. *The overall promotion and tenure system has reasonable credibility.* How does one judge reasonable credibility? Senior academic administrators must listen carefully to complaints. Those who lodge the strongest complaints do not necessarily have the strongest cases, and they may take an inordinate amount of time and patience, but the listening process is nonetheless an important aspect of credibility.

Fairness is an integral part of credibility. How does one define fairness? Certainly it is in the mind of the beholder, but it is more. While not explicitly definable in terms of a particular campus, over time there develops on a campus or in a college an opinion about the fairness of a promotion and tenure system. If experienced faculty members and departmental chairpersons are not generally favorable toward an established system, they may cleverly twist the system to provide the fairness that they believe it lacks.

At least three approaches may be useful in judging credibility. The number of court cases may be one test; comparisons with benchmark institutions may be helpful. If such comparisons show considerable variance from the mean number of serious cases at benchmark colleges, an institution would do well to review its promotion and tenure system. A second approach may include annual or biennial reviews of the institution's academic personnel policies and procedures by deans or unit chairpersons. A third approach may involve a "kitchen cabinet": a senior administrator may seek the opinions of a small group of trusted faculty members on the system's credibility.

This chapter began with some general characteristics of today's promotion and tenure systems, noting that these systems emerge from a number of small but significant policy and procedural changes made over time, rather than from planned efforts. The chapter also touched on faculty perceptions and attitudes toward promotion and tenure policies and procedures. Citing some of the very little research that exists on this subject, one can say that a sizable minority of faculty members and chairpersons, at least in the fields studied, are dissatisfied with their system. More study of this important matter is needed.

The chapter also considered some weaknesses in promotion and tenure systems. The murkiness of institutional missions may foster confusion at the college and department levels or lead faculty members to work around the system to serve their own ends. Some institutions may not be paying sufficient attention to the details involved in developing the files that will be presented for promotion and tenure.

Ten characteristics of effective promotion and tenure systems are suggested. Gleaned more from experience than from research in view of the paucity of the latter, the list is suggestive rather than inclusive. I hope it will inspire more thinking and research on this conceptual approach.

Two

Guidelines for Improving
Evaluation Systems

Logan Wilson wrote in 1942 (p. 112) "that the most critical problem confronted in the social organization of any university is the proper evaluation of faculty services." This is no less true today; in fact, with the problems created in the burgeoning 1960s likely to bear fruit in the 1990s, one can make the case that proper evaluation of faculty services is needed today more than before.

Teacher evaluation and the subsequent personnel decisions, far from being new, have been common for many centuries. In Antioch (a city in Asia Minor) in about 350 A.D., for example, a father who suspected his son's teacher of inferior performance had the right to have the son examined by another authority. If the examination confirmed the teacher's negligence, the father could enter a formal complaint against the teacher. If a panel of teachers and laymen confirmed the teacher's neglect, the father was permitted to transfer his fees and patronage to a new teacher. Such proceedings were important to teachers because they earned their incomes from these fees.

At about the same time a similar practice emerged whereby the students themselves paid fees directly to their teachers. This form of student instruction continued through the Middle Ages and into the eighteenth century; some tutorial disciplines such as music and dance continue this practice today. Promotion and tenure decisions in earlier times were quite simple. Parents voted with their coins; students, with their coins and their feet. Other historical sources describe the evaluative selection of teachers. For example, it was common in the first cen-

14

turies after Christ for a teacher to be appointed to a chair only after a rhetorical contest in which he demonstrated his familiarity with the subject and his speaking ability.

The present and the decade ahead may see a great reappraisal as we challenge all ways of doing things in higher education. In the sixties the simple systems model—goals, programs, resources, evaluation—came upon the public school educational scene, a spinoff from sophisticated models developed in the national space and weaponry businesses. At that time postsecondary education was running at full speed just to build enough classrooms and to find instructors to teach in them, and it was not operationally interested in detailed approaches to faculty evaluation. Postsecondary interest in systematic evaluation picked up in the seventies, perhaps exemplified by the title of a 1973 speech by Earl Cheit (pp. 2-3): "The Management Systems Challenge: How to Be Academic Though Systematic."

Our current emphasis on academic evaluation was given a push at the beginning of this decade by some industrial leaders who believed that America was rapidly becoming second-rate in producing high-quality products. Main's article in *Fortune* (Dec. 29, 1980), "The Battle for Quality Begins," was a catalyst for this effort. Subtitled "U.S. Industry Is Rousing Itself to Meet the New World Standards Set by the Japanese," the article galvanized the thinking of some corporate leaders. For example, at a special seminar at Cornell University in the spring of 1981 the corporate heads of Ford Motors, AT&T, and IBM were guest speakers; each had read and digested the *Fortune* article and clearly embraced its message.

In the mid-eighties, postsecondary education has clearly taken seriously the messages of planning and program evaluation. One of the useful panel reports (no. 71, 1986, p. vi) of the American Council on Education, entitled *Campus Trends, 1985,* reported that "almost all of the nation's colleges and universities have procedures in place for long-range planning (87 percent) and for program review (83 percent). . . . More than half of the institutions have developed procedures for systematic faculty planning."

This very brief overview of postsecondary education reinforces the view that the early stages of a great reappraisal of postsecondary education are upon us. Administrators and faculty members may be expected to become more conversant, sophisticated, and comfortable with evaluation, not only with summative evaluation but with evaluation as feedback and guidance (the title of the 1967 yearbook of the Association for Supervision and Curriculum Development). Greater attention may be given to feedback, which has not received sufficient notice in discussions of academic evaluation although the concept is basic to technology. One of the oldest technological feedback devices is the water-level control in the reservoir tank of the common household toilet, which dates back to ancient Rome. Truxal (1986, p. 18) notes that "feedback, in a general way, measures the actual system output, compares this with a desired output value, and forces the output to change until it reaches the desired value. A feedback system is, therefore, a goal-seeking system."

Definitions of Evaluation

Evaluation has been defined by Michael Scriven (1981, p. 53) as "the process of determining the merit or worth or value of something, or the product of that process." Evaluation is regarded by the authors of *Taxonomy of Educational Objectives: Cognitive Domain* (Bloom, 1956) as the highest level of cognition and is placed at the apex of a pyramid of cognitive functions. They write that "evaluation represents not only an end process in dealing with cognitive behaviors, but also a major link with the affective behaviors where values, liking, and enjoying (and their absence or contraries) are the central processes involved" (p. 185).

Charles Feasley (1980, pp. 7-13) has written about nine possible uses of evaluation—as measurement, as professional judgment, as a measure of the extent to which performance reaches stated objectives, as the basis for making decisions, as a goal-free process, as conflict resolution, as complacency reduction, as an agent of change, and as ritual. Of these possibilities, evaluation is most frequently used as professional judgment and as the basis for making decisions. Evaluation for improvement is a dominant formative purpose that is not included in Feasley's work.

Purposes of Faculty Evaluation

The two basic, well-known purposes of faculty evaluation are to improve faculty performance (a formative function) and to assist in making equitable and effective academic personnel decisions (a summative function). Faculty evaluation can also serve, according to the Southern Regional Education Board (1977, p. 2), "to promote expansion of the scope and quality of basic and applied faculty research, and to keep alive a sensitivity to the needs of the local, state, and national community." A few colleges use faculty evaluations as a way of providing students with ratings of all professors, presumably to help them make better course selections. One prominent private liberal arts college maintains an up-to-date notebook of these ratings in its library. With less faculty mobility, there may be greater use of faculty evaluation as a diagnostic process for tenured faculty members. This point was made by Sommer (1981, p. 226): "Having taught at some university for a long time, I am able to use other faculty members' evaluations longitudinally." For example, by comparing a single professor's ratings over time, one may be able to detect burnout or boredom from teaching the same courses.

Some controversy has arisen over whether one evaluation system can be used for both formative and summative purposes. Advocates of two systems contend that the fundamentally different formative and summative purposes cannot both be met by one system. On the other hand, advocates of one system can point to some single systems that are currently serving both purposes satisfactorily. Perhaps a dual system would be ideal; however, limitations of time, money, and personnel to process and use two systems' results favor concentration on one system with both formative and summative dimensions.

This concentration does not negate the importance of either faculty development programs or individualized developmental efforts, such as videotaping, in improving faculty performance. A number of formative systems enhance individual development, and some aspects of summative systems can also be useful for formative purposes.

The key consideration today and tomorrow in making summative evaluations is the best use of reliable and valid data to make fair and effective decisions. Since these decisions are the most important ones made by colleges and universities, emphasis on data needs to be tempered with the understanding that evaluation requires judgment as well as measurement.

Changes in Faculty Evaluation Practices
Over the Past Decade

By understanding better the immediate past, we can bring the present and future into clearer focus. Some of the changes of the past decade are judged to be positive, while others are questionable. The positive changes will be considered first.

1. *Systematic use of faculty evaluation has significantly increased.* Although there is general agreement among careful observers of developments in faculty evaluation on this increase, almost no recent research data exist to substantiate the claim. Yet the increases that are ascribed to the past decade probably were not true for the 1960s. John Gustad's classic study (1967, p. 270) found that in the five years between his 1961 study and a replication in 1966 the use of "systematic student ratings" dropped dramatically among eighteen criteria. While Gustad did not discuss possible reasons, perhaps the college teacher shortages created by the building boom caused the quality of teachers to become less important than their quantity.

The phrase *systematic use* needs brief elaboration. All colleges and universities have ways of evaluating professional performance of faculty members, but the extent to which they are systematic is open to question. Probably two-thirds to three-quarters of postsecondary institutions have a systematic procedure, which can be defined to include written policies and procedures, routine operation, and agreed-upon uses of evaluative results. About one-quarter are too casual, informal, and irregular in their procedures to be considered systematic. In its 1975 survey of 536 institutions in Southern states, the Southern Regional Education Board (1977, p. 12) concluded that in those states "detailed and systematic evaluation practices are most likely to exist in large, doctoral level institutions"—a finding that is likely to be as true today as in 1975.

2. *Faculty development (formative) programs have come into use more than summative evaluation systems.* Some approaches to faculty development are not new; gatherings of scholars to discuss matters of mutual academic interest predate ancient Greece by a thousand years or more. Other faculty development approaches, such as pedagogical assistance, technological aids, career guidance, and personal counseling, are relatively new. The most noticeable improvements in faculty development during the past decade have been made in these areas. The extent to which colleges and universities are using their faculty evaluation systems for development is not known, but Judith Aubrecht (1984, p. 88) concludes that "very few institutions are making good use of their faculty evaluation systems for developmental purposes." Just how few is "very few" is debatable, but there is general agreement among observers that the number is small.

3. *Broader data bases have been used to make academic promotion and tenure decisions.* Data from Peter Seldin's book (1984, p. 50) indicate an increase in the number of significant sources of data for evaluating teaching in private liberal arts colleges. (See Table 1.) Only three sources—colleagues' opinions, chair evaluation, and dean evaluation—earned a mean score of less than 2.00 in the 1973 study; in the 1983 study, five sources —the same three plus systematic student ratings and self-evaluation—earned a score below 2.00. (The lower the rating, the greater the use.) This increase in the number of sources with low mean scores suggests that private colleges are using a wider range of sources in evaluating faculty performance. Although similar longitudinal data are not available for public colleges and universities, Seldin's data seem relevant to these types of postsecondary institutions as well.

4. *Functional systems for faculty evaluation have devel-*

Table 1. T-Tests of Differences in Mean Scores of Sources of
Information Considered in Evaluating Faculty Teaching
Performance in Private Liberal Arts Colleges, 1973 and 1983.

Sources of Information	1973 (N = 410) Mean Score	1983 (N = 515) Mean Score	t^a
Systematic student ratings	2.20	1.45	13.57[b]
Informal student opinions	2.04	2.35	−6.40[b]
Classroom visits	2.98	2.48	8.99[b]
Colleagues' opinions	1.76	1.69	1.42
Scholarly research and publication	2.30	2.28	0.31
Student examination performance	2.95	3.03	−1.47
Chair evaluation	1.22	1.26	−0.87
Dean evaluation	1.19	1.33	−3.40[b]
Course syllabi and examinations	2.56	2.21	6.41[b]
Long-term follow-up of students	3.13	3.13	−0.08
Enrollment in elective courses	2.79	3.09	−6.07[b]
Alumni opinions	3.09	3.05	0.97
Committee evaluation	2.17	2.06	1.38
Grade distributions	3.05	3.04	0.23
Self-evaluation or report	2.58	1.95	9.24[b]

[a]The test used was a t-test for differences in independent proportions.
[b]Significant at 0.01 level of confidence.
Source: Seldin, 1984, p. 50.

oped. A decade ago the literature and conversations about faculty evaluation discussed a number of separate evaluative policies and procedures. Today, these are seen as parts of an integrated evaluation system. A system considers each part and how it meshes with the whole; the whole should be greater than the sum of its parts—a tenet of Gestalt psychology. A faculty evaluation system might include parts such as these:

• Explicit instructions are written for administering the classroom teaching evaluation instrument to students.
• Information is given on expected turnaround time for the results of classroom evaluation.
• Participants know who sees the results of evaluation.
• The weighting of the evaluative criteria is known and discussed.

- The roles of the various constituencies in the decision-making process, such as colleagues, chairperson, designated committees, dean, and the chief academic officer, are known to everyone.
- Developmental and operational costs are known.
- Grievance procedures are available to faculty members.

The systems approach requires much more planning at both the conceptual and operational levels than does developing a series of separate procedures. This complexity augurs well for the usefulness, credibility, and durability of a system. It does, however, require more or less constant monitoring and procedural adjustments along the way because its complexity also means that more things can go awry.

The trend toward evaluation systems also reflects increasing sophistication in using faculty evaluation. More people today know much more about faculty evaluation than was the case twelve years ago. Much greater use of computers has also made these systems easier to manage.

5. *The quality of student rating forms for appraising classroom teaching performance has substantially improved.* Some earlier forms were excellent and enjoyed widespread use and acceptance. Examples include the Purdue Rating Scale that was developed by Remmers and the various rating scales for classroom teaching that have been used at the University of Washington since 1924. E. R. Guthrie's (1954) report on faculty evaluation, primarily about the University of Washington's program, remains insightful and useful.

Recently developed student survey forms are machine scored or optically scanned, and they usually ask questions more relevant to the components of teaching and learning than the "kitchen sink" approach that typified many earlier efforts. This approach followed the dictum, "When in doubt about the value of a question, include it." Greater understanding of the teaching and learning processes, as well as significant refinements in related fields such as interpersonal communications, have allowed constructers of student rating forms to ask more relevant questions about the teacher-learning interactions and about learning environments while often asking fewer questions altogether.

6. *Court cases have improved the quality and fairness of academic personnel decisions.* The number of court cases on irregularities and inequities in making academic personnel decisions may have peaked, but a steady stream of such cases may be expected to continue. In the State University of New York (SUNY) system in the seventies, the threat of litigation became so commonplace that one administrator, when threatened with a suit by a faculty member, replied: "Get a ticket and stand at the end of the line!" On the whole, legal action has improved the process of faculty evaluation over the past decade.

7. *Use of the research/scholarship criteria in making academic promotion and tenure decisions has increased.* In comparing 1978 and 1983 data on the use of thirteen criteria in evaluating overall faculty performance, Seldin (1984, p. 39) found that a substantial increase was in the use of the research/ scholarship category, which increased from 25 percent in 1973 to 33 percent in 1983. The importance of publication as an aspect of scholarship increased from 19 to 29 percent. In interpreting these findings, Seldin (p. 74) suggests that "public colleges in particular may be emphasizing research and publication in the drive to impress state legislatures and other public bodies that control the purse strings." In another interpretation of these findings, Eble (1984, pp. 97-98) speaks about "a return to what a majority of faculty probably regard as 'traditional' values. I refer to the increasing weight given to research, publication, and professional activities and to the increasing use of outside referees of scholarly productivity, as well as less attention being given to advising, committee work, and personal attributes." The greater weight given to scholarship and research in evaluating overall faculty performance also may be related to better policies and procedures for appraising them. Many more colleges and universities have detailed procedures for this process today than in 1974.

This decade has also seen some questionable changes in the area of faculty evaluation that may not result in positive developments and improvements.

1. *"Rush to press" has seriously flawed some evaluation systems.* Some mandates to develop evaluation systems have allowed faculty and administrators insufficient time to investigate and to reflect; a mediocre product is likely to result. This has been most evident at the state level and in the two-year colleges. The amount of time recommended for developing or extensively restudying a faculty evaluation system or a promotion and tenure system is about one academic year plus a summer.

2. *Use of the wrong models may have increased.* Some small colleges and regional public universities have inadvertently or otherwise placed as much emphasis on research and scholarship as research-oriented universities. This may stem from an effort to impress and perhaps also from subconscious feelings that bigger is better. The tendency of regional comprehensive public universities to overemphasize research and scholarship may also be due to a tendency to follow the patterns and practices of the more prestigious land-grant universities even if these patterns are not particularly relevant to their own nature and mission.

3. *Reliance on quantification can become excessive.* The "if you can't count it it doesn't exist" point of view has led to excessive reliance on numbers and numerical weightings. Certainly appropriate quantification is desirable and necessary if large batches of data are to be processed quickly, but these data always need to be buttressed with reasoned judgment. Perhaps the quantification problem and its humanistic amelioration were stated most succinctly by Enthovan (1970, p. 51): "It is better to be roughly right than precisely wrong."

4. *An antiintellectual backlash has hindered development of some faculty evaluation systems.* Anyone who has gathered chalk dust on his or her sleeves knows of the art of teaching—to use the title of a thoughtful little book by Gilbert Highet. He wrote (1950, pp. vii–viii): "I believe teaching is an art, not a science. It seems to me very dangerous to apply the aims and methods of science to human beings as individuals." The teaching-learning process is indeed difficult to capture with words or on a rating scale, yet objective treatment of it is fairer and more defensible than mystical pronouncements about it. It would be

a mistake, however, for those advocating more objective and systematic faculty evaluation systems to take lightly Highet's argument and other objections to faculty evaluation and the objections to student ratings of classroom teaching.

Four Institutional Approaches to Student Evaluation of Classroom Teaching

The various natures and needs of different types of institutions require considerably different student evaluation systems. Four basic alternatives are suggested; many variations can be found within each approach. One approach uses a single form that is required of all students in all courses. This omnibus approach offers simplicity, interunit comparability, impartiality, and many summative evaluation data, but it sometimes lacks flexibility, individualization, and formative evaluation. At the other end of the continuum is a "nonsystem," in which there are very few policies and procedures for using or reporting student evaluation results. The decision is left to the individual instructor. This approach provides maximum flexibility, individualization, and formative evaluation, but it offers minimal individual accountability and weak summative evaluation. In addition, it is more vulnerable to legal action.

The "cafeteria" approach was developed at Purdue University in the early 1970s. It is used in a number of other institutions, particularly in the Big Ten universities in the Midwest. The Instructor and Course Evaluation System (ICES) developed at the University of Illinois is an example. (See Appendix B for information on this system.) The cafeteria is a catalogue or list of numerous evaluative items from which the individual instructor can select to create a student rating form. Its advantages include greater flexibility, individualization, and some comparative statistical data; its disadvantages are cost, complexity, and limited summative evaluation data. Ory, Brandenburg, and Pieper (1980, p. 252) studied faculty attitudinal and behavioral characteristics that were considered important by instructors selecting items from the ICES catalogue. They found that "the more-highly rated faculty in the study were apparently more interested in collecting feedback about their students' outcomes than about their management of the course." This finding is compatible with Feldman's finding (1976b) that student outcomes were at the top of his list of instructional dimensions most highly associated with superior college teachers.

A modified cafeteria rating system has a standard section of items applicable to all courses and instructors, with an additional section of optional items chosen by individual instructors from categories listed in a catalogue. The Arizona Course/Instructor Evaluation Questionnaire (CIEQ) developed at the University of Arizona is an example. (See Appendix B for information on this system.) This approach allows flexibility, individualization, and formative evaluation assistance while providing summative data for organizational purposes. Both the cafeteria and the modified cafeteria approaches use computerized answering forms; optical scanning technology reduces costs and speeds turnaround, but the basic operational and technological costs can be a disadvantage to some types of institutions.

A fourth approach is typified by the University of Washington's Instructional Assessment System (IAS). Six different forms are tailored to provide diagnostic information for six different types of courses: large lecture courses, small lecture-discussion courses, seminars, problem-solving courses, skill acquisition courses, and quiz sections. (See Appendix B for information on this system.) This approach allows rating forms to be adapted to the mode of instructional delivery, yet summative organizational needs can be met. However, it does not allow flexibility or individualization within a designated type, and the cost may be a problem for some institutions.

Guidelines for Developing and Evaluating
Faculty Evaluation Systems

General faculty evaluation guidelines need to be identified, for they are the ground on which promotion and tenure decisions are made. Some guidelines suggested here are quite

obvious, and others are controversial; yet each may be worthy of consideration in the complicated and sensitive task of developing and reviewing faculty evaluation systems.

1. *Faculty evaluations have always taken place,* in a vast number of ways and places ranging from the comments of students in a residence hall to the informal exchanges in muted tones of colleagues at a cocktail party. There is no reason to expect these personal ways of judging performance to diminish appreciably in the future.

But these highly informal approaches, if they see the light of a committee meeting, can do gross injustice to an individual's professional career because they may be based on personal vendettas, false information, or half-truths, and they can lead the administration straight into the courtroom.

2. *Systematic faculty evaluation is here to stay.* This is a hard reality for some professional educators who mistrust such systems. Stories about very poor systems, less than ethical application of a good system, or misuse of data can be recalled by almost every administrator and professor. Excesses and misuses of any system can be found. Until someone develops a credible and manageable way to evaluate faculty performance that is also a significant departure from current approaches, do we have any realistic alternative but to improve what we have?

Some people believe that this "evaluation itch" will pass; they may know something that has escaped many others, or they may be living in a world that no longer exists. Many who believe that systematic evaluation is here to stay also believe that we need to improve the process as a way of making more equitable and effective promotion and tenure decisions.

3. *There is no such thing as a perfect evaluation system.* Perfection is a realistic goal in many academic fields. In scientific measurements, in appendectomy operations, and in accounting calculations there is very little margin for error. In the social sciences, however, a systematic approximation often may be the best that can be attained.

Those who are developing faculty evaluation systems should strive for systematic, reliable, and valid policies and procedures rather than for perfection. Those striving for perfection

in these systems may be on a collision course with disappoint-
ment. Or they may have a more subtle, Machiavellian motive,
calling for a degree of perfection that they know can never be
achieved in order to sabotage the whole effort.

4. *Faculty evaluation systems are designed to improve
performance.* Some people may consider this guideline to be
empty rhetoric, believing that the bottom line is the use of faculty evaluation for academic promotion and tenure decisions.
If it is empty rhetoric, and one cannot deny that it is at some
institutions, then administrators and faculty members may want
to examine the system. Operational and successful models can
be found in which faculty evaluation is used both for faculty
development and for making academic promotion and tenure
decisions.

5. *Faculty evaluation data provide significant input into
promotion and tenure decisions.* This guideline confirms the obvious; namely, that faculty evaluation serves a summative function as well as the formative one articulated in the preceding
guideline.

Administrators want evaluation systems that are equitable and effective and that are operated in a systematic and impartial manner. A laissez-faire, informal system would be more
eclectic and uneven, and therefore more unfair, than a more
formal one. In defense of informality, one hears that it means
less red tape and therefore less time spent on the process. It also
places one's professional life in the hands of a very few persons
who may have personal biases and who have incomplete data.
And informal decision-making procedures are more likely to
result in lawsuits by those who believe that they have been dealt
with unfairly.

6. *The faculty evaluation system includes several sources
of data, and these sources are clearly communicated.* Using just
one source of data, such as student ratings of classroom performance or the chairperson's or dean's evaluation, is not recommended. Fortunately, this is not an issue because almost all
postsecondary institutions use many sources of data. On the
other hand, too many sources can be cumbersome without add-
ing validity to the final decision. As a rule of thumb, five or six

data sources are manageable yet still allow a checks-and-balances system to operate.

7. *Evaluation procedures are individualized and flexible.* Individualization can take place in a number of ways. An individual contract between the instructor and the department chairperson is used primarily in small or medium-sized institutions. Individualization can also be achieved by using a weighting system whereby the individual instructor and the department chairperson agree on the weight, or degree of importance, that will be given to teaching, research, service, and other elements included in the system. This approach is found most often in community colleges.

In a milieu as complex and diverse as that found on any campus, administrators are challenged to find avenues for individualizing instruction and bringing flexibility to professional workloads. Small, individualized adjustments can give credibility to the administrator's efforts to allow each individual to bring his or her unique abilities to the classroom or to a research project.

8. *Individualization considers the institution's nature, directions, and priorities, the department's needs, and the individual's interests.* These components are listed in order of the age of each sector. Almost all of our 3,200-plus colleges and universities are much older than any one of their members. Faculty members, however, are the lifeblood of programs and the source of academic knowledge, and in that sense they are as important as the mere length of existence of a postsecondary institution.

In times of institutional cutbacks in human and material resources, all facets are open to scrutiny, and the right of the institution to survive with dignity takes precedence over the right of any person or department. This hard message has been upheld by the courts, provided the institution's procedures for making cutbacks have not violated its own policies and procedures, have not been capriciously applied, and have not violated constitutionally protected individual rights.

9. *Faculty evaluation is conducted regularly—for everyone.* Posttenure evaluation promises to be one of the controversial subjects in faculty evaluation in the nineties. The issue is

whether tenured full professors should be evaluated on some regular basis. The American Association of University Professors (AAUP) has taken the position, expressed by Jordan Kurland (1983, pp. 1-14), that the current procedures for faculty evaluation are adequate and that posttenure evaluation is not necessary as a special focus. It is likely that professors at large research-oriented universities do not see the value of posttenure evaluation, but those at two-year colleges generally do not question its use in their institutions. John Bennett and Shirley Chater (1984, p. 38) conclude: "Systems of post-tenure evaluation provide an excellent way to preserve the strengths of tenure while also allaying public suspicions about tenure and concerns about faculty vigor and accountability. Failure to address these increasing public concerns will inevitably increase the likelihood of external regulation." The excellent booklet on posttenure evaluation by Licata (1986) is an important contribution to the meager literature on this topic. Posttenure review is discussed further in Chapter Six.

10. *An annual academic performance review (AAPR) is done for each faculty member.* This review, involving the chairperson and each faculty member, may be undertaken in the spring. The purpose of this forty-five- to sixty-minute scheduled meeting should be to review the past academic year's activities, to discuss its good and not-so-good aspects, to talk about plans for the coming year, and to consider ways in which chairperson and instructor together can improve the department. The AAPR requires careful preparation, documentation, and written follow-up. All of these take time; but if people are a high institutional priority, the time is well spent. The AAPR is discussed further in Chapter Nine.

A final note on evaluation: A grain, or several grains, of common sense and perspective may be in order. Walter Adams (1974, p. 124) points out that "it would be ludicrous to improve the efficiency of a symphony orchestra by pruning the oboe players (who for long periods are doing nothing), or streamlining the violins (many of whom are playing the same notes and are thus guilty of duplication), or eliminating some of the musical passages (many of which are repetitious and hence redundant)." Howard Bowen (1976b, p. 10) writes in a similar vein about the American home: "From a narrow pecuniary point of view, the typical American family is grossly inefficient. It wastes housing space. It provides specialized rooms for sleeping, eating, work, and recreation which are unused most of each day. . . . Indeed, we applaud these inefficiencies by calling them a high standard of living."

Three

~~~~~~~~~~~~~~~~~~~~~~~~~~~~~~~~~

Evaluating Teaching:
The Role of Student Ratings

At the heart of most promotion and tenure decisions is some evaluation of a teacher's performance. Student evaluation is generally agreed to have the most influence on these decisions, although both the views of peers and self-evaluation can be valuable also. The nationwide as well as professional interest in better classroom teaching that is evident today provides both an encouraging and a challenging backdrop.

What Is Good Teaching?

Is there anything new to say about good teaching? The answer is both yes and no. It is no according to the school of thought that believes "there is nothing new under the sun." Philosophers in the golden age of Greece carried on serious dialogues about teaching and learning, and the teachers in the Egyptian schools of Alexander the Great also discussed these subjects. The voluminous modern materials on teaching and learning include many hundreds of articles and booklets, reprints from countless workshops, and records of discussions at almost every postsecondary institution.

The answer also is yes. Indeed, teaching is a whole new world both to those just entering the teaching profession and to those who are "becoming," or trying to improve. It is ironic that those teachers least in need of improvement are the ones most often found at seminars and workshops on the subject (Centra, 1976a).

Each generation of teachers needs to rediscover its own

truths about teaching. Rediscovery does not mean starting as a *tabula rasa* but approaching in an open manner the best literature and experience on the subject. Each teacher, as a unique human being, needs to discover the teaching styles and approaches that best suit his or her personality, knowledge, and values. In this sense, good teaching is an exciting journey that never ends, and the good teacher never becomes stagnant or stultified.

A number of excellent materials on teaching have recently been developed. This literature includes books by Eble (1983) and Joseph Lowman (1984) and Wilbert McKeachie's perennially popular *Teaching Tips* (1986). In attempting to simplify and to present the essence of good instruction, one should not lose sight of the intricacies of teaching, as Rhodes and Riegle (1981, p. 16) point out: "Few concepts are as complex as 'effectiveness' or occur so frequently in talk about teachers and teaching."

McKeachie (1986, p. 53) suggests that a teacher functions as expert, formal authority, socializing agent, facilitator, ego ideal, and person. Table 2 summarizes some of the different goals and typical behavior that characterize each of these six functions.

Lowman (1984, p. 9) analyzed the various questions on student rating forms to discover what students find satisfying or dissatisfying in their teachers, drawing upon studies by Feldman (1976a, b), Mannan and Traicoff (1976), Marques, Lane, and Dorfman (1979), and Tennyson, Boutwell, and Frey (1978). Lowman concluded that the most important student concern was for clarity of presentation. Also important was the instructor's ability to stimulate students' thinking about the material rather than simply encouraging them to absorb it. A third factor was the instructor's ability to stimulate enthusiasm for the subject.

Kenneth Eble (1983, pp. 103-104) wrote that the seven deadly sins of teaching are "Arrogance, Dullness, Rigidity, Insensitivity, Vanity, Self-Indulgence, and Hypocrisy. Pride is clearly operative in most of these; Sloth should probably be included, though, like Lust and Anger, I leave it as more appropriately among humankind's general sins." Turning from the outside experts, ask yourself, as an administrator or teacher,

Table 2. Six Aspects of Teaching.

The Teacher's Roles	Major Goals	Characteristic Skills	Major Sources of Student Motivation (and Fear)
Expert	To transmit information, the concepts and perspectives of the field	Listening, scholarly preparation, class organization and presentation of material; answering questions	Curiosity, need for achievement; intrinsic interest in content (fear of being/appearing stupid; fear of being snowed)
Formal authority	To set goals and procedures for reaching goals	Defining structure, and standards of excellence; evaluating performance	Dependency; getting a good grade (fear of flunking, of being lost and pursuing irrelevant activities)
Socializing agent	To clarify goals and career paths beyond the course; to help students prepare for these	Clarifying rewards and demands of the major, the field, and academic area	Need to clarify one's interests and calling; desire to be "in" (fear of being rejected by field or having options reduced)
Facilitator	To promote creativity and growth in student's own terms; to help overcome obstacles to learning	Bringing students out, sharpening their awareness of their interests and skills; to use insight and problem solving to help students reach goals, avoid blocks	Self-discovery and clarification to grow in desired direction (fear of being/becoming a puppet or grade-grubber; fear of not developing a clear and useful identity)
Ego ideal	To convey the excitement and value of intellectual inquiry in a given field of study	Demonstrating the ultimate worthwhileness of or personal commitment to one's material/educational goals	The desire to be turned on; the desire for a model, a personification of one's ideals (fear of being bored, unmoved, and cynical)
Person	To convey the full range of human needs and skills relevant to and sustained by one's intellectual activity; to be validated as a human being; to validate the student	Being self-revealing in ways which clarify one's totality beyond the task at hand; being trustworthy and warm enough to encourage students to be open as well	The desire to be known as more than a student; the desire to have one's life cohere (the fear of being ignored or treated as a "product")

Source: McKeachie, 1986, pp. 65–66.

what is your definition of good teaching? Such a personal exercise may be interesting and revealing for you. It was for me over eighteen years ago. As a professor, I asked myself that question and crafted this definition: "Good teachers are open to ideas and innovation. They personify enthusiasm, not only for their areas of competence, but also for their students—and life itself. They know their subject, can explain it clearly, and are willing to do so—in or out of class. They approach their areas of competence and their students with an integrity that is neither stiff nor pompous, and their attitude and demeanor are more caught than taught." Now, I would update this definition to include "a sense of humor."

Evaluating Classroom Performance

Methods of evaluation include student rating forms, classroom visits by peers, written appraisals, achievement tests, interviews, alumni ratings, and more informal ways. While each can be useful, the student rating form is the most widely used approach, with classroom visits by peers a distant second.

Student Rating Forms

Seldin's study (1984, p. 48) found that the percentage of private liberal arts colleges that "always used" systematic student ratings in evaluating teaching performance increased from 29 percent in 1973 to 53 percent in 1978 and 67 percent in 1983. While comparative evidence is not available for public colleges and universities, there is reason to believe that a similar increase occurred.

Choosing instruments for student appraisal of teaching has received little attention in the literature, yet it usually demands considerable time from almost every committee established to consider faculty evaluation. Committees often choose to invent their own rating scales or to modify one that they already have or that someone else has developed. The many hours required to develop a new instrument may be well spent if they make the final product more acceptable, but one usually has no assurance of this. The committee also should have, as Aleamoni pointed out (1981, p. 116), "the benefit of advice and consultation with experts in questionnaire design." This point is an important one.

The development of some student rating forms begins with a dragnet or popularity approach, or with the questions to be asked the students rather than with the purposes or objectives of the student rating forms. The faculty is asked to provide items for inclusion in a student rating form, which are then computerized and rank-ordered. Interestingly, lists of items prepared this way do not differ appreciably from more conceptually derived statements, and they may be more politically viable because their preparation has involved many people. The final selection of value descriptors on the rating scale, however, should have the benefit of psychometric expertise.

In another approach, a committee selecting an evaluation survey form may consider one of the several established rating scales that have a research base. Another strategy is to borrow an instrument from a peer institution. The commercially developed instruments offer ease of scoring, since the company handles this, and the availability of comparative data, but they are usually more expensive. See Appendix B for information about several successful student rating forms.

Adapting or devising a form might begin with a definition of good teaching; various rating scales can then be scrutinized to see how their categories relate to this definition. Halsted (1970, p. 625) wrote that an adequate rating scale should contain four components: an underlying theory of instruction or a model of the instructional process, a translation of the theory or model into one or more operational definitions, development of a rating scale consistent with these definitions, and assurance that student raters understand the criteria.

A number of features are recommended in student rating forms. First, the form should be short, no more than one page in length; no more than twelve questions are needed to cover the areas that students are in a position to assess. Comparisons of the medium-length and short versions of the Berkeley instrument used on the Davis campus of the University of

California indicated that the short form of one page did almost everything the longer one did (Wilson and Dienst, 1971). The short form is less likely to cause evaluation fatigue for students, who may be filling in several forms per semester. Because it takes less time to process, it is slightly less expensive.

A second feature is the opportunity for flexibility and individualization. Most postsecondary institutions have developed or have chosen forms that include room for additional questions and handwritten comments.

A third feature of a good form is that it asks questions that are within the scope of the course and the experience of the students. There are five areas in which students are uniquely able to answer questions on rating forms because of their direct classroom contact with the teacher; each of these areas should be covered by at least one question on the form.

1. *Pedagogical methods* can best be judged by the students who are in regular classroom contact with the professor. Students can tell whether the teacher merely lectures, doing little to get across his or her ideas, or carries on a deliberate, sustained, and effective search for ways to convey knowledge and attitudes.

2. *Fairness* is of great concern to students. For example, they rarely confront directly the professor who uses "pop" quizzes, believing that discretion is the better part of valor and protecting themselves against retribution, but they uniformly detest what they consider a sneaky and negative way of evaluating them. They tell observers that professors who believe that they have to "keep the students on their toes" with such surprises usually do not offer much in the way of enthusiastic, positive, and trustful teaching.

3. *The teacher's interest in the student* as a person can be judged firsthand from the relationships in and out of class, provided the class is not a large lecture course. Even here, however, the teacher can elicit sincere and directed interest whenever possible, and word of this attitude moves through the grapevine. The lead lecturer in a large lecture class elicits interest from students through his or her expectations and direction of the course assistants. Colleagues and department chairpersons glean

ideas and information about a colleague's interest in students from unsolicited student comments as well as from the teacher's comments; great caution should be exercised, however, in using such information to make academic personnel decisions.

4. *The teacher's interest in the subject* can be judged quite accurately by students and colleagues as well as the department chairperson. For colleagues, this interest manifests itself in many little ways and in questions that a professor asks or does not ask. Doing research, presenting professional papers, and writing are also evidence of professional interest.

5. *Normative teaching judgments* known as global ratings can be made best by students. Centra's research (1979, p. 153) found that "only some 12 percent of a national sample of almost 400,000 teachers received less than average ratings from students." The use of comparative data, as pointed out by Aleamoni (1981, p. 134), "can serve to counteract the positive response bias, resulting in a more accurate and meaningful interpretation of the ratings."

Normative or global questions usually come at the end of a student survey form. One type asks the student to compare the overall competence of the instructor with others in the department or with all instructors. Another type of global question, less competitive but still normative, asks the student to rate the course in general or as a whole. Global questions are summative in nature and have the most value in making academic personnel decisions. Other questions on the rating form, although not devoid of normative implications, are most useful in diagnostic and formative types of evaluation.

A fourth recommended feature of student rating forms is clear, unbiased, and concise introductory statements and instructions to the student. Some collegiate evaluation committees take great pains to develop the questions and the instrument but give little or no thought to the introductory statement, which is written almost as an afterthought. Such an oversight can sabotage an otherwise excellent effort.

A seven-point rating scale with endpoint and midpoint verbal descriptors is a fifth feature. The five-point scale commonly used has the advantage over the seven-point scale of

being simpler to complete and probably somewhat more reliable. But the five-point scale may unconsciously bias the rater
toward a higher rating. For example, if the scale uses 5 as the
highest rating, 3 as the middle, and 1 as the lowest, the rater has
only one choice between the highest and the middle rating.
Raters may be reluctant to use the highest rating except for exceptional individuals; yet since the "average" or middle rating
seems too low, the most plausible alternative is a 4.

The seven-point scale allows the rater, while reserving the
highest rating for the truly exceptional, to give the teacher a 6
(highest-high) or a 5 (high-competent); hence the rater can be
more precise in making judgments. A ten-point scale allows even
greater differentiation, but then the element of complexity
comes into play, and reliability may suffer slightly.

Research on the use of verbal labels by French-Lazovik
and Gibson (1984) found that the misuse of labels can significantly influence the raters. For example, in an analysis of the
student rating of the word *average* in a list of thirty-two verbal
labels, they found that "students judging teaching behaviors
characterize significantly less than 50% of their teachers by the
word 'average' " (p. 56). Their research also found a lack of
symmetry in the use of balanced sets of terms such as *very good*
and *very poor*. The 121 students in their study gave the top
first, second, and third ratings to "exceptional," "superior,"
and "outstanding"; the middle three ratings were "compares
well with the average," "middling," and "competent"; and the
lowest ratings were given to "very low," "very ineffective," and
"very poor."

A seven-point scale with labeled endpoints and midpoint
is used in the rating scales in Appendix A. Results of the study
by Lam and Klockars (1982, p. 321) indicate that "scales with
only the endpoints labeled produce results similar to scales with
equally spaced response labels. The researcher interested in obtaining an interval scale may thus be able to eliminate the effort
of labeling all points on the scale in favor of labeling only the
endpoints." However, since the rating scale in Appendix A uses
seven points rather than five, the midpoint is labeled also. The

verbal indicators chosen, based upon research by French-Lazovik and Gibson (1984, p. 52), are "exceptional" (7), "moderately good" (4), and "very poor" (1). The midpoint is not described as "average." As French-Lazovik and Gibson point out: "When ratings of human behaviors are made, the term 'average' may be pejorative; people typically do not like to be described by this term" (p. 50).

Three components of teaching can be evaluated by both professors and students. Students as freshmen are not in a good position to judge the *content mastery* of their teachers; this is also true for students taking courses in academic areas outside their major. After students have had several courses in their major, they can answer questions about the content of courses in that area on a normative basis, but professional colleagues theoretically are still in the best position to answer questions about content mastery. The word *theoretically* is used because compartmentalization by academic specialty may make it difficult to judge the knowledge of colleagues accurately. In small colleges where staffing patterns require professors to teach several different courses, the assessment of someone's knowledge in a single area is also difficult. In view of the many problems in obtaining clear data from any one source, it is common to ask both students and colleagues about the teacher's mastery of the course content.

Both students and colleagues can offer important insights into *course organization*. The students can judge the day-to-day course organization effectively; they are in a poor position to judge how the organization of the course relates to the overall academic program.

Students and professors can also be asked essentially the same question about *course workload*. Their answers, however, may well vary. Students may say that Professor A acts as though he believes that his course is the only one that they are taking. Professors are in the best position to compare the workload to that of other courses in the program. It may be that Professor A represents the program norm and his syllabus reflects what others are doing. On the other hand, a lackadaisical department with relaxed workload requirements may resent an energetic young professor who wants to move the students' knowledge too far ahead of the department's expectations.

Written Appraisals

Most student rating forms include a space for a written appraisal, providing students with an opportunity to use their own words, though many students may choose not to use it. Some students do not want to take the time to write an appraisal. Fear of a professor's retribution deters other students from writing negative comments, and with some reason. An occasional professor will go to great lengths to identify the authors of negative appraisals. This fear can be eliminated if all written comments are typed by a secretary and returned to the professor in this form. If secretarial assistance is not available, the chairperson or an assigned senior professor can be asked to summarize these comments and to destroy those rating forms with written comments after the numerical ratings have been recorded on another form. At one university, evaluation forms designed by students are administered by faculty but returned to student committees for analysis. Faculty members do not see the forms until the semester is over. However, retribution is still possible in this system if a student who has written negative remarks takes another class from the same professor.

Almost no colleges and universities use only a written appraisal. A few smaller private colleges ask seniors to write a general appraisal of their overall collegiate experience. The arguments against widespread use of written appraisals include their lack of comparability, the time they require from both the students who complete them and the faculty and administrators who read them, and the difficulty of coming to generalizations from the various written comments.

These caveats should not preclude consideration of the written appraisal. A few colleges have used structured student interviews for formative and summative evaluations of teaching performance. The work of Braskamp, Brandenburg, and Ory

(1984, pp. 56, 58) is recommended in an exploration of these alternatives.

Alumni Ratings

Alumni ratings of college teaching have received very little attention, with a notable exception. In 1983, President Reynolds of Baylor University sent a "Dear Baylor Graduate" letter to every alumnus in the classes of 1957, 1962, 1967, 1972, 1977, and 1982, with this introductory paragraph: "One of the ways we can continue to strengthen our faculty is to gain knowledge of the results of the work of the faculty in the lives of our alumni. Consequently, it is very helpful to know how you view your instruction at Baylor from the perspective of your years away from the campus." The following three pages listed the names of all professors by college. Raters were asked to rate the *total* performance of those who had taught them on a five-point scale. The reliability of student ratings of instructors over a period of time is well established; asking alumni to add their perspective therefore has credibility. Furthermore, the public relations advantage of this approach does not go unnoticed.

Achievement Tests

In some academic fields, such as accounting and the natural sciences, achievement test scores can be useful for evaluation. The social sciences may use this approach for introductory courses in areas such as psychology. Any academic course with multiple sections and common examinations can develop longitudinal data about the extent of student content mastery under various teachers. After using appropriate statistical procedures and correcting for special circumstances, we can try to discover why students of certain teachers score higher on content mastery. Is it better teaching, a more suitable class time, the teacher's better content mastery, or some other factor? Both the results of student rating forms and content achievement scores can provide useful data. It is possible that these teachers stress content to the exclusion of other skills, such as critical thinking, that students are expected to acquire.

Achievement tests such as the American College Testing (ACT) Program's College Outcome Measures Project (COMP) will be used substantially more in the near future to verify improvement or the lack of it in many areas. A number of states have mandated that outcome measures be developed for assessing student achievement. The trend is away from prescribing a single outcome measure for an entire state; educators consider diverse outcome measures to be preferable to a single test or measurement package.

The effect of greater use of outcome measures on teaching evaluation is not yet clear. It is likely that greater use of achievement measures in general will condition members of postsecondary institutions to have less fear of surveys for evaluating faculty. A contrary trend may also develop, however; misuse of institutional or statewide outcome measurements might turn people away from all measurement by tests, including surveys for faculty evaluation.

Special Incidents

It has been mentioned that special care must be taken in considering informal student opinion. Such opinion should not be ignored, however. A category called *special incidents* may be used to handle these data openly and systematically. Special incidents may include laudatory or negative comments about aspects of an individual's teaching (such as an unusually fine course syllabus or course preparation) or a student delegation to the dean's office to protest a teacher's alleged incompetence. Care must be taken that these incidents do not assume undue importance and that they are investigated with care if related to sensitive matters. A written form that may help in structuring these incidents is suggested in Appendix A (p. 182).

Alternatives to quantified student ratings of classroom teaching continue to be explored. These approaches usually include multiple data procedures that involve collecting several different types of data in addition to student ratings (Carlson,

1975; Fowler and McKenzie, 1975; and Smock and others, 1973). In their comprehensive computer-assisted search of the literature on multidata alternatives to quantified student ratings, Greenwood and Ramagli (1980, p. 674) found that "sixteen percent focused on peer or colleague evaluation, 12 percent on direct measurement of student achievement, and 12 percent on instructor self-evaluation. Two percent of the literature was on integrated multiple data systems, while the largest amount (25 percent) examined the interrelationships among different types of data (e.g., peer ratings versus administrative ratings versus self-ratings versus student ratings)." Explorations of multiple data approaches should continue, although their cost, the time required to develop and administer them and to synthesize the results, and the complexity of their interpretation continue to be major problems.

Common Questions About Student Ratings

Some professors question whether college students have the maturity to make fair and sound judgments about classroom teaching. In addition to research evidence that indicates that students can make valid and reliable judgments if asked the right questions, there is a commonsense answer to this question. Students are professional teacher-watchers by the time they enroll in college, having watched teachers since nursery school. One of the most common approaches to stimulating dinnertime conversation during the early years is a parent's question, "How was school today?" Our children over many years are thus urged or nudged to give evaluative descriptions of schooling and teaching. Children and young adults also talk among themselves about teachers, grades, courses, and problems. A college teacher standing before a class of first-year students is thus exposed to experts! During an average academic term a class of twenty or twenty-five students will accumulate about seven or eight hundred teacher-watching hours. It seems reasonable to believe that, if asked relevant questions that are within their experiential background, students can make fair and sound judgments about teaching.

"Do not confuse me with facts; my mind is made up." This expresses the views of a few (maybe not so few) college teachers on student rating forms. Interestingly, some college professors who are very careful in relying upon data and research in their academic fields have no reservations about making sweeping generalizations quite contrary to research findings on aspects of student ratings of classroom performance. They may feel their expert status comes from having been associated firsthand with students for a number of years and perhaps having served on several committees. These experiences can be valuable, but they should not lead one to ignore the considerable body of experiential data and research findings that exists on most major aspects of using student rating forms in classrooms.

A number of excellent research summaries are available on the most controversial and important issues involving student ratings. These include the following: Guthrie, 1954; Costin and Associates, 1971; Miller, 1974; Feldman, 1976a; McKeachie and others, 1979; Cohen, 1980a; Aleamoni, 1981; Centra, 1979; Millman, 1981; Benton, 1982; Marsh and Overall, 1981; Lowman, 1984; Feldman, 1984; McKeachie, 1986; and Gleason, 1986. One of the most extensive summaries and one that still commands respect is Costin and Associates (1971). The following section develops conclusions, based on an extensive analysis of historical and contemporary research and data, about eleven variables related to student ratings. These are class size, feedback, gender, grades received, overall instructional improvement, reliability of ratings, research and teaching, teacher personality, teaching and aging, uses of evaluation, and validity of evaluation.

Class Size

Perceptions about class size are closely related to the size and style of the institution. If students are reminded of the virtues of small classes, as they usually are by teachers and administrators at small colleges, one should not be surprised to find them favoring small classes. Then, classes that were considered large when some of the earlier research on class size was conducted may well be considered medium-sized today.

The findings on the influence of class size on student evaluations are mixed. Gleason (1986) reports that Feldman's review of thirty studies (1978) found that about one-third reported no relationship between class size and ratings. The other two-thirds suggested a modest relationship, from 1 to 8 percent variance in ratings, which is "not enough to use large classes as an excuse for low ratings" (Gleason, 1986, p. 12).

The size of the class depends somewhat on the subject. A science course, for example, lends itself to lecturing more than a discussion-oriented course in philosophy or a language course that requires active student participation. McKeachie (1971, p. 2) writes that "our analysis of research suggests that the importance of size depends upon educational goals. In general, large classes are simply not as effective as small classes for retention, critical thinking and attitude change." In short, more research is needed to assist us in understanding better the intricate relation of class size to teaching and learning.

Feedback

According to Cohen's excellent meta-analysis (1980, p. 323), there are at least four possible explanations for the failure of instructors to improve teaching following student rating feedback. First, the feedback may not provide new information. Centra (1979, p. 39) found that when instructors' self-evaluations were considerably better than their students' ratings, changes in instruction occurred after only half a semester. Second, instructors may have difficulty implementing changes in the short span of one term. Third, normative data may be needed to help instructors determine their teaching strengths and weaknesses. Finally, instructors may not know how to change their teaching techniques after they receive student rating feedback.

The kinds of feedback used have a significant effect on research findings. Abrami and others (1979) and Rotem and Glasman (1979) found that student rating feedback in general has little overall impact on increasing instructional effectiveness. On the other hand, McKeachie and others (1979), Aleamoni (1978), Stevens and Aleamoni (1985), and Menges and

Binko (1986) found that student ratings plus consultation have a positive influence. There is general agreement among the various authors with the findings of Menges and Binko on the role of consultation as an integral part of constructive feedback.

Gender

The majority of the studies that have investigated differences in teaching evaluation by male and female students and differences in student ratings of male and female teachers have found that no significant overall rating differences exist based on the sex of either the student or the teacher (McKeachie, 1959; Walker, 1969; Aleamoni, 1979; and Centra, 1979). But there is some contrary evidence with respect to specific characteristics. McKeachie and others (1971) found that female teachers were rated more effective than their male counterparts; Centra's research (1972) found that female teachers were more likely to be aware when students did not know the material, were more concerned with student progress, made more comments on papers and examinations, and generally made better use of class time. Courses taught by male teachers were rated more stimulating and more difficult.

Grades Received

The grades that students receive in a course have no correlation or a modest positive correlation with how they rate the teacher. Aleamoni and Hexner (1980), as reported by Aleamoni (1981, p. 115), found that "some 22 studies have reported zero relationships. Another 28 studies have reported positive relationships. In most instances, however, these relationships were relatively weak, as indicated by the fact that the median correlation was approximately .14." Centra (1979, p. 32) found that the correlation between grades and ratings "is usually in the .20 range," which is considered low.

The modest positive correlation that is found in a number of studies would be expected. Students who earn better grades generally attribute some of their success to both the teacher and the course; their ratings therefore reflect this positive view. But no study has found a high correlation between grades and ratings. One can conclude that students' ratings of their teachers are very moderately influenced, in a positive way, by the grades they receive from these teachers. In other words, students who receive low grades do not subsequently give their teachers poor teaching evaluations.

Overall Instructional Improvement

Very few studies have asked whether the systematic collection and use of student ratings over time makes a difference in the overall instructional quality of the institution. Murray (1983, p. 8) concluded that "after 12 years of mandatory summative evaluation, faculty members (at the University of Western Ontario) continue to have generally favorable attitudes toward student evaluations of teaching . . . ; and the mean level of teaching effectiveness . . . has improved substantially over the past 12 years, presumably due, at least in part, to the incentive and selection functions of summative evaluation of teaching." Salzberg and Schiller (1982, p. 84) reviewed the results of student evaluation of teaching from 1970 to 1980 in the department of mathematics at Rhode Island College. They found "no evidence that the use of student evaluations produced improved ratings over the decade though faculty already rated highly tended to improve further while those initially rated low showed downward trends. . . . All this is taken to support the continued use of student ratings in the evaluation process."

One way to learn more about the long-term effects of evaluations would be to pool individual case studies at institutions. In one case study, Sommer (1981, p. 226) reports on his twenty years of recorded teaching evaluations. In general, these evaluations were helpful to him in pointing out his strengths in large class presentations compared to seminars, indicating which courses he taught best, and calling attention to some annoying mannerisms. He concluded: "Although there are few surprises in the evaluations that I now collect, I find them still useful in deciding which portions of a course are to be emphasized the next time it is taught, in selecting textbooks and audio-visual aids, and for evaluating non-salient aspects of the course. I also feel that collecting student ratings keeps me honest as an instructor."

Clearly very little research evidence exists for a positive correlation between teacher evaluation and overall instructional improvement over time. This should be expected in view of the paucity of research studies on this topic. Yet there may be a logical basis for believing that teacher evaluation positively influences overall instructional quality by transference. In symphony orchestras and athletic teams, we know that rigorous and persistent evaluation does lead to overall improvement. While there are many differences in intensity and scope of purpose, it is, nevertheless, not unreasonable to believe that some similarities can be drawn.

Reliability of Ratings

Reliability refers to the consistency of measurement. Unless measurement is reasonably consistent on different occasions or in different examples of a single type of performance, little confidence should be placed in the results. The research findings (Drucker and Remmers, 1950; Centra, 1979; Marsh and Overall, 1981) strongly agree that the scores that teachers receive on student rating forms generally are significantly correlated over a period of time. Centra (1979, p. 26) concluded that "student ratings are not elastic yardsticks. Their reliability or consistency, as indicated by numerous studies is very good, provided enough students in a class have made ratings." Yet Millman (1981, p. 113) warns "that wherever student rating forms are not carefully constructed with the aid of professionals, as is the case of most student- and faculty-generated forms (Everly and Aleamoni, 1972), the reliabilities may be so low as to negate completely the evaluation effect and its results." The evidence strongly indicates that if statistically reliable survey forms are used, students can be expected to assess classroom teaching by individual teachers reliably one, five, or ten years later.

Research and Teaching

More heat than light has been generated on this issue over the years, and the obfuscation continues. Bresler (1968) found that the instructors at Tufts University whom the students rated best were those who had published articles and who had received or were receiving government support for research. Yet the research by McDaniel and Feldhausen (1970), based on a sample of 76 professors and 4,484 students at Purdue University, found no relationship between book writing and effective teaching. They found that the most effective instructors wrote no books and limited their work on papers and articles to second authorships; there was no relationship between research activity, as indicated by grants, and instructional effectiveness. Aleamoni and Hexner (1980, p. 72) reported that Aleamoni and Yimer (1974), Guthrie (1954), and Linsky and Straus (1975) found no significant relationship between instructors' research productivity and students' ratings of their teaching effectiveness. Webster (1985, p. 62) concluded that "there is little or no positive correlation between teaching effectiveness and research productivity."

Finkelstein (1984, p. 126) reached a somewhat different conclusion: "To the extent that judgments of teaching effectiveness are based largely on its intellectual competence dimension (and this appears to be the preferred criterion of faculty), then research productivity and the expertise that it engenders or the general ability that it signals does bear a fairly small, consistently positive relationship to good teaching. To the extent that judgments of teaching are based on socioemotional aspects of the learning situation (and students appear more disposed to this criterion), then the expertise developed via research activity appears a largely irrelevant factor. That good research is both a necessary and sufficient condition for good teaching, then, is not resoundingly supported by the evidence. Resoundingly disconfirmed, however, is the notion that research involvement detracts from good teaching by channeling professional time and effort away from the classroom."

The difference that Finkelstein points out between faculty and student opinions of what constitutes good teaching is another dimension that needs exploration. Others have made the following argument about the importance of research to teaching. Research brings new intellectual and innovative challenges, and it forces teachers to be more curious as they are spurred by the perplexities of their problems. Is it not likely that the mental processes of investigation and problem solving that are necessary to research carry over into the classroom, where students are sensitive to the teacher's interest in the subject? And is it not likely also that the mental outlook that motivates research manifests itself in the classroom as a greater interest in the subject? These are promising areas for future research. Currently available studies, however, show little relationship between the quantity or quality of one's research and one's teaching performance.

Teacher Personality

Ryans's classic research (1967, p. 47) on the X, Y, and Z teacher personality types found that no single teaching style is equally effective for all students. The considerate and understanding X, the organized and responsible Y, and the stimulating and imaginative Z all have their followings among students. Yet in spite of this diversity, some common elements in good teaching exist. Enthusiasm, for example, can be quiet or overt and still be recognized by students as enthusiasm.

A number of studies have investigated the relationship between teacher personality and student ratings. Guthrie (1954, p. 7) found that "an examination of the names of the 62 teachers in the top percentile of the annual ratings [at the University of Washington] revealed a certain outgoing interest not unlike the interest of an actor or musician, coupled with a friendly interest in students, and, most important, an industry and interest in the subject that insures his own preparation for every class period." On the other hand, Isaacson, McKeachie, and Milholland (1963, p. 115) sought to determine whether five personality traits that are generally considered relevant to teaching—leadership, agreeableness, dependability, emotional stability, and culture—correlated with effective college teaching. They found that the only high correlation (.48) was between the peer rating of culture and student rating of effectiveness. And Lewis (1964) concluded that effective teachers cannot be differentiated from less effective ones on the basis of personality variables.

The "Dr. Fox phenomenon" grew out of a widely discussed and criticized study by Naftulin, Ware, and Donnelly (1973, p. 634) in which a professional actor gave one graduate-level lecture with eloquence and conviction but with a contrived lack of content. The graduate students, who were not familiar with the subject of the lecture, rated Dr. Fox's performance highly. This led the researchers to conclude that "given a sufficiently impressive lecture paradigm, an experienced group of educators participating in a new learning situation can feel satisfied that they have learned despite irrelevant, conflicting, and meaningless content conveyed by the lecturer." The criticisms of the study centered on the graduate students' unfamiliarity with the subject and the likelihood that it would be much more difficult to fool the students about content for an entire semester.

General agreement exists between the 1971 findings of Costin and Associates and the 1986 report by Gleason (p. 13). The latter concludes that students "can and do tell the difference" between personal popularity and teaching effectiveness. Other things being equal, an engaging and pleasant instructor is likely to receive a slightly higher rating. But if other things are not equal—for example, if the teacher is poorly prepared or unfair in evaluations or not interested in students—then personality becomes an insignificant factor in student ratings.

Teaching and Aging

This is the title of an excellent recent publication by Mehrotra (1984, p. 1), which begins: "This is the age of aging." Recent geriatric studies of aging and mental powers reveal that the mind loses very little of its intellectual power until well into the sixties, and then in different ways for different people. Some gradual losses before this time may well be compensated for by experience and confidence. In other words, there is very little scientific evidence to indicate that student ratings need be influenced by the effects of age on a teacher's mental ability.

The major effects of age are psychological, such as burnout and boredom, and physical, such as diminished energy. These factors may profoundly affect teaching competence, as may attitudinal differences that often develop with age—the generation gap, for example. Differences in views of the world and life can significantly change teaching styles and attitudes and thereby affect student ratings. But most of these conclusions are conjectural because we have few studies of the teaching and research performance of teachers over fifty years of age.

Early research by Heilman and Armentrout (1936) and Downie (1952) found little or no difference in student ratings based upon age. Centra (1979, p. 33), however, found that teachers with over twenty years of experience received lower ratings than those with twelve years of experience. In a related finding, Centra and Creech (1976) found that the best student ratings come between the third and twelfth years of teaching. Clearly more research is needed on the teaching effectiveness of those over fifty years of age in view of the increasing number of professors over fifty and the end of mandatory retirement at seventy.

Uses of Evaluations

Do students evaluate teachers differently depending upon what they know about the use that will be made of evaluation results? In other words, are students inclined to be more sympathetic (and therefore to give higher ratings) if they are told that their ratings will have a significant influence on promotion and tenure decisions rather than be used only for instructional improvement?

Analyses of the research evidence reach conflicting conclusions. Murphy and others (1984, p. 53) found that "the purpose of rating does not have a general effect on rating accuracy.

Raters who believe that their ratings will be used in making important decisions do not appear to be more generous in observing or in evaluating behavior than those who believe that ratings will have little or no impact upon the rated individuals." Quite different conclusions were reached by Aleamoni and Hexner (1980, p. 67) in their comparison of the effects of different sets of instructions on student evaluations of the course and the instructor. They found that "the results indicated that the students who were informed that the results of their ratings would be used for administrative decisions rated the course and instructor more favorably on all aspects than students who were informed that the results of their ratings would only be used by the instructor."

In their research synthesis, Murphy and others (1984, pp. 45-46) concluded that studies by Berkshire and Highland (1953), Heron (1956), Sharon and Bartlett (1969), and Sharon (1970) suggest that ratings for personnel decisions might be more lenient than ratings having no impact on these decisions. On the other hand, Centra (1976b) found the effects of purpose on the ratings to be weak and inconsistent; and Meier and Feldhausen (1979) found no such effect on the leniency of ratings. More carefully controlled research is needed.

Validity of Evaluations

Validity can be defined as the extent to which student rating forms serve their purposes. Do they measure what they are supposed to measure? Valid evaluations take all relevant variables into account and judge them objectively.

The two standard references on studies of the validity of student rating forms are the conclusions of Costin and Associates (1971, p. 530) and McKeachie and others (1971, p. 444). The latter study concluded: "Our results . . . do not invalidate the use of student ratings as one source of evidence about teaching effectiveness, but they are less convincing than we had hoped for." On the other hand, Rodin and Rodin (1972, p. 1166) reject the use of student evaluations, stating: "If how much students learn is considered to be a major component of good teaching, it must be concluded that good teaching is not validly measured by student evaluations in their present form." The Rodins' methodological design and conclusions were questioned by Centra (1973), Frey (1973), Gessner (1973), and Menges (1973).

The literature on the validity of student evaluations of classroom teaching is extensive and conflicting, and sometimes it does not rise above conceptual and methodological mediocrity. A cautious generalization might be that students can provide acceptably valid opinions on good teaching if asked questions that are on subjects within their experiences (pedagogical effectiveness, course organization, interest in the student, interest in the subject, and evaluation fairness), that are clearly and concisely written, and that refer to commonly accepted aspects of good teaching.

Student rating forms for evaluating classroom teaching can be expected to do only certain things, and their strengths as well as limitations need to be considered carefully. Technical questions related to constructing these forms can be important, such as whether to use verbal descriptors on anchor points and which descriptors to use. Sometimes these considerations are considered trivial, but psychometric research on rating scales does not agree.

Some of the most heated debates about student ratings of classroom performance swirl around such eternal questions as the validity of the ratings, the role of the teacher's personality in the use of ratings, and whether students who receive poor grades in turn give the teacher poor ratings. On most issues a substantial body of respectable research can be found, but one needs to analyze the evidence carefully where conflict exists. Many factors can account for opposed conclusions, such as the samples, the variables used, the reliability of the instruments, the instructions given about the research, the research design, and the way that conclusions are drawn from available data. We do not always find answers in the research findings, but they nonetheless warrant careful attention.

The literature on teaching and learning is extensive, and there is evidence that concerns about quality and techniques existed in antiquity. Individuals and generations need to discover their own definitions of good teaching; the process involved in this journey of discovery will shape and educate one both through an understanding of history and through new insights about oneself. And somewhere along the way, teaching will be improved.

Four

Evaluating Scholarship
and Service

This chapter discusses scholarship, which encompasses professional presentation, publication, and research, and professional
and public service. Scholarship, service, and teaching constitute
the three basic criteria for evaluating professional performance.

Scholarship

The word *scholarship,* defining a broader concept than
research, is appropriately applied to the activity at smaller liberal arts colleges and two-year colleges, where research is not
the norm as it is in research-oriented universities. But what is
scholarship? Obviously, it belongs to a scholar, but who is a
scholar? The pipe-smoking, white-haired, pensive, slightly un-
kempt professor comes to mind—and there are many models
around any campus to confirm this stereotype; yet one can also
find young men and women scholars in fashionable clothing
hurrying about more like stockbrokers or young executives.
Scholarship, in essence, is a state of mind—one that was captured by President Johnson in his 1965 inaugural address, when
he spoke of human improvement in the United States: "It is the
excitement of becoming—always becoming, trying, probing, fall-
ing, resting and trying again—but always trying and always gaining." And it is also accomplishment.

But how does one measure a state of mind? Colleagues
who daily brush shoulders with one another and have countless
bits of conversation can develop a fairly accurate general picture
of scholarship, which may include these dimensions:

- content mastery, including both knowledge and understanding;
- an inquiring, puzzling-through attitude;
- dispassionate and rigorous examination of all evidence;
- passion about accuracy in use and interpretation of data;
- willingness to discard the old for the new, or as Charles F. Kettering noted: "The world hates change, yet it is the only thing that has brought progress"; and
- productivity.

The rating form for professional growth that is included in Appendix A (p. 172) has a question on the general dimensions of scholarship. Three specific aspects of scholarship—professional presentation, publication, and research—are discussed below.

Professional Presentation

There are few models for appraising professional presentations, which include speeches, panel participations, professional demonstrations, and workshops. Some criteria for assessing professional presentations, such as their frequency, are obvious. A numerical tally, however, can miss equally important considerations, such as the importance of the occasion, the subject of the presentation, and the location and prestige of the institution. Some professional fields, such as business administration and education, may offer more frequent opportunities for presentations than the humanities. Institutions located in or near busy urban areas and airports provide greater opportunities for professional presentations. And the population of an area affects the number and size of potential audiences.

The importance of the assignment usually is considered. An address to a local historical society, as important as it is to local people, does not have the same professional prestige as an address to a state or national historical association. Serving on a panel at the national meeting of the association is easier to arrange and requires less preparation than addressing a large group at a conference of professors in an academic field. Judging the quality of a presentation may be difficult. For example, at a presentation on a very controversial issue, two sides will inevitably disagree, with concomitant negative reports.

More has been said about exceptions than about concrete guidelines for judging presentations; very few precedents for making judgments are available. Yet professional presentations are important in some fields and at some institutions; therefore, systematic procedures for appraising this dimension are needed. The rating form for professional presentations in Appendix A includes items about audience evaluation, media accounts, and other professional reactions.

Publication

Publication is generally subsumed under research. This practice has a number of problems, however. For example, some important studies—such as final reports of sponsored projects or agricultural extension reports—that may be based on the best research are never published in professional journals or by offset presses; in order to serve a specific audience the publications are written simply and packaged plainly. Other important publications are thought pieces that are more insightful than systematic.

A numerical count of publications may be part of an institution's system of appraisal. This approach invites a number of questions. How much personal time and effort does a piece reflect? Does one long piece count for more than two shorter ones? Is the piece cited by others? Citations indicate something about the piece's impact, but caution needs to be used in evaluating them. As Cole and Cole (1967, p. 380) pointed out: "(1) Work of the highest significance often becomes common knowledge very quickly and is referred to in papers without being cited. (2) Citations may be critical rather than positive. (3) The various scientific fields differ in size. If we wish to compare the work of scientists in different fields, we must take into account the number of people actively working in these fields. (4) The significance of scientific work is not always recognized by contemporaries."

Counting only pieces appearing in "refereed" journals as bona fide publications creates hardships for scholars in fields which have a limited number of such journals, or where the lag between an article's acceptance and its actual publication may be as long as two years. In most scientific fields refereed journals are virtually the only outlet for publications, but in some professional fields, such as business and education, there are nonrefereed publications that have excellent visibility and professional respect.

The quality of the piece should be an important criterion. Gustad's 1961 research, outlined in Table 3, raises some questions about whether common practices sufficiently consider quality. Although the sole study on the topic is more than twenty-six years old, there is little reason to believe that the types of data gathered for evaluating publications have changed much.

Gustad (1961, p. 14) noted that "faculty yardage—the resume or publications list and the reprints sown in strategic places—is the principal basis for evaluation. It would appear that colleagues, chairmen, and deans are the ones who evaluate this material. *Some* chairmen, *some* colleagues, and a *few* deans are probably doing so."

Evaluating publications is also complicated by the way various disciplines view the different categories of publications—books, chapters in books, monographs, periodical articles, and special reports. Centra's research (1979, p. 123) found that "research and scholarship in the humanities and social sciences are generally slower to develop compared with the natural sciences; moreover, they more frequently result in book publication. For this reason, departments that emphasize research in the humanities and social sciences put more weight on the publication of books than do natural science departments. . . . The number and quality of journal articles and grants received are especially critical to the evaluation of natural science faculty members." Appendix A contains a rating scale for publications that considers the opinions of colleagues both inside and outside the department, the opinion of the chairperson, the reputation of the publisher, citations and reviews, and the author's evaluation.

Table 3. Data Gathered for Evaluating Publication.

				Types of Institutions, by Percentages			
Source	*Liberal Arts Colleges*	*Private Universities*	*State Universities*	*State Colleges*	*Teachers Colleges*	*Junior Colleges*	*Technical Professional Colleges*
Faculty résumé	28	37	50	28	48	28	42
Committee evaluation	2	22	17	6	10	0	5
National reputation	3	15	17	2	4	0	3
On-campus reputation	10	13	17	2	7	0	5
Journal quality	8	12	10	8	0	0	8
Chairman evaluation	10	18	30	14	7	0	18
Dean evaluation	22	13	30	14	10	0	18
Reprints	32	21	27	34	24	8	24
Other	2	0	3	6	7	0	0

Source: Gustad, 1961, p. 14.

Research

It seems that two senior professors were reading a colleague's obituary notice on a bulletin board when one com-
mented: "Poor Jones, he published and published but he still
perished." The issue is less humorous to young college instructors, who must strike an acceptable balance among teaching,
scholarship, and service.

Research ordinarily is not an end in itself but a means to
other ends, such as satisfying curiosity, solving problems, proving or testing hypotheses, and enhancing professional growth.
It is also a way to improve one's chances of professional mobility, but this purpose should be subordinate to the others in
order to increase the probability that the work will be of a high
quality and that research will not taper off significantly after
the first six years. Research in the natural sciences falls off after
about six years, according to Centra's research (1979, p. 124),
although a similar pattern is not evident in the humanities and
in the social sciences.

Most faculty members do not think of themselves as researchers (Fulton and Trow, 1974), with the exception of those
working at land-grant and large, research-oriented universities.
About 150 research-oriented universities are members of the
National Association of Universities and Land-Grant Colleges
(NASULAC); others are members of the American Association
of Universities (AAU). On the other hand, the approximately
twelve hundred two-year colleges are solely teaching institutions. In generalizing about American higher education, one
needs to keep in mind the vastly different clienteles that are
served by the more than three thousand colleges and universities. A mother of four who developed the entry-level typing
skills at a community college that allowed her to support her
family and to move into a supervisory position at work has at-
tended her Harvard.

The productive researcher, as defined by Finkelstein
(1984, p. 98), "holds the doctorate; is strongly oriented toward
research; began publishing early, perhaps prior to receipt of the
doctorate and received 'recognition' for scholarly contributions;

is in close contact with developments in his or her field via interaction with colleagues and keeping abreast of the literature; and spends more time in research, less time in teaching, and is not overly committed to administrative chores (although this may vary over institutional prestige strata)." It has been estimated that about 90 percent of the research is done by less than 20 percent of the faculty. A study of faculty research productivity by Bourgeois (1967) at the University of Southwestern Louisiana found that 10 percent of the faculty did 90 percent of the research.

Measures of research can be grouped into quantitative, qualitative, peer judgment, and eminence (prestige) dimensions. Creswell's excellent summary (1985, p. 54) of how the research criteria listed by four authors fit into these four categories is shown in Table 4.

Several factors may be relevant to evaluating research and publications, such as the reputation of the publisher in a particular academic field, ratings by departmental colleagues, ratings by colleagues and recognized authorities in other institutions, ratings by department heads, the number and tenor of reviews, and the extent of citations. In addition, the individual faculty member may complete a self-evaluation form, answering questions such as: Are the goals of the project well-defined; are they realistic with respect to time and resources; which obstacles have been overcome, and how; have resources been adequate; are the institution and department receptive to the work; and has the research changed or modified the investigator's position or perspectives? Rating forms for both colleague and self-evaluation of research are included in Appendix A (pp. 178-179).

The extent and quality of research and publications tell something about one's zeal to communicate what one believes should be said, to share the results with colleagues elsewhere, and to keep options open for professional mobility. Beginning faculty members are hard pressed for time to do research and to publish, yet the longer they find reasons not to do it, the less likely it is to get done. Their long-term options for professional mobility are limited if they do not publish. This decision, of course, is their free choice, but one should have no illusions

Table 4. Measures of Research in Faculty Evaluation Studies.

Jauch and Glueck (1975)	Centra (1976); Seldin (1984)
	Quantitative Measures	
Number of papers, books, and technical reports published; number of papers presented at professional meetings	Publications in all professional journals; papers at professional meetings; books, sole or senior author; books, junior author or editor; monographs or chapters in books; grants or funding received; unpublished papers or reports
	Qualitative Measures	
Index of journal quality; citations to published materials; success rate of proposals for research support	Articles in quality journals; citations to published materials
	Peer Judgments	
Peer evaluations; self-evaluations	Peers at institution; peers at other institutions; self-evaluation; departmental chairs; deans
	Eminence Measures	
Referee or editor of scientific journal; recognition-honors and awards from profession; officer of national professional association; invited papers and guest lectures; number of dissertations supervised	Referee or editor of scientific journal; honors or awards from profession

Source: Creswell, 1985, p. 54.

about the possibility of appointments in research-oriented and land-grant universities if one does not publish. And in these institutions, academic advancement is determined more by a research and publication record than by any other single criterion.

In sum, scholarship is essential for every collegiate teacher. On this point there should be agreement. No such agreement exists, or should exist, on the categories of presentations, publications, and research. How these categories are used and how they are weighted depends substantially on the nature of the institution. Two-year colleges have a mission fundamentally different from that of research-oriented universities—not better or worse, but different; thus one would expect them to use different criteria for evaluating scholarship. Two-year colleges themselves differ widely in size and type. But in any case, systematic academic policies and procedures for evaluation that are tailored to the nature and circumstances of each institution are essential to making effective and fair academic personnel decisions.

Professional and Public Service

The passage of the Morrill Act, the founding of Cornell University, and the development of the Wisconsin Idea were nineteenth-century innovations that led universities toward commitment to public service. Postsecondary education's involvement in public service stems from two different sources. One is the deep tradition of service in American society. The traditional role of the university in providing leadership for this service is well established and accepted. It has been particularly critical in wartime, but it tends to languish somewhat at other times.

This passive peacetime role was strongly challenged by Walter Lippmann in a 1967 keynote address to the American Council on Education: "The thesis which I am putting to you is that the modern void, which results from the vast and intricate process of emancipation and rationalization, must be filled, and that the universities must fill it. This is high destiny. But it must be accepted and it must be realized" (p. 103). Clarion calls for enlightened public service by the higher education community have been sounded recently by Newman in *Higher Education and the American Resurgence* (1985), by Bok in *Beyond the Ivory Tower: Social Responsibilities of the Modern University* (1982), by Bowen in *The State of the Nation and the Agenda for Higher Education* (1982), and by Boyer and Hechinger in *Higher Learning in the Nation's Service* (1981). The latter authors wrote: "We believe higher education remains one of the best hopes for social progress and its leadership is urgently required" (p. 8).

Partnerships between business and postsecondary institutions are entering a period of heightened activity, stimulated by the nation's historical sense of service and the demands of the information revolution as well as by monetary rewards. The theme of the American Council on Education's 1985 conference was "Corporate/Campus Cooperation," and the *Chronicle of Higher Education* ran a three-part series on this theme (Jaschik, 1986a, 1986b, 1986c). Two-year colleges in particular see the industrial connection as a way to boost sagging enrollments. The need for the expertise of postsecondary personnel has never been greater, and it can be expected to grow.

Another reason for postsecondary education's involvement in public service was captured by Herbert Spencer's classic question: "What knowledge is of most worth?" The information revolution is forcing change on individuals and organizations. Radical reorganization of a given body of knowledge can be expected not once in a couple of decades but at intervals of five or ten years. Commenting upon this problem, R. B. Rogers wrote in 1985 that we are drowning in information and starving for knowledge. Expertise in higher education provides the best hope for finding ways to help society cope with the information explosion.

Professional Service

This refers to activities such as participating or holding office in professional associations and societies and to professional status as viewed as oneself and by others. The relative weights of various activities in this category are difficult to determine because little attention has been given to the matter in higher education literature. How does one weigh service as, for example, a newsletter editor for a state, regional, or national newsletter; an editor or reviewer for a professional journal; and an officer for a state or national professional association? Only a fine line may separate a narrow definition of professional service from the broader category of public service. In the interests of manageability, most institutions combine professional service and public service into one category for evaluation, although the use of two categories in initial considerations may enable clearer differentiation of the forms of service. Appendix A includes a rating form for professional service (p. 143).

Extramural proposals. Where does proposal writing fit into the academic reward system? For instance, a community college instructor writes a customized training program that requires much time, expertise, and thought; a professor in a research-oriented institution writes a "request for proposal" (RFP) for a federal program that also requires a great deal of effort. It would be difficult to say that one effort was per se more important than the other, but they are different. And is an excellent proposal that fails to receive funding rewarded differently from an average one that is funded? Generally speaking, success is rewarded over lack of success, but the effort involved in an unsuccessful attempt should not go unnoticed. Many extramural competitions are highly competitive, and in a few cases the contest is "wired," or the winner is predetermined in a clandestine way. It is not necessary to establish a form or mechanism for evaluating the quantity and quality of extramural proposals; the evaluative process can be handled informally at the chairperson's or dean's level. Work on extramural proposals needs to be recognized and evaluated, however, if only to avoid giving an impression of indifference that would in effect discourage persons from undertaking future efforts.

Public Service

What is public service? To begin with, it is not, according to the useful monograph by Elman and Smock (1985, p. 13), "work which fulfills one's 'civic duty', work for professional organizations, or work for committees within the academic institution." They define professional (public) service using these five categories: applied research, consultation and technical assistance, instruction, products, and clinical work or performance (p. 20).

Professional consultation—an important if controversial aspect of public service—can be expected to increase in the next several years. Patton and Marver (1979) reported that three out of five academics engage in some form of consulting; two of these three are paid. Finkelstein (1984, p. 127) wrote that although a significant segment of the professoriate derives significant supplementary income from consulting, "only about one out of five faculty members devotes more than a half day and only about one out of twenty faculty devotes more than one full day per week to consultation activities."

Are faculty members who consult shirking their responsibilities on campus? Boyer and Lewis (1985, p. v), in their excellent research summary, write: "The available evidence clearly suggests that those faculty who do consult are, on average, at least as active in their other faculty roles as their peers who do not consult. Faculty who consult, compared to their peers who do not, teach as many courses and devote as much of their professional time to teaching and research, pay more attention to issues of national importance, publish more, subscribe to more professional journals, are more satisfied with their careers and their institutions, and are at least as active in departmental and institutional governance."

How often should consulting be expected or allowed? It depends on the academic area as well as on the institution, but one day per week is the accepted rule of thumb. Some colleges and universities have set up rather elaborate rules to regulate the time that faculty members can spend on these activities. The amount of time and energy that administrators put into developing such policies may be counterproductive if faculty members believe that the administration is motivated primarily by the view that faculty members are cheating the institution out of its fair portion of their time. Administrators would be better advised to take advantage of the enthusiasm and knowledge gained from professional consultation than to seek ways to catch the very small percentage of faculty members who may be giving too much time to consultation.

Differences of opinion exist about whether paid consulting should be included in one's reporting of service. One point of view contends that only unremunerated consulting should count. This position, however, overlooks the value of consulting to the professor. It implies that monetary rewards are inferior to nonmonetary values, and it thus invites the question:

"Is a token honorarium a lesser evil than a large one?" Most postsecondary institutions allow paid consultations to be included among forms of public service.

Evaluating public service often is done without systematic attention, if it is done at all. Centra's survey (1979, p. 133) found that only 2 percent of the department heads surveyed considered public service to be a critical factor in evaluating faculty members, while one-third said it was not a factor at all. Most said that it was a minor factor. Seldin (1984, p. 43) found greater support for public service in approximately one hundred public liberal arts colleges that were asked to rate public service as one of thirteen factors to be considered in evaluating overall faculty performance. In 1973, public service was rated as the sixth most important major factor (28 percent) and in 1983 it was rated seventh (35 percent).

When public service is a criterion in evaluating faculty performance, we have very little evidence on how to use it. The study by Gustad (1961, pp. 14–15) sought out the data that were collected for evaluating public service; the results are shown in Table 5. In analyzing the responses, Gustad notes that "the ubiquitous faculty resume is high on the list; that is, the faculty members tell someone, usually the chairman or dean, what they have been doing. This presumably is about as informative as a publications list. From it, one knows that the faculty member is not entirely cloistered and that someone is presumably interested enough in him to invite (or permit) him to venture into the market place" (p. 15). There is little evidence that attitudes or practices have changed much since Gustad's study. Appendix A contains a rating form for public service (p. 177).

In evaluation of public service, Elman and Smock (1985, pp. 22, 43) write, the service "must be of the same quality as that expected in teaching and basic research. Furthermore, the structural mechanism for evaluating the level of quality must be the same as, or at the very least, compatible with the mechanisms for evaluating teaching and research. . . . They are documentation, evaluation (who evaluates and what criteria are

Table 5. Data Collected for Evaluating Public Service.

Source	Types of Institutions, by Percentages						
	Liberal Arts Colleges	Private Universities	State Universities	State Colleges	Teachers Colleges	Junior Colleges	Technical Professional Colleges
Faculty résumé	30	37	67	42	48	36	34
Faculty committee	0	4	3	2	7	0	3
Chairman evaluation	10	21	20	4	17	4	13
Dean evaluation	10	10	23	6	10	0	11
Public reaction	5	9	3	10	4	0	3
Public relations office	18	6	13	18	7	24	11
Nature of the organization	0	2	3	0	4	0	3
General knowledge	18	9	10	12	7	12	0
Other	0	6	3	6	7	0	0

Source: Gustad, 1961, p. 15.

used) and the application of relative weights." For reasons mentioned earlier, public service will become more important in the years immediately ahead. It may be advisable, therefore, for postsecondary administrators and others to review their approaches to this activity.

Five

Assessing Other
Important Aspects
of Professional Effectiveness

The evaluative criteria discussed in this chapter are advising, classroom visitation, faculty service and relations, professional growth, self-evaluation, and teaching materials and procedures. Almost all systems for evaluating faculty performance include one or more of these criteria along with teaching, scholarship, and service, although their use may be obscured or included under a larger heading.

Advising

The Study Group on the Conditions of Excellence in American Higher Education stated in their publication *Involvement in Learning* (1984, p. 31) that "advisement is one of the weakest links in the education of college students. Many faculty members do not participate in advisement, and those who do often treat this responsibility perfunctorily." In a similar vein, Alexander Astin (1985, p. 165) wrote: "Academic advising seems to be one of the weakest areas in the entire range of student services." These statements are consistent with the findings of a study conducted jointly by the National Center for Higher Education Management Systems (NCHEMS) and the American College Testing Program (ACT), which surveyed 947 colleges and universities on student retention and attrition (Beal and Noel, 1980, p. 43). Table 6 summarizes part of this important study. Among the seventeen negative campus characteristics linked to

Table 6. Negative Campus Characteristics by Type of Institution (in Average Ratings).

	2-Year Public	2-Year Private	4-Year Public	4-Year Private	Total
N =	294	55	221	377	947
Inadequate academic advising	2.93	2.33	3.58	2.93	3.03
Inadequate curricular offerings	2.69	2.60	2.91	2.91	2.81
Conflict between class/job	3.82	2.13	2.86	2.05	2.80
Inadequate financial aid	2.37	2.49	2.61	2.99	2.63
Inadequate extracurricular programs	2.49	2.88	2.34	2.58	2.61
Inadequate counseling-support system	2.56	2.29	2.76	2.82	2.59
Inadequate academic-support services	2.40	2.14	2.80	2.53	2.52
Inadequate cultural/social growth	2.40	2.13	2.52	2.63	2.51
Inadequate career-planning services	2.59	2.19	2.73	2.36	2.49
Inadequate student-faculty contact	2.37	1.61	2.97	2.06	2.33
Insufficient intellectual challenge	2.29	2.06	2.40	2.29	2.30
Inadequate part-time employment	2.38	2.10	2.45	2.12	2.27
Lack of faculty care and concern	2.29	1.59	2.86	2.00	2.26
Unsatisfactory living accommodations	2.01	2.28	2.25	2.41	2.25
Low quality of teaching	2.20	2.00	2.44	2.12	2.21
Lack of staff care and concern	2.23	1.71	2.51	2.07	2.20
Restrictive rules and regulations	1.35	2.62	1.58	2.09	1.78

Note: Ratings are on a scale of one (low) to five (high).

Source: Beal and Noel, 1980, p. 43.

attrition, inadequate academic advising was the most important. High quality of advising was ranked fifth in importance in another table of positive contributors to student retention. The importance of good academic advising is well established, and some institutions, particularly the small and medium-sized ones, have made a good deal of progress in this area.

Two relatively new kinds of students are placing additional burdens on college advising. One is the adult part-time student. These students require as much or more advising time than full-time residential students, and their advisers often need to have a broader knowledge of the institution. Planning and working out individualized programs for part-timers is more complicated and adapting schedules and programs to adult learners is more difficult.

The second kind of student is described by such terms as *disadvantaged, culturally deprived, underprepared,* and *high-risk.* Cross (1981) describes these students as white sons and daughters of blue-collar workers, although a significant number are from ethnic minorities. These new students are unlikely to find rewards for good performance within the school system. They do not seek intellectual stimulation from their classes, nor do they expect to discover the joy of learning; they just hope to survive and to protect themselves against obvious failure. They learn job-related material well because it is usually concrete and its usefulness is apparent.

The problem of adequate student advising is quite evident at large public universities, where few, if any, brownie points are given to professors for taking the time necessary for constructive, informed advising. Commenting on this issue, Paul Dressel (n.d.) wrote that "academic advising suffers at the undergraduate level because few of our faculty in the present day have any conception of what undergraduate education is all about. The horizon of each professor is limited by the barriers thrust up around the disciplines, and the large number of courses piled helter-skelter inside these barriers impedes discussion and understanding of the curriculum offerings even within the discipline. . . . If faculty members are to accept academic advising as a really important function, they are going to have to spend time on it, and administrative officials are going to have to recognize that time is necessary."

Effective general academic advising requires a good comprehension of general education, a knowledge of the institution's policies and procedures as well as those of the department and college, a knowledge of career patterns, and an interest in advising. And advisers need to recognize the human tendency to favor their own subjects. As Solmon, Bisconti, and Ochsner (1977, p. 165) pointed out: "The danger for a professor of classical literature if he recommends that his students sample psychology or business is that the students might decide that psychology or business is either more interesting or more marketable than classics. The classics professor could lose a student rather than gain a student who knows classics but has broader skills."

The Study Group on the Conditions of Excellence in American Higher Education (1984) suggests these practices to make guidance and advising more effective:

- Using academic administrators to serve as advisers. Each academic administrator, from department chairs on up, should advise a few students. . . . It provides administrators with very direct means of finding out what is happening to students.
- Using the telephone to check in and talk with student advisees. The personal office visit is not the only way to cover the territory.
- Providing short but intensive training periods or workshops for advisers.
- Assuring continuity and focus. While some students will seek advice from many sources, having one individual who follows the student through the college career works better than having three who are responsible for advising at different points in the college career [1984, pp. 31-32].

Helping students analyze their career interests is an important dimension of the advising and counseling function. Yet how many advisers keep abreast of occupational trends? Gilford's classic research (1975, pp. 424-425) developed information on the postsecondary plans of sixteen thousand high school seniors in the spring of 1972. He found that 45 percent wanted to go into professional work; yet in 1970 only 14 percent of the labor force was in the professional and technical occupations, and the projection for 1980 was only 16 percent. In other words, there was a considerable mismatch between student aspirations and employment opportunities. Such a discrepancy can create genuine problems for students and counselors in high school and college. The excessive amount of floundering that accompanies choosing a career field suggests that current postsecondary advising and counseling programs should be evaluated more frequently and more rigorously than often is the case.

Colleges and universities determine academic advisee load and assign advisees to faculty members in a variety of ways. Each institution might begin by examining the extent of its commitment to the advising and counseling program; organizational and advising procedures will follow from basic philosophical and policy commitments. How academic advising and personal counseling are provided depends on a number of factors that should be determined by each institution or unit. Student input is important; Appendix A includes a form for obtaining a student perspective (pp. 161-162).

Evaluating advising and counseling effectiveness also can be facilitated by raising a series of questions: (1) To what extent are academic advisers informed and up to date about academic programs, procedures, and requirements? New advisers must be adequately informed and veteran advisers must be updated; and the institution should have an updated handbook for advisers. (2) Are advisers accessible, and what procedures for arranging appointments are most effective? (3) How does an institution identify those who are most interested in advising and those who are most effective at it, and should an instructor with little interest or ability nonetheless have an advising load? (4) How does an institution provide every student with access to at least one faculty member with whom problems and concerns can be discussed? (5) What recognition is given to the time and expertise required for effective advising?

Classroom Visitation

Classroom visitations allow teachers to see themselves through the eyes of colleagues. The experience, while inherently threatening, can provide insights that may escape other types of classroom teaching feedback. Classroom visitations usually serve either formative or summative purposes, although some combination is possible.

For formative purposes: Menges (1986, p. 5) concluded that the "effectiveness of colleagues as consultants in the teaching improvement process has yet to be validated experimentally in terms of student outcomes. As far as faculty participants are concerned, however, findings are clear. Participants report high satisfaction, increased motivation, renewed interest in teaching, and increased interaction with other faculty members." To be most effective, the process should be mutual, open, and relatively unthreatening and should end with a structured critique by the observers. Too often, the final step is approached casually. Such spontaneity has merit, but some structure is needed to lessen misunderstandings while the intricacies of teaching and learning are delved into.

The secondary school literature on classroom observation is more fully developed than the postsecondary literature. McGreal (1983, p. 97) has suggested four tenets for either formative or summative observational evaluation of classroom teaching:

1. The reliability and usefulness of classroom observation are directly related to the amount and type of information supervisors have *prior* to the observation.
2. The narrower the focus supervisors use in observing classrooms, the more able they will be to describe accurately the events related to that focus.
3. The impact of observational data on supervisor-teacher relationships and on the teacher's willingness to fully participate in an instructional improvement activity is directly related to the way the data are recorded during observation.
4. The impact of observational data on supervisor-teacher re-

lationships and on the teacher's willingness to fully participate in an instructional improvement activity is directly related to the way feedback is presented to the teacher.

For summative purposes: The use of data from classroom
observations requires more attention when the results will be
used in making academic personnel decisions. Some people
question the validity of these data, contending that results from
classroom observations are highly suspect. Little research exists
on the validity and reliability of class visitations. Centra (1979,
p. 75) reported that colleague ratings are not statistically reliable; the average correlation among ratings by different colleagues was about .26 for each item used in his research. Centra's study also reported that colleague ratings of an instructor
were more favorable than ratings by students.

Some research is available on the relation of peer review
to the process of making academic promotion and tenure decisions. While this process usually does not include classroom visitation, the fact that both involve comparisons among raters provides some degree of commonality. Bergman's extensive research
summary of peer rating (1980, p. 19) concluded "that until
peer rating systems are developed that are reliable and valid,
their use should be strictly supplementary, or on an experimental basis." While the cautionary note sounded by Bergman and
others should be heard, carefully planned classroom visitations
can be helpful in appraising classroom teaching performance.

The process used for the visitation is the key to an effective evaluation. The following procedure combines successful
practices found in small liberal arts colleges. The visiting team
should consist of at least two persons—one a colleague in the
teacher's own discipline or (in the case of a small college) a related field, the other a respected, tenured faculty member from
another discipline. Three team members would be better than
two, but the additional time this would require makes it imprac-
tical in most situations. Members of the team should be selected
by the dean, in consultation with the department chairperson
and the teacher to be observed. Planning for the visitation
should include conversations with the teacher to be visited, and

the visitation date should be set principally by the teacher. It is likely that he or she will choose a strong topic for the chosen day, naturally wishing to be judged on his or her strengths. An unannounced visit is highly questionable for several reasons, including the possibility of observing a dull review session or a quiz, but more from the negative psychological connotations that it conveys.

The teacher to be observed should submit, at least one day in advance, an outline for the class period and any other appropriate materials. An observer rating form, such as the one included in Appendix A, may be useful (p. 166). A standard rating form makes comparing data easier and permits a more systematic and objective consideration of teaching variables than a more informal approach might allow. A structured critique between the teacher and the observers should take place in a quiet and private environment no more than five days after the classroom visit. The discussion should include the observations and conclusions of the visiting team and provide the teacher with an opportunity to respond. A final report should be filed with the dean, the department head, and the teacher, who should have an opportunity to respond in writing.

Braskamp, Brandenburg, and Ory (1984, p. 66) state that "at least three or four classroom observations for a given class over a single semester are needed to ensure adequate representation. An observation is suspect if only one classroom visit is made." This recommendation creates a dilemma: while one visit may not be enough, the amount of time required for three or four visits usually is not practical.

The national use of classroom visitation systems has not increased as rapidly as some predicted it would a few years ago. The process is so subjective that some people mistrust it. It can easily become overly bureaucratic and it can lose credibility if misused by a few individuals who have a personal ax to grind. If any system is to remain credible it should be easy to manage; it should have established procedures, specified uses, and outcomes spelled out in some detail; and it should be operated with common sense as well as with carefully crafted guidelines.

Faculty Service and Relations

The academic community is a very human one, and it probably is neither more nor less controlled by human feelings than the business or governmental communities. Gustad (1961, p. 9) found that personal attributes were the third most influential factor in faculty evaluation (see Table 7). Second in importance was the category labeled "other," which deals with factors such as cooperation, loyalty, Christian character, and compatibility—all of which could have been included under personal attributes. If the "other" category is combined with that of personal attributes, the combined category becomes the most important factor after classroom teaching. There is little reason to believe that a 1987 study would produce findings significantly different from Gustad's.

Seldin (1984, p. 72) asked the liberal arts deans of private and public colleges to indicate the importance of nine factors that are considered in evaluating college service; his results are shown in Table 8. Seldin (p. 73) found minimal change during the 1978–1983 period in the influence that academic deans accorded these factors. Service on college-wide committees and academic advising are cited by more academic deans than any other factor; service on departmental committees and departmental administrative duties are important considerations. Liberal arts colleges give the least weight to willingness to teach undesirable courses and to do service as student recruiters. Student advising and nonacademic student counseling receive greater recognition at private colleges than at public institutions. Participation in campus symposia has become more important, especially at public colleges.

Considering the de facto importance of faculty relations and, to a lesser extent, faculty service in academic personnel evaluation, one wonders why more institutions do not have some written criteria for making judgments about them. The courts will respect the use of such criteria if they are part of the written statement of academic policies and procedures. A rating scale for this category might include questions on acceptance

Table 7. Factors Considered in Evaluating Faculty Members.

Type of of Institution

Factor	Liberal Arts Colleges		Private Universities		State Universities		State Colleges		Teachers Colleges		Junior Colleges		Professional and Technical Colleges		Total	
	Mean	Rank	Mean	Rank	Mean	Rank	Mean	Rank	Mean	Rank	Mean	Rank	Mean	Rank	Mean	Rank
Classroom teaching	2.97	1	2.96	1	2.91	1.0	3.00	1.5	2.97	2.0	3.00	1	2.95	1	2.97	1
Supervision of graduate study	.94	13	1.70	10	2.35	5.0	1.42	11.0	1.42	11.0	.13	14	1.55	11	1.36	11
Supervision of honors	1.14	12	1.25	13	1.35	12.0	.90	14.0	.86	14.0	.57	12	.61	14	.95	14
Research	2.02	8	2.53	3	2.82	2.0	1.95	8.5	1.66	10.0	.78	10	2.31	3	2.02	5
Publication	2.08	6	2.41	4	2.70	4.0	1.95	8.5	1.76	8.5	.96	9	2.21	5	2.01	6
Public service	1.72	10	1.54	11	1.77	9.5	1.79	10.0	1.79	7.0	1.61	8	1.68	10	1.70	10
Consultation	.93	14	1.22	14	1.31	13.5	1.22	12.0	1.24	12.0	.52	13	1.37	12	1.12	12
Professional society activity	2.00	9	1.88	7	1.86	7.5	2.04	6.0	1.83	6.0	1.65	7	1.92	7	1.88	8
Student advising	2.40	4	2.21	5	1.86	7.5	2.37	4.0	2.14	4.0	2.52	4	1.95	6	2.21	4
Committee work	2.03	7	1.87	8	1.77	9.5	2.14	5.0	1.93	5.0	2.09	5	1.84	8	1.95	7
Length of service in rank	2.17	5	1.82	9	1.45	11.0	1.98	7.0	1.76	8.5	1.78	6	1.76	9	1.82	9
Competing offers	1.19	11	1.35	12	1.31	13.5	1.03	13.0	.93	13.0	.70	11	1.08	13	1.08	13
Personal attributes	2.49	3	2.15	6	1.98	6.0	2.49	3.0	2.28	3.0	2.61	3	2.29	4	2.33	3
Other	2.91	2	2.57	2	2.86	3.0	3.00	1.5	3.00	1.0	2.86	2	2.88	2	2.87	2
Total Mean	1.93		1.96		2.02		1.95		1.83		1.56		1.89		1.88	
Total Variance	4.13		4.11		4.44		4.19		3.71		3.27		3.93		3.87	

Source: Gustad, 1961, p. 9.

Table 8. Relative Weight Assigned to Factors Considered in
Evaluating College Service Performance in Liberal Arts Colleges, 1983.

Factors	Private Colleges (N = 515)		Public Colleges (N = 96)	
	Major Factor %	Not a Factor %	Major Factor %	Not a Factor %
Service on department committee	46.2	4.3	55.2	1.0
Service on collegewide committee	82.9	0.6	84.4	0.0
Academic advising	80.2	1.2	59.4	6.3
Nonacademic student counseling	21.2	14.2	8.3	35.4
Willingness to teach undesirable courses	16.9	23.3	11.5	31.3
Adviser to student organizations	21.2	9.5	18.8	12.5
Service as student recruiter	12.8	20.0	7.3	31.3
Departmental administrative duties	45.6	5.4	43.8	6.3
Participation in campus symposia	25.0	11.7	29.2	10.4

Source: Seldin, 1984, p. 72.

of college assignments (does the faculty member accept college
assignments willingly and volunteer occasionally?), performance
of college assignments (how effective is the faculty member in
carrying out college assignments?), cooperation with colleagues
and others and assistance with their problems (is the faculty
member a good team player?), and professional behavior as it
relates to professional activities and the goal and nature of the
institution (does the faculty member act responsibly?). Appendix A includes a rating form for appraising faculty service and
relations (p. 168).

Professional Growth

Bowen and Schuster (1986, p. 23) remind us that "learning is the chief stock-in-trade of the professoriate. It occurs in
all fields, it takes place in diverse settings, and it serves varied
clienteles." Professional growth may be defined as an attitude
toward self, others, and work that looks toward improvement—
toward becoming. It is difficult to measure professional growth,
but there is general agreement that it is essential for the best
professional performance.

In their survey of 372 faculty members, Eble and McKeachie (1985, p. 165) found that "having too much to do" was the most prominent concern, listed by 66 percent. This concern should not be surprising; faculty members work the most hours of any of the twenty-three occupations studied by Caplan and others (1980). Other concerns found in the Eble and McKeachie study were conflicts between teaching, scholarship, and service responsibilities (54 percent), salary (53 percent), lack of administrative support (32 percent), job insecurity (19 percent), lack of independence (10 percent), and monotony (10 percent).

Some confusion may exist about similarities and differences between faculty development and professional growth because the two concepts and activities are closely related. In his study of faculty development activities at over one thousand institutions, Centra (1976a, p. 47) used six groups of faculty development practices: emphasis on assessment, grants and travel funds, instructional assistance, publicity activities, traditional teaching practices, and workshops and seminars. These activities received the highest ratings:

1. Specialists assisting individual faculty in instructional or course development by consulting on course objectives and course design 75%
2. Specialists helping to develop teaching skills such as teaching or leading discussions, or encouraging the use of different teaching-learning strategies such as individualized instruction 70%
3. Specialists assisting faculty in constructing tests or evaluating student performance 69%
4. Assistance to faculty in using instructional technology as a teaching aid (such as programmed learning or computer-assisted instruction) 65%
5. Workshops, seminars, or programs for acquainting faculty with the goals of the institution and the types of students enrolled 65%
6. "Master teachers" or senior faculty working closely with new or apprentice teachers 61%

7. Faculty with expertise consulting with other
    faculty on teaching or course improvement 60%
8. Visiting scholars program bringing people to the
    campus for short or long periods 58%
9. Specialists on campus assisting faculty in the
    use of audiovisual aids in instruction, including
    closed-circuit television 58%
10. Workshops or program for helping faculty im-
    prove their academic advising and counseling
    skills. 57%
11. Periodic reviewing of the performance of all fac-
    ulty members, whether tenured or not. 55%

This ranking provides a useful national picture, although a replication in 1987 might find less attention given to the use of technological aids and more to assessment and workshops.

     Eble and McKeachie (1985, p. 14) place professional
growth under the umbrella of faculty development (improvement) in this manner: "The most extensive activities within faculty development programs are those in support of individual
faculty members' professional growth. Grants, fellowships, or
leaves (including sabbatical leaves) are typically intended to enable faculty members to carry out research or scholarly activities that will enhance competence in their disciplines. While not
excluding such direct assistance of research and scholarship
from faculty development, many programs emphasize kinds of
professional development that seem likely to have a positive impact on teaching. That emphasis has not drawn a sharp line between scholarly development and increased teaching competence. But it has stressed that professional growth involves an
enlargement of teaching capacity fully as much as improving research productivity."

     Appendix A contains a rating form that may be used to
appraise professional growth (p. 172). It can be used for self-
analysis as well as for the annual academic performance review
(AAPR) of each faculty member by the chairperson. The form
inquires about participation in content seminars and workshops,
participation in pedagogical seminars and workshops, personal

projects and efforts to enhance scholarship, personal projects and efforts to enhance teaching and advising, and professional journal subscriptions.

Self-Evaluation

Self-evaluation for professional improvement differs from self-evaluation as input into personnel decisions about oneself. Research on self-evaluation for either professional improvement or personnel decisions is spotty in quality and short in quantity. An early study by Webb and Nolan (1955, p. 45), reporting on the results of supervisor ratings, student ratings, and self-ratings at the Jacksonville Naval Air Technical Training School, found a high correlation of .62 between student ratings and instructor self-ratings. However, the supervisor's ratings showed no significant correlation with any of the other measures, which were intelligence, level of schooling, teaching experience, and desire to teach.

Studies in academe by Doyle and Crichton (1978, p. 824) compared the self-ratings of fourteen teaching assistants in an introductory communications course with their student's ratings and ratings by colleagues. They found that these three groups "gave ratings that were fairly similar in mean, range, distribution, and skew." Marsh, Overall, and Kesler (1979, p. 154) found a correlation of .49 for fifty-one social science teachers and their students. Centra (1979, pp. 48–49) reported a modest correlation of .21 between self-ratings by 343 teaching faculty from five colleges and their students' ratings, but when he calculated the item mean responses for students and faculty the correlation jumped to .77, indicating that both groups tend to see the same relative strengths and weaknesses among teachers.

Blackburn and Clark (1975, pp. 249–250) compared forty-five instructors' self-ratings with ratings by colleagues and students, finding that "colleague judgments about teaching performance are positively related to their judgments about the overall contribution of a faculty member. Professor and student judgment about teaching performance are in substantial agreement." Research findings support some confidence in the positive correlation between student ratings and teacher self-ratings, but more extensive reliance upon self-ratings as indicators of classroom teaching performance is highly questionable.

Self-evaluation for teaching improvement is something that effective teachers do informally after every class, asking themselves quickly, almost subconsciously, such questions as: How well did the class go? Did I cover what I had planned? Did the students understand a complicated concept? What do I need to review during the next class that did not seem to be understood today? How did so-and-so behave (referring to a problem student or two)? Did anything new develop—any surprises? Was there an acceptable level of interest? Was I "on my toes"? If not, why not?

Audio and video recordings can be used to help one see the teaching act as others see it. Care needs to be taken, however, that teachers enter into the video recording process voluntarily, because this approach is not for everyone. A teacher who has some fears about the process may be adversely affected by the experience. Also, we know that some studies lend themselves more readily to effective video recording than others. For example, it is more difficult to develop useful videotapes of teaching in art classes than in chemistry classes. The teaching of art often includes some "dead spaces," moments when silence allows the student to ponder over a painting or a piece of sculpture, or when the camera needs to focus on both the piece being studied and the student who is talking. Lectures in the sciences often use experiments and models that are set up in the front of the room and are explained by the teacher. Since the model is the primary focus of attention and most of the talking is done by the teacher, the film is usually more straightforward and keeps a steady pace and continuity; it therefore usually comes across more clearly on tape.

Giving students a rating form at the end of the first two weeks of classes is another useful approach to teacher self-evaluation. These forms, for the instructor's eyes only, may point out something that has missed the instructor. For example, the teacher may be moving too rapidly through the material or may not have made the course expectations, including evaluation procedures, sufficiently clear. Sometimes the instructor will use the same rating form as the students and score it while the students score theirs. Items rated lower by the students than by the teacher are likely to receive further consideration, possibly resulting in some teaching improvement.

Self-evaluation for personnel decisions is a standard procedure used by almost all colleges and universities, and the forms are often known by some nickname such as the "rainbow sheets" or the "brag sheets." The role of self-evaluation in academic personnel decisions depends on how effectively the files are presented and the extent to which the candidate is able to project a positive image without boasting.

Teaching Materials and Procedures

This category includes materials that the teacher distributes to the class, such as course outlines, reading assignments, and examinations. The quality of student papers written for the course also may be considered. Some postsecondary institutions require an outline for every course; the outline is then made available in the departmental office or library. This procedure can be helpful to students and it may slightly reduce the casualness of some professors' outlines.

Based in part on an excellent summary by Braskamp, Brandenburg, and Ory (1984, pp. 110-111), the following list of items might be considered in evaluating teaching materials and procedures.

Course Organization

1. The course objectives are congruent with the department curricula.
2. The course objectives are clearly stated.
3. The syllabus adequately outlines the sequence of topics to be covered.
4. The intellectual level of the course is appropriate for the enrolled students.
5. Time given to the various major course topics is appropriate.
6. The course is an adequate prerequisite for other courses.

7. Written course requirements, including attendance policies, are included in the course syllabus.

Course Content

1. The required- or recommended-reading list is up to date and includes works of recognized authorities.
2. Readings are appropriate for the level of the course.
3. The texts used in the course have been well selected.
4. A variety of assignments is available to meet individual needs.
5. Laboratory work, if a part of the course, is integrated into the course.
6. The assignments are intellectually challenging to the students.

Course Evaluation

1. The standards used for grading are communicated to the students in the course syllabus.
2. The written assignments and projects are chosen to reflect course goals.
3. The examination content is representative of the course content and objectives.
4. The examination questions are clearly written.
5. The examinations and papers are graded fairly.
6. The grade distribution is appropriate to the level of the course and the type of student enrolled.
7. The examinations and papers are returned to the students in a timely fashion.
8. Students are given ample time to complete the assignments and take-home examinations.
9. The amount of homework and assignments is appropriate to the course level and to the number of credit hours for the course.

Appendix A includes a rating form for teaching materials and procedures (p. 183).

Although the category of teaching materials and procedures is not usually included in teaching appraisals, at least not in a formal manner, it can be a useful addition. The departmental chairperson or an established departmental committee might logically be responsible for appraising this category.

Chapters Three, Four, and Five discussed nine criteria that cover the range of alternatives that might be used in evaluating faculty performance; Chapter Five focused on some criteria that are not used as frequently as teaching, scholarship, and service. Herein may be a dilemma for some institutions. Faculty service and relations, for example, often are not included in promotion and tenure decisions, yet the research that is available as well as experiential evidence indicates that this category is second in importance only to teaching and scholarship. Would not institutions who place this criterion in a catchall category, such as service, want to study whether this practice causes distressful uncertainty among young faculty members, or even leaves the system vulnerable to legal action? The less frequently used criteria in Chapter Five may be useful as a checklist as colleges and universities undertake studies of their faculty evaluation systems.

Six

Understanding Purposes
and Procedures
of Academic Promotion
and Tenure

The most important decisions that are made by postsecondary institutions are people decisions. This very simple truth is not unique to education; it holds for all fields of organized endeavor. In an age of sophisticated high-tech hardware and software, it is easy to depend more and more upon computerized data until, without realizing it, we are letting the data make the human decisions. A dramatic example of this seductive tendency was described in *Business Week*'s September 19, 1983, cover story on Texas Instrument's $119 million loss. Strategic planner Lockerd said: "We had the tendency to substitute mechanics for thought" ("After the $119 Million Loss," 1983, p. 68).

Purposes

What are the purposes of the promotion and tenure processes? Many institutions have given little attention to basic purposes while acknowledging in very general terms the crucial importance of these decisions to the long-term growth and quality of the institution. A major reason lies in the tendency of an institution to focus on the tangible procedures for promotion and tenure rather than on the more nebulous concept of purposes. A statement of purpose can provide the context or framework for detailed policies and procedures. Individual institutions might benefit from examining their statements of purpose, using the following purposes as guidelines.

1. *Academic promotion and tenure decisions should assure students of sound teaching and learning opportunities by providing the most competent professionals.* This statement places students at the center of the educational process. Postsecondary institutions have improved their student services over the past decade, their innovations and creativity stimulated significantly by economics, but the golden age of the student, as suggested in the Carnegie Council on Policy Studies in Higher Education's report on *Three Thousand Futures* (1980, p. 53), has not yet come to pass. This first purpose provides a perspective which places students first among goals.

2. *The promotion and tenure process should provide a developmental period for new faculty members.* New faculty members have a hectic existence. Fresh from the Ph.D. struggles, they now must move into a new community and start in a new professional environment that has folkways, procedures, and expectations that may be quite different from what they are used to. And usually they are expected to turn their dissertations into an article or two. To complicate their lives further, they often are assigned the largest classes, in the least desirable rooms, and at the most unwanted hours. During this developmental period, they are scrutinized, usually obliquely but nonetheless intensely, by senior faculty members. The unfortunate part of this scrutiny in too many cases is the lack of direct and systematic professional feedback along the way, a lack that sometimes leaves the institution vulnerable to legal action.

The developmental period provides at least seven years of opportunity for professional improvement. If all goes well, professional work habits and motivation to improve will be enhanced during this period and will be maintained throughout the teacher's career. Little evidence exists, however, to confirm or deny this expectation. Research by Centra (1979, p. 124) indicates that the number of publications in the natural sciences peaks after about six years of teaching; in the social sciences and the humanities the curve of production is much more level, peaking between thirteen and twenty years.

3. *The promotion and tenure process should provide a time of mutual exploration for those who transfer professional experience from other institutions.* Faculty members accept new appointments with high expectations that are shared by the recruiting institution, which has spent several months and some money in the process. Newly hired faculty quickly focus on institutional promotion and tenure expectations in a way that was not possible during the campus visitation and interview process. Becoming familiar with institutional processes and procedures (along with the chairperson's assistance) provides critical guidance for new instructors; at the same time, colleagues and the administration have a basis on which to appraise the instructor's performance.

4. *The process should help the institution to choose the people who are best suited to its nature and directions.* Market realities enter into promotion and tenure decisions, and the dilemmas involved in these decisions have been discussed earlier. It will suffice to repeat here that this dilemma will continue to plague sensitive and dynamic administrators who need to guide the institution in the direction of powerful forces that are sometimes beyond their control, yet want to maintain a balance between the sciences and business on the one hand and the fine arts and humanities on the other.

The promotion and tenure processes allow the institution to encourage people who are compatible with its nature and directions. Some denominational institutions, for example, require prospective faculty members to sign an oath of allegiance or expectations before signing a contract. Smaller liberal arts colleges generally have an unspoken set of expectations that significantly affect new faculty members. However, these expectations are usually in the minds of senior professors rather than in written form. They may relate to life-style as well as to matters such as advising, collegiality, and professional emphasis.

The balance between research and teaching also affects the compatibility of the individual and the institution. It is not uncommon to read of court cases involving professors in research oriented universities who overtly placed teaching significantly above research. Institutions have the right to select faculty according to a written standard or general institutional expectations. If these standards have been consistently and equitably applied, court rulings usually have supported institutional positions.

5. *Promotion and tenure policies and procedures should strengthen the academic component of the institution.* Colleges and universities are judged substantially by academic achievement, notwithstanding those institutions with successful athletic teams; the academic personnel procedures are crucial to maintaining and improving quality. In its *Revised Report . . .* (1985, p. 2) on academic personnel policies and procedures, Vanderbilt University stated that "building institutional excellence requires the development of a strategy for faculty appointments. Each new appointment and tenure decision should serve as a building block toward demonstrably achieving the goal of faculty excellence."

Comparing Promotion and Tenure Criteria

The same criteria generally are used for promotion and for tenure. In CUPA's extensive promotion and tenure study of institutions in the four basic Carnegie institutional classifications (1980b, p. 25), it was found that 80 percent use "criteria for tenure decisions that are generally the same as those used for promotion. The remaining 20 percent of institutions establish some criteria—such as enrollment projections and tenure density—that are uniquely used in the tenure decision-making process."

Using common criteria, however, should not lead us to ignore important differences. Promotion criteria focus more on the *merit* of the instructor's professional and scholarly contributions and promise; the criteria for tenure decisions focus more on the long-term *worth* of the instructor to the institution. Certainly there is some overlapping between merit and worth. Lincoln (1983, p. 225) advocated judging merit and worth separately—the former by faculty committees and the latter by administrative ones. This separation is useful up to a point, but faculty members who serve on faculty committees usually make decisions on both merit and value in reviewing the entire array of professional activities that are included in colleagues' vitae. Administrative decisions, particularly at the level of the chief academic officer, also review both merit and worth, and the economic health of the institution may change the priority of these criteria. For example, in difficult economic times, younger professors in academic areas with high tenure rates may be less likely to receive tenure.

While both merit and worth are important, the past ten years have seen a somewhat greater emphasis on worth. Economic constraints and the need for a sharper focus on institutional missions and goals have been prime forces behind this subtle shift in emphasis. Administrators are sensitive to the delicacy of the balance. If merit is given too little importance, faculty quality may suffer; if worth is insufficiently considered, desired institutional directions may be difficult to sustain. It is not easy to discern the most likely tilt in the next ten years. Institutions may give more weight to self-interest, depending on their health and sense of direction. And because worth is favored in times of national economic stress, the national economy can be expected to have a significant influence.

Promotion

Promotion differs from tenure in one important way. Tenure is a one-time-only opportunity, while instructors can be considered for promotion more than once in most academic ranks. In larger institutions, it is not uncommon to find senior associate professors with tenure who have not been advanced to the rank of professor because of inadequate scholarship.

Clearly stated criteria for promotion assist both applicants and committees. Most institutions prefer fairly simple criteria with wording that is specific but not restrictive. The following criteria are based on those used successfully at several institutions.

Instructor: Possesses Ph.D. or equivalent or is well along in work toward the terminal degree. Some teaching experience is expected. Three to four years in rank are customary before promotion.

Assistant professor: Possesses Ph.D. or equivalent or has completed all degree work except the dissertation. Completion is expected within an agreed-upon time. The clock starts running in the countdown to promotion and to tenure. Promotion usually requires three or four years in rank. The candidate should be establishing a reputation for teaching, research, and service. Some research or scholarly endeavors should be published or well under way.

Associate professor: Possesses Ph.D. or equivalent and several scholarly endeavors, including publications and research, that are considered excellent by peers and others. Teaching and advising and professional service to the institution and the profession should also be judged excellent. (The balance among teaching, research, and service depends on the nature of the institution.) Three or four years in rank are customary.

Professor: Possesses Ph.D. or equivalent, and the candidate should be considered outstanding in two of the three areas of teaching, research, and service. Several significant research studies and publications should be rated outstanding; teaching and advising should be outstanding; and professional service to the institution and to the profession should be excellent. National or regional academic recognition should be evident.

Gaining promotion becomes increasingly difficult as a candidate moves up the academic ladder. It is not uncommon in many larger institutions to find departmental and college committees recommending promotion only to have the recommendation rejected by the chief academic officer. Sometimes the rejection relates to a projected long-term cost factor that weighs more heavily if the quality of the individual file is average. Generally speaking, the chief academic officer at many larger institutions frowns upon having files sent forward ahead of schedule. More time for the file to improve is the primary factor, although the cost factor may be a consideration.

Tenure

The concept of tenure is far from new. Metzger (1973, p. 94) traced its beginnings to 1158 A.D. when Emperor Frederick Barbarossa issued an edict promising scholars in his domain safe conduct in their journeys, protection from attack upon their domiciles, and compensation for unlawful injury—the "Authentica Habita," as defined by Koeppler (1939, pp. 606-607). With this precedent and example, the sovereigns of other lands followed suit, and for centuries the royal institution joined the far-reaching Roman Papacy to shield university scholars from their would-be plunderers and assailants—the country brigands and the city mobs.

Tenure returned to prominent attention in recent years after having high visibility in the early 1970s, spurred by the 1973 report by the Commission on Academic Tenure in Higher Education, known as the Keast Commission, co-sponsored by the Association of American Colleges (AAC) and the AAUP. At that time the interest was spawned by the student unrest and riots in the 1960s, causing some loss of public confidence in the professoriate, which was often viewed as neutral or supporting student causes; by a sharp downturn in the economy; and by professional concern that the rapid professional hiring in the 1960s may have been at the price of quality control.

In the 1980s a number of concerns have revived the tenure issue, such as the anticipated (if not realized) declines in student enrollment, the approaching retirement of large numbers of those hired in the 1960s, and the current unprecedented national concern about excellence.

Tenure Trends

Since the 1960s, tenure has gradually become more difficult to obtain. The Commission on Academic Tenure in Higher Education (1973, p. 7) concluded that "though the proportion of tenured faculty in 1972 appears to be just about what it was in the early 1960's, the prospects for the future are very different. . . . If institutions continue to award tenure to 60 to 80 percent, or more, of eligible faculty, and if faculty size does not grow proportionately, many will find themselves, within a few years, with tenured staffs so large that promotion for younger faculty will be increasingly difficult." Confirming this trend, Bowen and Schuster (1986, pp. 44–45) found that the percentage of full-time faculty that had tenure in the 1960s "was on the order of 50–55 percent, that this percentage rose to 63–68 percent by 1980, and that . . . as of 1985, over 70 percent—perhaps even 75 percent or more—of the full-time faculties are on tenure, the percentage being greater for public than for private institutions." Findings in a tenure survey of Maryland's state colleges and universities indicated that the percentages of full-time faculty members with tenure increased from 54 percent in 1975 to 65 percent in 1981 (Maryland State Board for Higher Education, 1982, p. 3). Eble and McKeachie (1985, p. 3) concluded that as higher education moves toward the year 2000, "college-age populations in many areas of the country will continue to support few openings with tenure opportunities for college faculty in many disciplines." Probably to deter legal actions (as well as to soothe the senior faculty's guilty feelings about applying more rigorous standards), Cornell University has in its "Procedures for Appealing a Negative Tenure Decision" this sentence: "A weak previous tenure appointment shall not by itself be taken to define the departmental standard" (Fries, 1986, p. 40). Clearly, the evidence favors tighter control of tenure in the nineties.

Advantages and Disadvantages of Tenure

The AAUP's 1915 policy statement formalized its position on tenure and developed procedures that have since been clarified but not fundamentally changed. Tenure has been an integral part of academe since World War II; about 85 percent of all colleges and universities in the United States have some form of tenure. Baratz (1980, p. 8), the former general secretary of the AAUP, contends that the essence of the case for tenure may be summarized in two sentences. Without tenure, "American higher education would fail genuinely to promote the common good in the absence of academic freedom"; tenure also provides "a sufficient degree of economic security to make the profession attractive to men and women of ability." Freedom from anxiety about employment allows full attention to be devoted to academic responsibilities and encourages risk taking by removing the most serious penalty for failure. A secure professor is more likely to encourage differing opinions among students and to differ himself or herself with colleagues and administrators.

O'Toole (1980, p. 8), however, states that "the practice of tenure actually *undercuts* academic quality, *abridges* academic freedom and *short-circuits* the chances of professors to have satisfying and productive careers." Others contend that tenure prevents flexibility in programs and staffing. It discourages professional mobility, which brings freshness and new perspectives, and encourages complacency. Tenure forces institutions to live with their mistakes; promising young scholars are lost to academe because positions are filled with tenured professors. It can foster individual interests to the exclusion of departmental and institutional participation.

Faculty productivity after tenure sometimes becomes an issue. Walden (1979, p. 217) asked 310 academics at a single university whether their own productivity and that of persons they knew had increased or decreased since tenure was approved. "About 95 percent of the tenured respondents . . . state either that tenure has made no difference in their level of productivity or that productivity has increased since tenure was awarded." Orpen (1982, pp. 61-62), studying the productivity of thirty-six pairs of tenured and untenured professors at an Australian university, found that the average productivity of the tenured group "was virtually the same" as that of the untenured group.

Alternatives to Tenure

Some postsecondary institutions have developed alternatives to traditional tenure. Options such as term contracts, extended probationary periods, suspension of the "up-or-out" rule, and tenure quotas are causing a restructuring of the traditional academic career. Martin Finkelstein (1986, p. 32) argues that this restructuring is along three lines, which are faculty immobility ("Once a place to 'hang one's hat,' a particular college or university has become a place to 'hang on to' "); insecurity, even for tenured faculty members; and the changing of the traditional tenured faculty into a cadre of "temporary not-tenure-eligible full-timers or a variety of individuals teaching something less than full-time" in regular tenure-track positions. Excellent discussions of the part-time problem can be found in Finkelstein (1986), Fries (1986), Heinzelman (1986), and Pollak (1986).

Term contract. Largely in response to a fiscal deficit in 1973–74 and dire predictions of declining enrollment, Curry College, a small, nonsectarian, coeducational liberal arts institution founded in 1879, abandoned its tenure system in 1974 for a three-year rolling contract. The new system was intended to provide greater flexibility in meeting fluctuating student enrollment and changing program needs. After several years of operation, Hill (1985, p. 54) found that the system had five major advantages: "It protects academic freedom and job security. It motivates faculty and provides them with established promotion criteria. And it brings some financial benefits to the administration." While the overall evaluation of the Curry plan is positive, there are some acknowledged shortcomings. The plan has not increased the college's financial and program flexibility; this point has not really been tested, however, because the anticipated decline in enrollment did not occur. Faculty evaluations continue to be a weakness; this problem is evident in many other small liberal arts colleges.

The use of term contracts has increased substantially in the past ten years, and further increases can be expected. Fiscal problems caused by uncertain enrollments, diminished state and federal financial support, and shifts in program emphasis have contributed to administrators' preferences for the flexibility provided by term contracts. Term contracts also can be useful in recruiting for specialized areas, such as music instruction, in which talented individuals are not necessarily interested in tenure-track positions and institutions cannot afford to hire them on a full-time basis.

There are many varieties of term contracts. They range in length from one semester to five years and may include full faculty rights (excluding benefits) and equivalent salary. Administrators must take care that program and unit continuity are not sacrificed by having too many people on term contracts. Large urban universities and community colleges are most susceptible to this problem.

Extended probationary periods. The Atelsek and Gomberg survey of 760 institutions (1980, pp. 16-17) found that private universities and colleges had a slightly longer average probationary period (6.0 years) than their public counterparts (5.5 years); the institutions expected to have probationary periods of 6.3 and 5.6 years, respectively, in another five years. The Commission on Academic Tenure in Higher Education (1973, p. 58) stated that "the probationary period should be long enough to permit careful consideration of the faculty member's qualifications but it should not be so long as to postpone unduly the faculty member's enjoyment of the full benefits of permanent status, keeping him in jeopardy of termination into middle life." Since its 1940 *Statement of Principles on Academic Freedom and Tenure,* the AAUP has held that the probationary period should be no longer than seven years. The national trend is toward slightly longer probationary periods.

Some institutions have developed their own plans. Chait and Ford (1982, pp. 93-105) write about several universities and colleges that have extended probationary periods to eleven or more years and eliminated the "up-or-out" provisions. These institutions include the University of Rochester, Columbia University, Princeton University, Vassar College, and the Harvard School of Business—to name just a few. In her study of probationary policies at twenty-three public and private research universities, Fries (1986, p. 38) found that a majority adhered to AAUP guidelines that mandate a tenure review in the sixth year. However, "several (including the University of California system and the University of Michigan) schedule the tenure review for the seventh year; several (including Yale, Harvard, and Columbia) raise the possibility of promotion to nontenured associate professor after the tenure review."

The value of the extended probationary period is not so

much in its sheer length as in how the extra time is used to help young faculty members acquire tenure—provided the institution has a reasonable intention of permitting them to do so. If the added years are more of the same, probationary faculty members may not benefit, although a longer probationary period statistically improves their chances of receiving tenure, according to a study by Luecke (1974, p. 279). The longer period also gives the institution an opportunity to make better plans for using its human and material resources. If the institution's system of planning is poor to begin with, however, more time will not improve it.

Suspension of "up-or-out" policies. This is a way of extending the probationary period, or rather of eliminating it altogether. It has been used effectively in a few smaller colleges, largely as a means of keeping competent younger faculty members while holding to an overall tenure quota. If an institution's governing board orders a limit on the percentage of tenured faculty, developing another category, such as "tenurable faculty," allows an institution to keep a portion of its faculty members in holding patterns until openings can be found. As a creative adjustment to a rigid quota system, suspending the "up-or-out" policy has both merits and liabilities. It does not provide security; when appointments become available elsewhere, marketable young professors—the ones that the institution wants to keep—will be the first to go. This practice may also create greater insecurity among faculty members in general.

Tenure quotas. Tenure quotas have not been as popular in the 1980s as they were in the 1970s, when the quotas instituted by Colgate University, the City University of New York (CUNY), and the New Jersey State Board of Higher Education received media attention. The deep recession of the mid-seventies, double-digit inflation from 1976 to 1981, gloomy forecasts of declining student enrollment, and predictions of tenured-in faculties in the 1980s motivated some colleges and universities to impose tenure quotas.

As pointed out by Chait and Ford (1982, pp. 132-134), this approach has the advantages of simplicity, flexibility, selectivity, prestige, diversity, and economy; its disadvantages are inequity, deemphasis of merit, transiency, controversy, and self-imposed constraints. Once the tenure limit has been reached, a college may be unable to add new permanent faculty to departments that have significant potential for growth. A college president may be forced to deny tenure to probationary faculty members who are stronger than most of their tenured colleagues. Marketable faculty members who cannot advance because of a filled quota may choose to seek promotion and tenure or the possibility of them elsewhere.

An institution that wants to avoid a tenure quota might consider a number of approaches. It can become more selective, grant "instant tenure" less often, give less credit for prior service, lengthen the probationary period, suspend "up-or-out" policies, appoint faculty members outside the tenure track, reevaluate tenured faculty members, and offer attractive early retirement plans. In the past there was a tendency to establish tenure quotas rather than to explore seriously and creatively a range of options. Because the quota system is simpler, gives the illusion of equity, and is easier to administer, it appeals to board members in particular, but it may not be the best alternative.

If an institution must consider drastic cutbacks to ensure its long-term vitality and effectiveness, there is no substitute for accurate institutional and regional data. Without five- and ten-year projections of human and material resources and institutional needs, decisions affecting the future can be based on little more than intuition and hope.

Removing Tenure

Tenure has been removed from more persons for more reasons than is generally realized. The extensive CUPA study (College and University Personnel Association, 1980b, p. 31) of 1,058 institutions found that between 1972 and 1977, 429 terminations of tenured faculty members were reported. This sample represents approximately one-third of the nation's postsecondary institutions. A simple multiplication gives a nationwide figure of 1,287 tenure terminations for the five-year period, or about 260 terminations per year. These figures are approximations, and caution should be exercised in extrapolating from them, but they represent the only comprehensive survey data of fairly recent vintage that is available. Table 9 summarizes the results of CUPA's five-part study.

The CUPA study (1980b, p. 30) found that 840 institutions, or 79 percent of the sample, had established policies or procedures for terminating tenured faculty members. The reasons for termination most commonly included in their policies are incompetency (85 percent); moral turpitude (84 percent); elimination of program (79 percent); financial considerations (76 percent); and neglect of established obligations (72 percent). Among the two-year colleges, falsified credentials (67 percent) was listed as well. Eighty-eight percent of the CUPA sample said that tenure (meaning permanent employment) could be revoked "for cause." Of this group, 96 percent would terminate for causes that included moral turpitude, incompetency, excessive absences, excessive outside employment, or a disciplinary matter; 83 percent would terminate "for cause" or for financial considerations; and 76 percent would terminate tenure "for cause" or because of program elimination.

The column in Table 9 labeled *percentage of total* shows that 43 percent of the dismissals of tenured faculty were for financial considerations (22 percent) or program elimination (21 percent); the latter reason is usually related to financial considerations. Only 22 doctoral universities cited financial reasons for dismissal (5 percent), which speaks to their greater overall affluence and the flexibility that larger budgets permit. Community colleges account for 45 percent of all dismissals for incompetence. According to the New York University Law Review Study (1979, pp. 840–841), incompetence is "a state of inability arising from a lack of talent, intelligence, training, motivation, or professionalism. Incompetence encompasses a teacher's classroom demeanor, teaching methods, physical ability, and ability to maintain an environment conducive to learning." The right of an institution to dismiss for incompetence has usually been upheld by the courts. Lovain (1983-84, p. 422) concludes that "where charges of incompetence, especially in teaching, are supported by substantial and relevant evidence,

Table 9. Reasons for Termination of Tenured Faculty.

| | Types of Institutions | | | | | | | | | | |
| Reason for Termination | Doctoral | | Compre-hensive | | Liberal Arts | | Community Colleges | | Total No. Termi-nations | % of Total | Rank Order |
	Public	Private	Public	Private	Public	Private	Public	Private			
Financial considerations	5	4	20	14	0	29	21	3	96	22	1
Program elimination	9	4	13	14	1	21	27	3	92	21	2
Incompetence	8	0	10	7	0	11	28	2	66	15	3
Neglect of obligations	11	2	13	6	2	5	20	2	61	14	4
Moral turpitude	5	2	7	4	0	4	8	0	30	7	5
Absence record	4	1	5	2	1	2	10	0	25	6	6
Falsified credentials	2	2	6	2	0	0	4	0	16	4	8
Plagiarism	3	0	5	0	0	1	0	0	9	2	9
Excessive outside work	4	1	1	1	0	1	1	0	8	2	9
Other	3	1	6	5	1	4	6	0	26	6	6
Totals	54	17	86	55	5	77	125	10	429		
TOTALS	73		141		82		13		429		

Source: Adapted from College and University Personnel Association, 1980b.

the courts will defer to the expertise of academic administrators."

Immoral behavior by tenured faculty members usually includes dishonesty (plagiarism), extreme vulgarity, and sexual harassment. The Commission on Academic Tenure in Higher Education (1973, p. 75) acknowledged that "dishonesty in teaching or research" is an adequate cause for tenured dismissal. The courts have upheld the right of an institution to dismiss faculty members for falsifying credentials. (See *Barszez* v. *Board of Trustees,* 400 F. Supp. 675 (N.D. Ill. 1975).) Sexual harassment, although difficult to prove, can constitute adequate cause for dismissal. (See *Lehman* v. *Board of Trustees of Whitman College,* 89 Wash. 2d 874, 576 P. 2d 397 (1978).)

Neglect or dereliction of duty usually involves disobedience of institutional rules and requirements or missing classes, office hours, and other commitments. Lovain (1983-84, p. 420) reports on *Shaw* v. *Board of Trustees of Frederick College,* in which two professors were dismissed for boycotting a faculty workshop and commencement ceremonies in protest of plans to abolish tenure at the college. The court held that the First Amendment did not give them the right to violate the terms of their employment. Lovain notes that faculty responsibilities extend beyond teaching duties; conditions of employment may include keeping office hours, filing required reports and agreements, and serving on faculty committees.

Terminating a tenured professor is never taken lightly by administrators, yet there are times when such a step must be taken in the best interests of the institution. In these circumstances, one may want to consider eleven procedural steps developed by Andrews and Daponte:

1. Because of the teacher's constitutional right to privacy, board members and administrators should refrain from discussing, writing, or distributing anything to anyone other than the management team with respect to any defects of a teacher.

2. Because of a teacher's freedom of expression guaranteed by the First Amendment, admin-

istrators should not engage in retaliatory acts following an instructor's criticism of the administration or the board.

3. Because of equal protection guarantees and the federal legislation supporting these guarantees, any act which could be construed as discriminatory on the basis of sex, race, age, or national origin should be assiduously avoided.

4. Although an evaluation is not always required to dismiss, administrators should avoid whitewashed evaluations if teaching deficiencies exist. . . .

5. Evaluations should be performed by a team of independent evaluators, chosen on the basis of their esteem in the profession. . . .

6. The board should actively seek that evidence which is most probative, and this means the testimony of experts. . . .

7. Evidence should not be based upon an isolated incident or incidents remote from the time of filing.

8. A board can avoid charges of partiality by designating a separate body to investigate a teacher's deficiencies and to make recommendations to the board.

9. To minimize the possibility of a personal liability suit under the Civil Rights Act of 1871 (42 U.S.C.A. 1983) based upon deprivation of the constitutional rights of a faculty member, the institution is well advised to establish a comprehensive legal education program for its middle and top managers. . . .

10. Counsel thoroughly familiar with statutory due process requirements in educational settings should be retained when a dismissal is first contemplated.

11. The need to dismiss tenured faculty can be reduced by more careful screening when hir-

ing, by non-retention of non-tenured faculty
when any doubt exists as to their competency, and by a sound program of faculty development [1981, pp. 25-27].

This chapter's discussion of tenure and promotion is intended to help readers to understand and to compare their system with the policies that the literature suggests. The following
checklist may be helpful in evaluating the quality and effectiveness of promotion and tenure policies and procedures. While
such a simplification has its dangers, succinctness may be a virtue in appraising the professional health of an institution's promotion and tenure system, or at least a good starting point.

- Policies and procedures have been seriously reviewed within
  the past three years.
- Review processes take into account where the *institution* is
  seeking to go.
- Review processes take into account where the *college or unit*
  is seeking to go.
- *College or unit* processes are compatible with institutional
  perspectives.
- Review processes deal with *short-term* realities.
- Review processes take into account *long-term* priorities and
  directions.
- The promotion and tenure review processes of at least two
  benchmark institutions have been studied. (A benchmark in-
  stitution is one that is roughly comparable.)
- Someone in the unit or college sees that promotion and tenure policies and procedures are scrupulously followed.
- The application of the system is taken seriously by committee members. Hard decisions are made on occasion.
- Members of the promotion and tenure committee(s) are
  given orientation prior to their assigned work.
- Review procedures provide for prompt feedback to recipients at each step of the process.
- The committee's chairperson carefully documents all meetings and all decisions.

Seven

Using Evaluation Results
in Promotion
and Tenure Decisions

Howard Bowen (1976a, p. 360) noted that "statistics are no substitute for judgment." One can say also that judgment is no substitute for statistics. Effective academic personnel decision-making processes blend the objectivity provided by statistics with judgments based on experience. An institution of higher education is both an organization and a community of people, and both aspects are considered in making academic personnel decisions.

Peer Reviews

Peer reviews are used in most reward systems, usually in one of four ways. Most commonly, a committee system is established for promotion and tenure. The composition of these committees varies considerably. A common pattern is a five-person elected or appointed committee. Often all five members are tenured, but some institutions use a committee consisting of three tenured and two untenured members. The inclusion of two untenured members recognizes the contributions of younger colleagues while acknowledging the institutional perspective and the experience of senior faculty members. Members of the faculty who are applying for promotion or tenure are not permitted to serve on the promotion and tenure committee for that year. In another arrangement, all departmental members form a committee of the whole. Some reservations about this approach are expressed in Chapter One.

Ad hoc, external reviewers, usually one or two outsiders, are commonly used by the larger research universities. Professional competence in highly specialized fields usually can be judged more accurately by individuals in the field than by a general committee.

The use of letters from external reviewers is relatively common for promotion to full professor. This approach has increased in recent years, although very little attention has been given to it in the literature. Some of the sensitive aspects of this process are pointed out by Poston (1984, pp. 44–46). He recommends the use of a standard letter such as the one included here:

> Dear _____:
>
> _____, an untenured Assistant Professor in this Department, is being reviewed this fall for tenure and promotion to the rank of Associate Professor. To assist us in our evaluation of the record, we would very much like to have your candid appraisal of [her, his] scholarship. I enclose a checklist of the items which would be sent to you.
>
> Should you be willing to write a report (1,000 words, perhaps), could we have such a report by September 5? We do not ask outside consultants for recommendations on promotion, since those decisions must ultimately rest upon a number of considerations, but solely for their candid evaluation of the written work submitted for their review. Your report will be read by departmental and university committees and administrative officers involved in the promotion process; with your name removed, it will be made available to _____ in accordance with a departmental policy which allows prospective candidates for promotion and tenure to read and, at their option, to respond to written evaluation of their work. We can offer you a modest honorarium of $100 for your report.

If, as I very much hope, you are able to respond affirmatively, the material will be sent to
you promptly. I look forward to your reply.

The use of these letters can pose some problems. As Poston observes (1984, p. 45): "A by no means uncommon occur-
rence in the profession is the arrival of a large and unexpected
file of reading material, accompanied by a letter asking the reviewer to read and respond within two weeks. Presumptuous in
the extreme, such a request does not invite a considered evaluation; what it ought properly to invite is a flat refusal to participate in the process."

In a fourth type of peer review, colleagues rate a department member. The logic of this approach is based on the ability
of colleagues to judge some professional dimensions better than
any other group. Cohen and McKeachie (1980, p. 148) list these
"teaching effectiveness criteria that colleagues are best qualified
to evaluate":

- Mastery of course content
- Selection of course content (knowledge of what must be
  taught)
- Course organization
- Appropriateness of course objectives
- Appropriateness of instructional materials—readings, use of
  media, and so on
- Application of the most appropriate methodology for teach-
  ing specific content areas
- Commitment to teaching and concern for student learning
- Student achievement based on performance on exams and
  projects
- Support of departmental instructional efforts

Colleagues also are in a good position to judge faculty service
and relations; and they can make some judgments about professional and public service, professional growth, and scholarship.
For these appraisals, a common written form is recommended
to allow a more accurate aggregation of data and to focus the

attention of colleagues on the same elements. The use of colleague evaluation should be carefully monitored for adherence to procedures and deadlines.

In their survey of sixty-six accredited graduate social work schools, Weinbach and Randolph (1984, p. 85) found that 60 percent considered peer review a very important part of tenure and promotion review, 24 percent considered it important, and only 12 percent did not use it. A broad acceptance of peer review was evident, although one cannot be sure who answered the questionnaires, because the deans to whom they were addressed may not have answered the inquiries themselves. Administrators can be expected to favor peer reviews because they are another source of evidence that usually supports whatever decision is made. We have no similar survey of faculty opinion on peer reviews, but one can speculate that it may be less favorable because faculty may view with suspicion the highly subjective nature of the process.

Weightings of Various Criteria and Inputs

Wilson (1942, pp. 100-101) summarized a report from the University of Minnesota that ranked the factors considered in promotions between 1913 and 1931 in order of importance: teaching (43 percent), productive scholarship (28 percent), student counseling (12 percent), administrative work (11 percent), and public service (6 percent). Today, the University of Minnesota, a major land-grant university, gives greater importance to productive scholarship. The explosion of knowledge, the complexity of new discoveries, the fundamental importance of research in organizing and understanding new knowledge, and the rapid increase of postsecondary institutions that are not research-oriented have combined to elevate the importance of research in land-grant universities. External demands have placed the burden of leadership in research on about 130-150 of our 3,000-plus postsecondary institutions. One should not be surprised, therefore, if the promotion and tenure criteria in these institutions value scholarship more than teaching.

The weighting of various criteria for evaluating overall faculty performance varies substantially by the type of institution and to a lesser extent by the external forces that are impinging on the institution. Table 10 shows one approach to weighting criteria. The percentages used are illustrative and are

Table 10. Weight Assigned to Criteria for Evaluating
Faculty Performance by Major Input Groups.

| Criteria | Input Groups | | | |
	Chair	Colleagues	Dean	Students
Advising	(15) Some	(10) Little	(5) Little	(70) Most
Classroom visitation	(10) Little	(90) Most	(0) None	(0) None
Faculty service relations	(50) Most	(40) Much	(10) Little	(0) None
Professional growth	(55) Most	(35) Much	(10) Little	(0) None
Professional service	(55) Most	(35) Much	(10) Little	(0) None
Public service	(50) Most	(35) Much	(15) Some	(0) Little
Scholarship	(30) Some	(65) Most	(5) Little	(0) None
Self-evaluation	(75) Most	(20) Some	(5) Little	(0) None
Teaching	(20) Some	(15) Some	(5) Little	(60) Most
Teaching materials	(15) Some	(80) Most	(5) Little	(0) None

Note: Numbers in parentheses represent percentage weighting; words represent descriptive weighting.

not intended to apply to a particular type of institution, although this type of weighting system is found most frequently in two-year colleges.

Individualizing Faculty Workloads

A number of approaches have been developed for tailoring the five major professional activities of teaching, scholarship, faculty service and relations, professional and public service, and professional growth to the interests of each individual for each year. For tenure and promotion decisions the range of variation in professional activities may be prescribed, but for the annual academic performance review (AAPR), discussed in Chapter Nine, some variation will exist among individuals. Faculty members who year after year allot the same percentages of effort to the various alternatives may be encouraged to move in some new directions. Of course the individual's yearly profile should reflect institutional and unit needs and priorities. Table 11 draws upon the excellent materials developed by Beaumont Technical College in Texas, J. Sargent Reynolds Community College in Virginia, and the Palm Beach Junior College in Florida. It can be adapted to a variety of postsecondary institutions.

The yearly workload should add up to 100 percent. To evaluate overall professional performance, the percentage of effort for each activity is multiplied by the score given for each activity. The score can be expressed as a percentage or ranked on a five- or seven-point scale. If a scale is used, a simple calculation will yield a composite rating if such a rating is desired.

An overall performance rating for the hypothetical Professor A can be determined using a quantified system as indicated in Table 12. The weight of criteria and the ratings of Professor A's efforts are determined by the chairperson, dean, and colleagues. Professor A's total effort is dispersed across four of the six areas, with 50 percent devoted to teaching. Each percentage of effort is multiplied by a criterion rating, which can vary from a low of 1 to a high of 7. Professor A's total raw score of 611 is divided by a total possible score of 700, yielding an overall rating of 87 percent. A difference of five percentage points or more between faculty members indicates a noticeable difference in overall performance.

One can see some immediate problems with any numerical weighting system. For example, determining the percentage of total effort can be difficult. Does Professor A have no advising responsibilities whatsoever, and does professional and public service claim none of his or her time? According to available research as well as experiential evidence, faculty service and relations is the most important criterion after teaching. It is un-

Table 11. Individualizing Faculty Workloads.

Activities	Self	Chair	Counselor	Learning Resource Director
Teaching Content mastery Instructional design Pedagogical skill Record keeping	50-80%	40-70%	0-10%	—
Advising Academic advice and record keeping for students Program assistance Referring students to other areas	5-15%	5-15%	—	—
College services Adviser to organizations Committee assignments Professional relations	5-20%	5-20%	5-20%	5-20%
Community services	5-30%	5-30%	5-30%	5-25%
Professional growth Academic advancement Attendance and partici- pation in professional meetings Professional courses Scholarship	5-30%	5-20%	10-30%	5-30%
Individual counseling Academic Behavioral Career planning Placement Referral to outside agencies	—	—	30-70%	5-15%
Group counseling Academic study skills Behavioral problems Career development Information dissemi- nation Personal and social skills	—	—	30-70%	5-15%
Administration	—	15-30%	5-15%	10-30%

Table 12. Determining an Overall Performance Rating.

Activity	Percentage of Professor A's Total Effort		Criterion Rating		Raw Score
1. Advising	—				
2. Faculty service and relations	20	×	6.2	=	124
3. Professional growth	10	×	6.1	=	61
4. Professional and public service	—				
5. Scholarship	20	×	5.3	=	106
6. Teaching	50	×	6.4	=	320
Total Raw Score					611
Overall Rating		611 ÷ 700		=	.87

likely that this criterion will be given the numerical weight appropriate to its importance. The same circumstance may be found with research, but for different reasons. Few professors move ahead significantly in research-oriented universities without solid credibility in research. Yet it is unlikely that many such institutions will want to acknowledge the weight that research has in promotion and tenure decisions. Parents and board members probably would not be happy with a written statement that makes research even slightly more important than teaching.

Considering these problems with numerical weighting systems, what are their value? They provide greater clarity in describing professional responsibilities (even considering the caveats that have been mentioned) than a general approach that might include high, medium, and low ratings on research, teaching, and service. Such generality works to the advantage of administrative decision making by permitting decision makers greater flexibility. But from the point of view of faculty members, clear workload expectations and evaluative bases are desirable; therefore, a differentiated system is preferable. Such a system also permits more variation in professional responsibilities from year to year. And legal considerations favor a differentiated system because it is easier to determine accountability and professional obligations when requirements are described specifically.

Flow of Promotion and Tenure Procedures

Vanderbilt University (*Revised Report...* , 1985) gathered data about the procedural flow for promotion and tenure that is used in twenty nationally prominent universities. Some generalizations can be made from an analysis of these data:

- Most of the colleges in a single institution follow similar tenure procedures. There are two exceptions.
- The initiative for the tenure procedures is always within the department or division of the college.
- The processes for making decisions on applications for tenure vary widely among the universities; no simple model can accurately describe every process. The most general pattern is this flow: Department → College Committee → Dean → University Committee → Senior Administrative Officer → President → Board of Trustees.
- The president of the governing board has the final decision-making authority in seventeen of the twenty universities.
- Twelve of the twenty universities have tenure committees consisting only of faculty members; six universities have committees consisting of both faculty and administrators. One university has faculty and students represented on its committees, and at another university both faculty and outside experts are represented.
- The appointment or election of tenure committees varies widely among these institutions; there is no predominant pattern in this sample.
- Nineteen of the twenty universities have options for the appeal of negative decisions.

Table 13 outlines a general procedural flow similar to that currently in place in many postsecondary institutions. An occasional comprehensive review of the procedural flow at any

Table 13. A Tree of Academic Advancement.

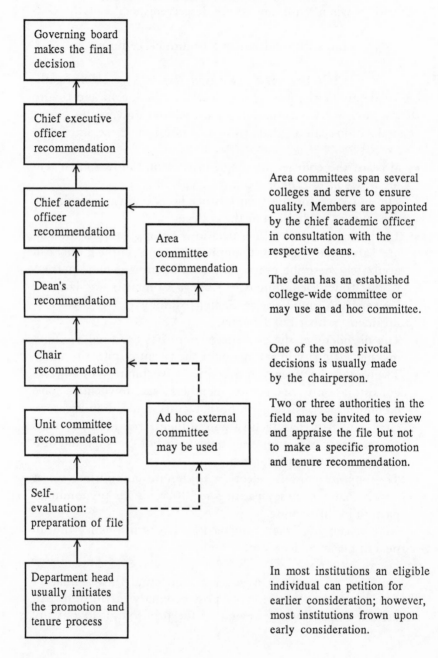

Area committees span several colleges and serve to ensure quality. Members are appointed by the chief academic officer in consultation with the respective deans.

The dean has an established college-wide committee or may use an ad hoc committee.

One of the most pivotal decisions is usually made by the chairperson.

Two or three authorities in the field may be invited to review and appraise the file but not to make a specific promotion and tenure recommendation.

In most institutions an eligible individual can petition for earlier consideration; however, most institutions frown upon early consideration.

institution can be useful in improving the system or confirming its effectiveness.

Committees at Work

Very little attention in higher education literature has been given to promotion and tenure committees at work. In some ways, they function better than we have the right to expect considering their casual and sometimes poorly organized operations. This section focuses on the first committee, which is at the departmental level. About 85 to 90 percent of the decisions made at this level are sustained through the remaining processes. Some institutions' promotion and tenure policies prevent the candidate's file from receiving further consideration if it is not approved by this committee.

The work of promotion and tenure committees requires confidentiality, yet the frequency and intimacy of daily contact among colleagues and the intensity of the environment make this difficult to achieve. Confidentiality has been described as something that faculty members share only on a one-to-one basis. Because of the need for confidentiality and the importance of maintaining collegiality in daily relationships, making difficult and sometimes negative decisions about colleagues can be personally painful and trying. Even if the results of committee deliberations as well as voting records are in the public domain, the actual deliberations need to be confidential so that candidates may be given full consideration. (This applies only to selected committees and not to processes where the unit sits as a committee of the whole.) To assist committees in their decision making, the following guidelines are suggested.

1. Committee members can profitably review the role of their recommendations in determining future directions and quality.
2. Committee members can benefit, even if they have served during the previous year, from reviewing (a) the role and functions of the committee, (b) the university context and

relevant policies and procedures, and (c) the committee's history.

3. Documentation of committee deliberations and recommendations should be complete and clear. Casualness is a fault in many instances, especially on the part of senior professors who carry around in their heads the history of the committee and the department. Court proceedings, always in the background of personnel actions, have prompted more thoroughness in documentation.

4. Time for unhurried reading and consideration of each file can be arranged. Busy faculty members may not allow sufficient time for the process, thereby forcing meetings to be concentrated and considerations to be hurried.

5. After recommendations, a postmortem committee meeting can be useful to the following year's committee by recommending adjustments and changes.

Examining promotion and tenure decision making is essential in the constant effort to make these decisions—the most important personnel decisions made by colleges and universities—more equitable and defensible. In this spirit many institutions would benefit from such examinations at regular intervals.

Eight

Monitoring Compliance
with the Law

The higher education community with its often casual and collegial approaches to academic personnel policies and procedures has allowed many well-meaning members of academe to flounder in a morass of legal requirements designed for a fair and balanced relationship with faculty members. In *Worzella* v. *Board of Regents* (1958) the court made the following observation regarding academic tenure: "Its vaporous objectives, purposes, and procedures are lost in a fog of nebulous verbiage." It is clear today that an understanding of the legal system and its impact on higher education has become essential to successful academic leadership. As Kaplin (1985, p. ix) notes: "The law has arrived on campus. Sometimes it has been a beacon, other times a blanket of ground fog. But even in its murkiness, the law has not come 'on little cat feet,' like in Carl Sandberg's 'Fog'; nor has it sat silently on its haunches; nor will it soon move on. It has spoken forcefully and meaningfully to the higher education community and will continue to do so." The main reasons for the relatively recent involvement of the law in higher education have been the recognition of the need to balance the interests of faculty and students more precisely with the traditional interests of academe and the recognition that institutions of higher education should not be exempt from societal goals set forth in current law.

Historical Perspectives

Barbara Lee (1985, p. 38) writes that because of the "unique, specialized" nature of higher education, it has "long

119

been afforded a special status by the judiciary." She points to a change in attitude that began with the civil rights movement and to other societal changes in the 1960s. Sloviter (1982, pp. 19-20) indicates that before 1970 the lawsuits initiated by faculty members primarily concerned questions of academic freedom. She writes: "Litigation involving faculty in the federal courts in the last decade seems to have arisen primarily out of suits brought under Title VII claiming discrimination on the basis of race, sex, or ethnic background, and suits challenging individual personnel decisions on the ground that the procedure utilized was unauthorized or unconstitutional." A report issued by the National Association of College and University Attorneys (1984, p. 4) also found that faculty nonreappointments, layoffs, and dismissals were ranked first by in-house legal counsel of colleges and universities among ten categories showing a net increase in workload.

Formerly, the law favored higher education by making it difficult for plaintiffs from academe to prevail over the institution unless "flagrant violations of some fundamental and unambiguous legal standard" had occurred (Hobbs, 1982, pp. 1-2). Litigation is more common and the probability of litigation is greater today because academe has more potential litigants, not because of a new wave of court intrusion into academe. The heightened awareness of the law's purpose and its influence on academic life may mislead some observers to feel that the courts are becoming less reluctant to exercise their powers in the academic arena.

Burnett and Matthews (1982, p. 206), saying that "a legalistic culture has become a part of the academic community of the 1980s," contend that the following elements are responsible:

- a "legal syndrome"
- the influence of state and federal government
- a widening scope of service on the part of the university
- a tight academic job market
- increasing concern and effort to reduce the arbitrary nature of administration and to recognize the rights of faculty and students

- an effort to democratize colleges and universities
- a conflict in role perceptions among students, faculty, and administrators
- collective bargaining, which has contributed to the adversary relationship between faculty and administrators
- increased costs for students, which have caused a demand for accountability

While all areas of higher education governance are vulnerable to litigation, this chapter focuses on litigation concerning policies and procedures for hiring, promotion, tenure, dismissal of faculty, and related matters, in the context of the historically recognized legal principle of academic freedom in higher education.

Academic Freedom

The basic legal principle guiding academic governance of faculty has been that of academic freedom, established by the First Amendment to the United States Constitution. John Brubacher (1971, p. 57) writes that "academic freedom is not just an internal affair of the school but its significance extends far beyond the campus to the intelligent conduct of social affairs in general." Supreme Court Justice Felix Frankfurter, in the landmark case *Sweezy* v. *New Hampshire* (1957), stated in a concurring opinion that "the four essential freedoms" for the university are "to determine for itself on academic grounds who may teach, what may be taught, how it shall be taught, and who may be admitted to study." The assessment and evaluation of faculty by students, colleagues, and administrators are involved in the first three freedoms outlined by Frankfurter; it should come as no surprise that litigation involving academic freedom and its role in higher education has a long history. This was enunciated by the United States Supreme Court in *Keyishian* v. *Board of Regents* (1967), in which the court called academic freedom "a special concern of the First Amendment."

Although the Supreme Court has led the way in recognizing the unique and important role of academic freedom in postsecondary institutions, the law does not support this principle uniformly. Academic leaders as well as faculty cannot use academic freedom to justify all their actions. Academic administrations should be cognizant of the fact that the legal system is designed to balance competing societal, institutional, and individual roles and interests within academe. This balance is intended to ensure fair treatment of faculty, and academic personnel decisions will be judged accordingly.

Recruiting and Hiring

The most critical phase of academic administration, from the legal perspective, is the establishment of relationships with faculty members. All too often the excitement of a faculty appointment causes both the new faculty member and the institutional employer to lose sight of their legal relationship. One of the first steps in recruiting faculty should be a review of the institution's affirmative action policies and the capacity for fulfilling them. Executive Order 11224, 30 Fed. Reg. 12319, as amended by Executive Order 11375, prohibits discrimination "because of race, color, religion, sex, or national origin" (Kaplin, 1985, p. 139).

The affirmative action efforts of colleges and universities have changed in the past few years; new state laws and regulations have affected both public and private institutions, and the political climate has changed with the national administration. An institution must ensure that efforts are made in good faith to meet all affirmative action obligations and that the institution complies with affirmative action goals and policies. These efforts will help avoid complaints filed by disaffected members of protected classes and subsequent review by federal and state agencies. Particular attention should be focused on the proper methods and procedures for recruiting minority and female faculty, including advertisements, interviews, and selection procedures.

When a faculty member begins an appointment, a contractual relationship exists that is often much more involved than it seems at first glance. There are many terms and conditions of this relationship that should be expressed as clearly as possible. The faculty member's rank should be stated, the university's published policies and procedures affecting faculty should be provided, insurance and benefits should be explained in detail, and tenure policies for tenure-track positions should be stated clearly. Other conditions of the appointment should be clearly defined, such as the completion of a Ph.D. or other requirements.

The new faculty member should be notified as soon as possible of the policies regarding the length of the probationary period, evaluation procedures, and dates of decisions, as well as other decision-making policies related to tenure. Many legal claims by faculty members involve specific claims of lack of notice or awareness of university policies. Although adequate notice can often be shown to have been given, the best defense against such a claim is a clear procedure for notification.

Probationary Faculty

Once a faculty appointment has been made, legal and other relationships begin and expectations arise between the individual and the institution. It is critical to successful academic governance that the faculty member be informed fully of evaluation, promotion, and tenure decisions. The courts require that any decision relating to the probationary faculty member be nondiscriminatory; this will be addressed later. The faculty member should be apprised of all the institution's policies affecting his or her position. Specifically, it is important that the institution adopt and follow precise and clear evaluation standards and procedures for salary and promotion decisions and make as clear as possible the expectations that departmental colleges and institutional officers have for faculty members. This is particularly true for evaluations leading to a decision about tenure.

A probationary faculty member's rights with respect to the institution are determined by his or her contractual relationships with the institution. In *Board of Regents* v. *Roth* (1972), it was determined that no tenure rights existed that due process was required to protect. However, each legal relationship between a faculty member and an institution has to be reviewed to determine whether the contract itself creates a contractual due process right arising from a possible expectancy of re-employment; in many cases, explicit or implicit contractual provisions covering probationary faculty (such as granting notice of nonrenewal, hearings, and other due process rights) may exist. An academic administrator should ensure that institutional policies on nonrenewal of probationary faculty are well defined, whether nonrenewal results from a denial of tenure or from dismissal for cause or for other reasons.

Tenure and Dismissal

Academic freedom is the philosophy or set of norms and values embodied in the law that protects a faculty member's freedom of intellectual expression and inquiry. Tenure is a contract; it is a set of procedural protections designed to guard faculty members against the negative consequences of unpopular beliefs. Tenure generally means that unless there is adequate cause for dismissal, a college or university will employ a faculty member until the faculty member has reached a mandatory retirement age. Tenure can also be viewed as a guarantee that any dismissal of a faculty member will be for conduct outside the scope of protected academic freedom. As Bowen and Schuster (1986, p. 46) point out: "Tenure is not an iron-bound contract. It may be annulled in cases of serious malfeasance on the part of individual professors and in cases of financial exigency on the part of institutions."

Tenure is a constitutionally protected property right when it is extended to a faculty member under private or state action; as a property right, it can be removed only by pretermination due process. This was the basis of the landmark decision by the United States Supreme Court in *Perry* v. *Sindermann* (1972). Academic administrators should ensure that their institution's policies and procedures for denial or removal of tenure fully comply with due process requirements. They should seek experienced legal counsel promptly if the dismissal of a tenured professor is being considered. Although the laws do not precisely enumerate the exact procedural steps to be taken, due process requirements have been developed in specific cases by the courts, and most postsecondary institutions have adopted or modified the AAUP's statement of principles on academic freedom, revised in 1940. The statement primarily addresses the principles of tenure and recommends certain standards for probationary periods and dismissal procedures. It states that tenured professors "should be terminated only for adequate cause" except in cases of retirement for age or under extraordinary circumstances because of financial exigencies. Adequate cause is not defined, but the statement refers to incompetence and moral turpitude as possible grounds. Generally, the AAUP statement leaves the definition of adequate cause to individual institutions.

Adequate cause has generally been found to include incompetence (*Chung* v. *Park,* 1974), immorality, including sexual harassment (*Lehman* v. *Board of Trustees of Whitman College,* 1978), neglect of duty (*Garrett* v. *Matthews,* 1979), and insubordination (*Stasny* v. *Board of Trustees of Central Washington University,* 1982), as well as conviction of a felony and physical or mental incapacity. Removal may also occur for noncausal reasons, specifically for financial exigency and program elimination, without infringing upon academic freedom. Tenure may not be removed for impermissible reasons, including protected exercise of free speech, or in violation of academic freedom.

The courts are properly protective of academic freedom and free speech in institutions of higher education; they also are sensitive and alert to evidence of pretextual dismissals and dismissals in retaliation for dissent, criticism of authority, or personal dislike. Academic administrators must be particularly aware of pressures for selective enforcement of rules regarding insubordinate behavior—one faculty member's behavior may be considered unacceptable while similar behavior by another may be ignored. As a consequence of these pressures, insubordinate behavior is the most difficult criterion of adequate cause to justify. The courts have consistently shown considerable deference to the expertise of the academy in personnel decisions. They acknowledge that dismissals of tenured faculty members should

be within the competence, as well as the authority, of colleges
and universities; unless there is violation of academic freedom
or unjustified disregard for ability or experience, such decisions
are proper. For further discussion of removing tenure, see Chapter Six.

Termination for Financial Exigency

Financial exigency is a relatively new term in higher education. It describes an institutional condition in which financial
problems are sufficiently serious to require the dismissal of tenured faculty. Financial exigency may be the result of a decline
in enrollment or declining state or federal support. In its 1976
recommendation for institutional regulations and academic freedom and tenure, the AAUP (1977, p. 17) defined financial exigency as "an imminent financial crisis which threatens the survival of the institution as a whole and which cannot be alleviated
by less drastic means" than the termination of tenured faculty
members. In *Lumpert* v. *University of Dubuque* (1977), the
court gave the following definition: "Financial exigency is defined as the critical, pressing or urgent need on the part of the
educational institution to reorder its monetary expenditures
within the institution in such a way as to remedy and relieve the
state or urgency within said institution to meet its annual monetary expenditures with sufficient revenue to prevent a sustained
loss of funds."

Because many colleges and universities have adopted or
adapted the AAUP guidelines, the courts have given them some
de facto validity, but they usually have not supported them
completely. Although financial exigency is clearly more than a
temporary or minor shortage, the courts have not required that
an institution be threatened with either bankruptcy or collapse.
The financial crisis need not be university-wide nor extend to
the capital assets of the institution. In *Browzin* v. *Catholic University of America* (1975), Catholic University's dismissal of
tenured professors in the school of engineering and architecture
was upheld; faced with severe budget reductions, the university
had reviewed the institution's current programs and made re-

ductions in areas in which the university had no great academic strength and could not hope to achieve strength under the new budgetary limitations.

The courts have required, however, that the institution demonstrate that its dismissals based on financial exigency are made in good faith. This finding was articulated in *American Association of University Professors* v. *Bloomfield College* (1974). Although Bloomfield College was on the verge of bankruptcy, the court based its decision on the existence of alternatives to the dismissal of tenured faculty that would be equally effective in balancing the budget. Specifically, the court cited as alternatives the sale of a tract of land and the hiring of twelve new and nontenured teachers to replace thirteen tenured faculty members dismissed earlier. The court considered the true motive for the dismissal to be the abolition of tenure, "not the alleviation of financial stringency" (M. 858). This case confirms that policy statements issued by the AAUP do not have legal status in themselves nor do they necessarily offer legal precedent. Saunders (1984, p. 12) cautions that "an institution that clearly adopts in its faculty contract or handbook the AAUP definition of financial exigency as articulated in its 'Recommended Institutional Regulations' has generally been locked by the courts into a more rigid determination of financial exigency than institutions with original or no policies."

Academic administrators should review their financial exigency policies to ensure that they will receive good-faith judgments if tested in court. Some factors showing good faith are a genuine fiscal crisis, faculty review and consultation, uniform treatment of affected faculty, the necessary minimum of due process, and use of remedial measures short of dismissal; other factors may be deemed rational on legal examination.

The courts have held that under circumstances of financial exigency minimal due process is sufficient and that the amount of due process required for dismissal for cause is not needed. In *Johnson* v. *Board of Regents* (1974), the court set forth the necessary procedures required by the Fourteenth Amendment to the United States Constitution: "Furnishing each plaintiff with a reasonably adequate written statement of the basis for the initial decision to lay off; furnishing each plaintiff with a reasonably adequate description of the manner in which the initial decision had been arrived at; making a reasonably adequate disclosure to each plaintiff of the information and data upon which the decision-makers had relied, and providing each plaintiff the opportunity to respond." Tenure clearly does not provide immunity from dismissal if a bona fide financial case exists for reductions in faculty or programs. Courts have clearly found that program and faculty termination during a financial crisis is an implied or inherent power that can be exercised in a fair and impartial manner.

David Figuli (n.d.) outlines some academic personnel policies and procedures that do not require due process: "Faculty need not be integrated into the process of selection of the departments or individuals to be discontinued or terminated; neutral or impartial review is not required; hearing need not precede decision to terminate a particular individual; an appeal from hearing need not be provided; there is no requirement that the institution present witnesses for cross-examination; institution need not follow contractual nonrenewal procedures where financial exigency motivates nonrenewal decision; and no particular selection process is mandated by the constitution, or, non-tenured need not be terminated before tenured."

The burden of proof of bona fide financial exigency has not yet been clearly allocated by the courts. Saunders (1984, p. 16) suggests that the burden should be divided between the faculty member and the institution. The institution is responsible for demonstrating that the alleged exigency is indeed real, and the faculty member should bear the burden of proving any bad faith on the part of the institution. The procedures should ensure that faculty terminations are made equitably and that the terminations are motivated by a bona fide institutional need. If the alleged exigency is deemed pretextual, or if arbitrary procedures were employed in the termination, the institution is likely to bear the burden of proof in any litigation.

Sex Discrimination

In the past few years the courts have been confronted with numerous claims of discrimination in academic personnel decisions. In 1972 the United States Congress amended Title VII of the Civil Rights Act of 1964 to cover educational institutions (Equal Employment Opportunity Act of 1972). The statute makes it unlawful to discriminate against a person who is a member of one of the defined protected classes of race, religion, sex, or national origin. Thus faculty members who suspect they were denied promotion or tenure because of their race, religion, sex, or national origin can bring suit against the institution under Title VII (often after exhausting internal grievance procedures at their institution), alleging that some apparently neutral practice of the institution has a disparate impact on an affected faculty member, or that they were intentionally subjected to disparate treatment because of one of the protected factors.

Under the disparate impact claim a plaintiff must demonstrate that a facially neutral criterion, such as a Ph.D. or publication requirement, has a disparate impact. Courts have required plaintiffs to prove with clear and convincing evidence the exactness of a substantiated discriminatory effect before they will apply a disparate impact analysis. Disparate impact analysis has rarely been used in promotion and tenure because the uniqueness of a faculty position and the small number of qualified applicants make it difficult to establish the statistical foundation needed for proof. Also, courts generally hold that universities are best able to determine their own selection standards as part of the traditional tenure process. Primarily for these reasons, the courts have utilized the disparate treatment analysis more often.

The disparate treatment analysis requires a step-by-step approach as set by the United States Supreme Court in *McDonell Douglas Corp.* v. *Green* (1973). First, a faculty member claiming discriminatory treatment must establish a prima facie case of discrimination. The courts recently have applied the normal elements of a prima facie case in a claim against a university. A number of courts have articulated standards for such a prima facie case: the faculty member must establish that he or she is a member of a protected class, is qualified for promotion or tenure, and despite his or her qualifications was rejected.

Second, once a prima facie case is established by a faculty

member, the university has the burden of articulating some legitimate nondiscriminatory reasons for refusing to grant promotion or tenure. Specifically, the university can argue that a bona fide occupational qualification was not met or rebut the claim that race, sex, religion, or national origin influenced its decision by showing that the faculty member was not qualified. Courts have accepted justifications for denial of tenure based, for example, on tenure density (*Timper* v. *Board of Regents of the University of Wisconsin*, 1981), inadequate scholarship (*Lynn* v. *Regents of the University of California*, 1981), lack of collegiality, and unwillingness or inability to teach specific courses (*Perkins* v. *Todd*, 436 F. Supp 1101 (N.D. Ill. 1977)). In *Trustees of Keene State College* v. *Sweeny*, 569 F.2d 169 (1st Cir 1977) (vacated and remanded per curiam, 439 U.S. 24 (1978), aff'd. 604 F.2d 106 (1st Cir 1979), cert. denied, 444 U.S. 1045 (1980)), the court noted that the college need only come forward with enough credible evidence to rebut the faculty members' claims. The court also noted that the college only had to state the reasons for its denial of tenure and was not obliged to prove it acted without discriminatory intent.

Third, if the trial court judge determines that the university's stated reasons for refusing to grant a promotion or tenure are sufficient, the burden shifts back to the faculty member. At this step the faculty member is given the opportunity to prove by a preponderance of the evidence that if race, sex, religion, or national origin had not been considered, he or she would have been awarded the promotion or tenure; that the reason for rejection was pretextual, that is, a mask for unlawful discrimination; and that the decision was discriminatorily motivated.

The courts have explicitly acknowledged the unique and subjective nature of academic promotion and tenure decisions in universities. Although the courts are willing to correct procedural irregularities and proven bias, they have refused to reverse tenure decisions that could be viewed as unfair. They have deferred to qualitative judgments concerning teaching, scholarship, and research and refused to substitute their judgment in the complex decision-making processes involved in academic decisions.

In the future, the courts may well limit their judicial deference to universities' decisions in Title VII cases. The recommended approach for academic administrators is constantly to review and examine academic personnel policies and procedures as well as the individual decision makers. The traditional multilayered process for promotion and tenure decisions allows many opportunities to ensure a fair and impartial review of each faculty member's status and, for members of a protected class, a fair and nondiscriminatory decision.

Peer Review and Confidentiality

The concerns recently expressed in the literature about the courts and their determinations regarding academic peer review processes stem primarily from Title VII discrimination litigation. The courts have expressed both an understanding of and a need for peer review in the area of academic personnel decisions, and they are generally reluctant to interfere. Sloviter (1982, p. 21) cautions that "courts must be vigilant not to intrude into that determination, and should not substitute their judgment for that of the college with respect to the qualifications of faculty members for promotion and tenure. Determinations about such matters as teaching ability, research, scholarship, community service, and professional stature are subjective, and unless they can be shown to have been used as the mechanism to obscure discrimination, they must be left for evaluation by the professionals, particularly since they often involve inquiry into aspects of arcane scholarship beyond the competence of individual judges."

In a recent peer review case (*Zahornik* v. *Cornell*, 1984), the court took this position: "A decentralized decision-making structure founded largely on peer judgment is based on generations of almost universal tradition stemming from considerations as to the stake of an academic department in such decisions and its superior knowledge of the academic field and the work of an individual candidate. It would be a most radical interpretation of Title VII for a court to enjoin use of a historically settled process and plainly relevant criteria largely because they lead to decisions which are difficult for the court to review." On the same issue (*Clark* v. *Whiting*, 1979), the court said: "Courts are not qualified to review and substitute their judgment for these subjective, discretionary judgments of professional experts on faculty promotions or engage independently in an intelligent informal comparison of the scholarly contributions or teaching talents of one faculty member denied promotion with those of another faculty member granted a promotion; in short, courts may not engage in second guessing the university authorities in connection with faculty promotions; that is exactly what [Clark] seeks by his action to have the courts do. . . . In essence, what [Clark] thus argues for, if carried to its logical conclusion, is the judicial supervision of the most delicate part of every state educational institution's academic operations, a role the federal courts have neither the competency nor the resources to undertake."

The courts have been consistent in their support for peer review; judicial decisions in the area of confidentiality have been less supportive. In *In Re: Dinnan* (1981), a University of Georgia faculty member named James A. Dinnan served thirty days in jail and was fined for contempt of court for refusing to divulge his vote in a tenure review committee. Further, in *Franklin and Marshall College* v. *Equal Employment Opportunity Commission* (1986) the Supreme Court upheld a decision supporting the EEOC's right to inspect confidential recommendations, minutes, and evaluations, with names deleted.

Clearly, the responsibility of the courts to dispense justice to all will continue to impinge on the traditional role of peer review in academic personnel decisions. The question of confidentiality will continue to evolve and administrators will need to adapt to the new academic order in which traditional confidentiality is outweighed by the importance of ensuring that academic personnel decisions are made on a nondiscriminatory basis.

Modifications of Tenure and Conditions of Employment

Tenure, from the legal perspective, is essentially a contract. In *Taliaferro* v. *Dykstra* (1977), the court stated that "the specific rights and duties associated with tenure are to be found in the understandings of the parties." If there are not clear contractual definitions of the parties' relationships in a faculty member's contract that incorporates the university's policies and procedures, the courts will try to ascertain what the relationship shall be.

Prior to the extension of the Federal Age Discrimination in Employment Act to colleges and universities, a number of cases recognized the ability of an institution to establish or change a mandatory retirement age, as long as the resulting policy was reasonable, was uniformly applied, provided for reasonable transitional accommodations for faculty members, and provided for faculty input. Late in 1986, however, H. R. 4154 was signed into law, outlawing forced retirement at age seventy and including professors who will be seventy in 1994 (Palmer, 1986, pp. 1ff).

The courts look at the contractual relationship between faculty members and the institution to determine the exact contractual provisions. These are usually related to a college or university's policies and procedures; in certain instances these provisions have been created through collective bargaining and the adoption of the AAUP's 1940 statement. The courts have recently addressed issues of salary reduction, contract terms, office space, and other matters; each case is examined on its own merits so that a legally fair and proper decision can be reached. Academic administrators must be fully aware of contractual obligations in making departmental and college decisions on specific faculty matters.

Referring to legal issues in higher education, including those of academic personnel policies and procedures, Branton (1984, p. 19) observes that "the courts are deciding more and more of these matters because either the institutions involved have no rules designed to provide due process, or they fail to follow the rules they do have. In the latter case, any institution will be a certain loser in court."

Clearly, some institutions are very vulnerable because of their haphazard academic policies and procedures. Most institutions would do well to plan for a biennial checkup on their policies. The institution should start with a coherent and relevant statement of mission. While every college has some sort of statement of mission, the statement should be carefully protected against possible legal entrapments. A systematic and regular evaluation process is another necessary component of planning, which also should include a continual review of the legal safeguards established to avoid problems. Olswang and Fantel (1980, p. 30) suggest that periodic institutional review of planning and evaluation models can be helpful in a quest for excellence. If used systematically, such reviews can help meet the public's demand for accountability. In a discussion directed to probationary faculty but applicable to a wider audience, the Special Committee on Education and the Law of the Association of the Bar of the City of New York (1984, p. 330) writes that "clarity, consistency, and fairness" are goals to be sought in the equitable treatment of faculty. They urge that "good practice, embodied in regulations, may establish enforceable contractual rights" (p. 329). In support, Hobbs (1982, p. 3) counsels that "the key to avoiding legal problems is a passion for fairness." Kaplin (1985, p. 178) recommends having detailed written procedures for personnel decisions and making these procedures available. He also suggests (p. 215) that administrators should keep good records and documentation of policy. In *Mayberry* v. *Dees* (1981), the court upheld a tenure denial on the basis of collegiality because the institution had specifically listed collegiality as a criterion for tenure (Zirkel, 1985, p. 35).

Litigation avoidance is the preventive medicine approach to academic administration. It should be practiced in every institution of higher education by both administrators and faculty members. The inordinate amounts of time and money consumed in court proceedings often mean that no one really wins. The following points made by Balch may be helpful:

A. Litigation avoidance by faculty:
   • Be aware of and get to know the next highest person in administrative authority. When a problem arises, contact this person first.
   • Have a third neutral party present when dealing with a sensitive matter with either students or administration.

- Keep written memoranda and keep full notes.
- Utilize the student evaluation process of the institution, and for added strength, design self-evaluation forms for classes to respond to other types of questions.
- Keep up-to-date records from the time of hiring (contracts, terms of employment) in a chronological file.
- Do not attack verbally or in writing any member of the administration.
- Keep current about laws, regulations, and policies on legal matters.
- Do not use words such as "immoral," "behaviorally undesirable," or "incompetent."

B. Litigation avoidance by administrators:
- Keep up to date on legal aspects.
- Be aware of administrative roles in institutional evaluation policies and practices.
- Make certain that the evaluation process for each faculty member is job-related.
- Be sure that the faculty evaluations are not discriminatory in intent, application, or results.
- Be certain that evaluation forms contain precise and uniform language and are statistically valid.
- Guarantee that evaluators at the institution are trained in how to use and analyze evaluation instruments.
- Make certain that institutional policies on evaluation are communicated to all newly hired faculty members *before* they sign their first contract.
- Work for improved administrator-faculty communications.
- Employ competent, up-to-date legal counsel.
- Be consistent in applying policies and produres.

- Create a sense of fairness in facing evaluation problems [1980, pp. 40-42].

Litigation avoidance also has a legal art to it. Inexperi-
enced administrators may err on the side of specificity in developing academic personnel policies and procedures. Experienced
administrators—and experience comes very quickly, usually
after winning or losing a court case—want legal protection for
fundamental academic freedom and critical personnel policies
and procedures. But they also want some leg room, or enough
generality to avoid being pinned down by their own rhetoric.
For example, the quotation from Saunders (1984) stated that
an institution that adapts the AAUP definition of financial exigency is usually restricted by the courts into a more rigid determination of financial exigency than institutions that have their
own policy or none at all. (The latter approach is not recommended.) On this point, however, the administration may en-
counter faculty support for the AAUP interpretation, which is
written primarily to protect faculty rights and jobs. This faculty self-interest is proper and important, but so is the institution's health.

Finally, it is important to keep legal matters in perspective. The purpose of the academy is to help students grow in
knowledge, wisdom, sensitivity, and humanness. Legal aspects
allow greater fairness and equity to hold sway. Lawyers and
legal decisions are important, and administrators who take them
lightly do so at their own peril. Nevertheless, risk taking, innovation, and intuition are commonly identified traits of successful leadership. An overcautious, legalistic approach to academic
administration is not only dull but likely not to be very successful.

Nine

Administrative Roles
in Promotion
and Tenure Processes

"See, there is a professor! He is responsible only to God!"
(DeVane, 1968, p. 252). This is the punchline from a story told
by a former dean of Yale University about the new captain of
the naval ROTC unit who came into his office, a bit bewildered
by procedures in the university, and asked: "What is the chain
of command here?" At that moment a professor came by his
door, prompting the dean's response. Administrators who forget
that professors with tenure see deans and presidents come and
go do so at their own peril.

Yet the need for dynamic academic leadership has become increasingly evident in recent years. The findings of a
comprehensive study made by *Forbes* (Sept. 15, 1968, pp. 51-
52) are relevant: "The clear lesson of fifty action-packed years
of U.S. business is: If a company has nothing going for it except one thing—good management—it will make the grade. If it
has everything except good management, it will flop." The difference between short-term and long-term perspectives was the
focus of an influential and provocative article by Hayes and
Abernathy (1980, pp. 70, 77) titled "Managing Our Way to Decline." They wrote: "The key to long-term success—even survival—in business is what it has always been: to invest, to innovate, to lead, to create value where none existed before. Such
determination, such striving to excel, requires leaders—not just
controllers, market analysts, and portfolio managers. In our pre-
occupation with the braking systems and exterior trim, we may
have neglected the drive trains of our corporations."

Attention to leadership is prominent in three recent and widely read books on American business—*In Search of Excellence*, by Peters and Waterman (1982), *A Passion for Excellence*, by Peters and Austin (1985), and *The Change Masters*, by Kanter (1983)—and in a prominent book on higher education—*Academic Strategy*, by Keller (1983). *Searching for Academic Excellence*, by Gilley, Fulmer, and Reithlingshoefer (1986), contains a chapter titled "Leadership: The Critical Element." This chapter considers administration from a perspective that is both dynamic and sensitive, contextual and personalized.

Chief Executive Officer (CEO)

CEOs generally ride "above the waves" in academic personnel matters, trying not to become overinvolved in day-to-day operations. They should, however, be involved in formulating academic personnel policies, either directly or through the chief academic officer. It has been estimated that the average CEO spends only about 25 percent of his or her time on instructional and curricular matters, which does not leave much time for academic personnel matters in particular.

In an extensive study that included successful and unsuccessful colleges, Richard Anderson (1983, p. 8) reports: "Presidents and senior administrators at the most successful colleges and universities did intrude in personnel matters. The effective officers, unlike those at less successful institutions, were more likely to contravene hiring, promotion, and tenure decisions made in faculty committees. This intervention was not arbitrary nor taken without insufficient cause. All successful administrators preferred positive actions. The officers offered symbolic and material rewards for professional accomplishments." Michael Cohen and James March (1986, p. 110) point out that the nature of the school influences the president's interest in tenure. "Presidents of schools where turnover of faculty is low and where growth is modest or nonexistent would involve themselves more directly in tenure decisions than would presidents of high turnover and rapidly growing schools."

Probably the common denominator in promotion and

tenure matters for all types of institution is the policy of having these decisions made through established channels. At the penultimate step, recommendations are made to the chief academic officer, who, in turn, makes recommendations to the CEO. At this point, if not earlier, CEOs will want to know about the problem cases, usually in some detail, and they will want to spend some time with the recommendations and perhaps with selected files. It is unwise, however, for CEOs to be their own chief academic affairs officers; this sometimes happens almost automatically because most have been chief academic officers en route to CEO positions.

Guskin (1981, p. 2), the former chancellor of the University of Wisconsin, Parkside, an institution with approximately 4,000 students, contends that in order to foster high-quality teaching at his level, one "must first accept an important two-part assumption: faculty members on the whole are bright and desire to be good teachers, and the quality of their teaching is more dependent on the quality of their lives as faculty members than on the techniques of the teaching process." Guskin concludes (p. 12) that under desirable circumstances, the president's style can create an organizational environment that increases knowledge by sharing, increases faculty confidence by letting the faculty influence decisions, accentuates the positive without glossing over the negative, and, through incentives and encouragement, increases the likelihood that faculty members will focus on their roles as teacher-scholars.

With respect to academic evaluation and promotion and tenure, the CEO usually has several important roles.

Espousing and facilitating academic quality is an important function of the CEO, since academics are the raison d'etre for postsecondary institutions. The day-to-day monitoring and modifying functions, however, are normally the responsibilities of the chief academic officer.

Initiating studies, committees, and planning efforts is an important component of the CEO's job. Effective CEOs use the power of initiative carefully because faculty members already feel that too little time is their greatest frustration. Some new CEOs have overused this power by initiating too many studies and task forces without careful thought about the intended outcomes or the time involved in doing the studies.

Serving as the institution's last recourse on promotion and tenure decisions can be a sensitive and time-consuming task; the CEO must obtain as much information and impartial advice as possible.

Using fiscal resources to work toward institutional missions and goals can directly affect promotion and tenure decisions. The difficulty of meshing institutional directions and needs with those of individuals has been discussed. CEOs must carefully consider how promotion and tenure decisions will be affected by reallocating or reducing fiscal resources.

Making promotion and tenure recommendations to the governing board is an important function. Some faculty members believe that governing boards rubber-stamp recommendations from the CEO. This perception certainly is not shared by experienced CEOs. Of course, the board rarely delves into individual cases because this responsibility is delegated to the CEO, but experienced CEOs know of enough cases where board members have raised questions about a CEO's personnel recommendations to make sure that they have mastered the intricacies of any difficult cases or any possible personnel problems that will come before the board.

The precise role of the CEO in academic promotion and tenure policies and procedures varies considerably, depending on the nature of the institution, its history, and its current status. In affluent times CEOs tend to pay less attention to academic matters than when austerity measures are necessary.

Chief Academic Officer (CAO)

"Typical Chief Academic Officer: He's 50, earns $61,000, has been on the job 5 years, and wants to be a president," according to a summary by Beverly Watkins (1985, p. 21) of a national survey of 376 chief academic officers by R. I. Miller and Gary Moden. Usually the second-ranking senior administrative official, this officer has overall responsibility for academic personnel and programs. With respect to academic evaluation and promotion and tenure, the CAO usually has these roles:

Espousing, facilitating, and monitoring academic quality makes everyone's work with academic personnel matters a bit easier and more satisfying. This Pollyannalike statement will be nothing more unless an espousal of quality is consistently backed by actions that, over time, enhance quality. At some time during one's early tenure as a CAO, usually in the first or second year, some difficult promotion and tenure decisions will be passed on by the chairpersons and deans. Usually they are promotion or tenure cases that no one else wants to handle. Others will be watching to see what happens, and the CAO's recommendation to the CEO may say much more than words about a commitment to quality.

Initiating and facilitating faculty development and professional growth is an important encouragement that can improve the academic performance of faculty members. Even in fiscally austere times, when faculty positions are being eliminated, the CAO must keep alive academic conversations and activities designed to promote faculty development and growth. The amount of funds available for these activities may be only token, but keeping them accessible sends an important message.

Seeing that institutional promotion and tenure policies and procedures protect the institution as well as the individual requires some legal expertise and sometimes much thought about strategies for change. If academic personnel statements have become overprotective of individual rights at the expense of institutional needs, then some redressing may be in order. These efforts require the utmost cooperation between the CEO and the CAO and often careful communication between the CEO and the governing board.

Monitoring the institution's promotion and tenure policies, procedures, and practices is an important function for the CAO. The support and insight of the college and school deans are essential in this delicate task. More than one dean has been returned to the faculty ranks for not making difficult personnel decisions but passing them on to the CAO. Occasionally, a department that is guided by an institution-wise chairperson will try to finesse its promotion and tenure practices so that they appear to satisfy the requirements of the college and university while in fact avoiding them. For example, one academic department at a research-oriented institution took advantage of the inexperience of a new president and chief academic officer to slip through promotions for faculty members who did not meet the standards of the previous administration. Two years later, after the chief academic officer got his feet on the ground, this practice ended.

Anticipating difficult academic personnel problems can decrease surprises. It is estimated that 25 percent of the academic promotion and tenure decisions take 75 percent of the time the CAO devotes to this area. Sometimes the problem cases have histories of several months or years. To be forewarned is to be forearmed.

Seeing that faculty recruitment policies, procedures, and practices are as effective as possible means helping to put the institution's best foot forward, assisting search committee members in learning about candidates, and helping candidates to feel comfortable during their campus visits. While faculty recruitment is and should be primarily the province of the faculty, the office of the CAO should monitor the process to help ensure that the best-qualified candidates are offered tenure-track positions. Effective recruitment programs can help avoid many problems of retention later.

CAOs would do well to remember the quotation at the beginning of this chapter, and also to remember that power is like money in the bank—the more you use, the less you have. There are times when the exercise of the CAO's power is in the institution's best interests, but Ratner (1981, p. 24), at the time a vice-chancellor and dean of faculty, reminded us that "persuasion is the best tool . . . available to academic administrators as they seek to facilitate quality instruction as well as meet the other responsibilities of their office."

College and School Deans

"When the dossier finally reaches the dean's desk, the weight of middle management responsibilities becomes noticeable. . . . What to do with the committee's recommendations . . . takes on an element of urgency and seriousness not equaled elsewhere in the administrator's sphere of tasks" (Morris, 1981, p. 59). The college dean has a direct role in the academic personnel decision-making process, as Centra's survey (1977, p. 11) of 453 department heads from 134 institutions shows. Fifteen sources of information were ranked in order of importance:

- Chairperson evaluation   1
- Systematic student ratings   2.5
- Colleague opinions   2.5
- Committee evaluation   4
- Informal student opinions   5
- Dean evaluation   6
- Content of course syllabi and examinations   7
- Popularity of elective courses   8
- Self-evaluation or report   9
- Teaching improvement activities   10
- Student examination performance   11
- Colleague ratings based on classroom visits   12
- Alumni opinions or ratings   13
- Long-term follow-up of student performance   14
- Videotape of classroom teaching   15

It may be a little deflating to some deans to note that their evaluations of teaching performance are considered only the sixth most important. Other deans, however, may be pleased to see that they are not as deeply involved in the process as they thought they were.

An important role for the dean in the academic personnel loop is to make sure that the institutional, college, and departmental policies and procedures have been followed and that the recommendations are fair and equitable. They want no surprises and expect to be apprised fully in advance of possible problem cases. Deans sometimes become arbitrators between department committees and chairpersons when personnel disagreements are on the horizon or arrive full blown. CAOs expect deans to handle their own problems rather than to pass them upstairs. Deans are expected to make recommendations on promotion and tenure after careful study of the individuals' files and the recommendations of the departmental committee and the chairperson. Their recommendations support chairperson and committee recommendations perhaps 90 percent of the time, especially when the committee and the chairperson strongly agree.

In a few instances, deans are hired to take care of difficult personnel problems and to redirect a college. An unwritten agreement between the CEO or CAO and the dean sometimes is necessary in order to turn a college around. Such a role requires a dean to walk a very thin line, maintaining credibility in the college while moving in directions considered desirable by the CEO and CAO. The dean at times will need to place institutional priorities above the different agendas of individuals in the college.

Department Chairpersons

"An institution can run for a long time with an inept president but not for long with inept chairpersons" (Peltason, 1981, p. xi). An estimated 80 percent of all administrative decisions are made at the departmental level, according to Roach (1976, p. 13), yet most chairpersons are selected for reasons other than demonstrated managerial skills. In her research, Bragg (1981, p. 11) found that 82 percent of the thirty-nine department heads in a large land-grant university "reported no orientation of any kind. Most department heads were simply provided policy manuals and given instructions to call if they had any questions." In his 1977 survey of four hundred department chairpersons in the state university system of Florida, Allan Tucker (1981, p. 1) found that 68 percent had had no administrative experience, the turnover rate was 15 to 20 percent per year, and the average term of service was approximately six years. Forty-one percent had been elected by their colleagues and another 44 percent had been appointed by their deans with faculty consultation. A more recent survey could not be located, but there is no reason to believe that the figures are appreciably different today.

The chair is the "front-trench" position where its occupants are in day-to-day contact with both faculty and students, yet they are administrators. It provides a baptism by fire for those who want to test the waters of administration. As an army's strength traditionally depends on the efficiency and morale of its squads, so a postsecondary institution can only be as academically strong as its departments.

Centra's study (1977, p. 11) outlined earlier indicates the importance of chairpersons in making academic personnel decisions. Their evaluations are ranked as the most important single evaluation in all fields of study, except in the social sciences, where they are ranked second in importance. One can expect about 90 percent of the final institutional promotion and tenure decisions to concur with those made at the departmental level.

When Waltzer (1975, pp. 25-27) interviewed chairpersons at Miami University, he found that the most difficult and frustrating aspects of the position were "job overload, too many justification requirements, and too many record-keeping and data-reporting requirements." Yet the staff of the Committee on Program Evaluation (COPE) of the University of Illinois, Urbana, which evaluated almost all academic units on that campus, found that being "impressively systematic in managing unit functions" (Miller, 1979, p. 114) was the most evident common factor among departments rated the highest. An integral aspect of this effectiveness is having detailed departmental policies and procedures for making academic personnel decisions. New chairpersons would do well to review these elements carefully and, if no changes are made, to understand thoroughly how they work in theory and in practice.

Specifically, the chairperson usually is the one to notify individuals of the due dates for promotion, tenure, and merit files. Careful attention to such details is important. The chairperson also should provide departmental members who are being reviewed with technical assistance so that their files will be as strong as possible. After carefully reviewing the report of the department's personnel committee as well as the individual's file, the chairperson makes an appraisal and writes a recommendation for each applicant.

The annual academic performance review (AAPR) is one

of the most important appraisal and development functions of the chairperson. Some postsecondary institutions have established regular reviews; more should, in my opinion. They allow the chairperson and each faculty member to have at least one serious and structured conversation about professional performance each year. Their purpose should be improving academic performance. The chairperson might follow this structure and modus operandi:

1. Schedule these reviews at about the same time each year, probably in April.
2. Notify each faculty member of the time of the review in writing, providing also a statement of purposes.
3. Schedule reviews for one hour each, and do not schedule back-to-back reviews or more than four reviews in one day. A chairperson with a department of thirty faculty members will require about two weeks per academic year for reviews, as well as another ten to fifteen hours for preparation and follow-up. But if people are the most important part of a university, one hour of serious and systematic professional discussion per person per academic year does not seem unreasonable.
4. In the session itself, focus on three areas: What professional strengths and weaknesses have become evident during the current academic year? What would *you* like to do professionally next academic year to improve or to innovate? and, What can *we* do to improve the department?
5. Plan the review with data where appropriate. Be frank and professional. Personnel books in the management field spend some time on the appraisal interview; some dimensions of this interview are outlined in Table 14.
6. Send a written record of the conclusions or important notes from the review to the faculty member and invite comments.
7. File a final written report for each faculty member, if desired, with a copy to the faculty member.

Those who enter administration expecting to be powerful figures on campus may be disappointed if they do not realize

Table 14. Cause-and-Effect Relations in Three Types of Appraisal Interviews.

Role of interviewer	Tell and Sell	Tell and Listen	Problem-Solving
	Judge	Judge	Helper
Objective	To communicate evaluation. To persuade employee to improve.	To communicate evaluation. To release defensive feelings.	To stimulate growth and development in employee.
Assumptions	Employee desires to correct weaknesses if he or she knows them.	People will change if defensive feelings are removed.	Growth cannot occur without correcting faults. Discussing job problems leads to improved performance.
Reactions	Defensive behavior suppressed. Attempts to cover hostility.	Defensive behavior expressed. Employee feels accepted.	Problem-solving behavior.
Skills	Salesmanship. Patience.	Listening and reflecting feelings. Summarizing.	Listening and reflecting feelings. Reflecting ideas. Using exploratory questions. Summarizing.
Attitude	People profit from criticism and appreciate help.	One can respect the feelings of others if one understands them.	Discussion develops new ideas and mutual interests.
Motivation	Use of positive or negative incentives or both. (Extrinsic in that motivation is added to the job itself).	Resistance to change reduced. Positive incentive. (Extrinsic and some intrinsic motivation).	Increased freedom. Increased responsibility. (Intrinsic motivation in that interest is interent in the task).

(continued on next page)

Table 14. Cause-and-Effect Relations in Three Types of Appraisal Interviews, Cont'd.

	Tell and Sell	Tell and Listen	Problem-Solving
Gains	Success most probable when employee respects interviewer.	Develops favorable attitude toward superior which increases probability of success.	Almost assured of improvement in some respect.
Risks	Loss of loyalty. Inhibition of independent judgment. Face-saving problems created.	Need for change may not be developed.	Employee may lack ideas. Change may be other than what superior had in mind.
Values	Perpetuates existing practices and values.	Permits interviewer to change his view in the light of employee's responses. Some upward communication.	Both learn since experience and views are pooled. Change is facilitated.

Source: Chruden and Sherman, 1976. Reproduced by permission from Norman R. F. Maier, The Appraisal Interview (New York: Wiley, 1958).

that some of the fundamental responsibilities of administration involve service, cooperation, and fairness. Those who have served for extended periods as faculty members as well as senior academic administrators see both power and service as essential ingredients in a successful *student-oriented* institution. Without service and cooperation, the institution cannot come close to fulfilling its potential. Some conflicts and antagonisms inevitably arise when strong-minded, dedicated, and bright people are in daily contact, but the overall atmosphere must be one of working together for the successes that cannot be achieved otherwise.

Ten

Preparing for
Future Evaluation
and Personnel Needs

Thinking ahead of the problems and issues confronting higher education requires a solid grasp of the present and an ear to the past. Planning in the future will be complicated by the increasing complexity of the educational enterprise and by demographic changes. The information explosion will require administrators and faculty members to sift through more knowledge in their decision making. And a mild or severe economic recession may require major adjustments. These conditions make better planning in the future a necessity for more effective institutional management.

The following ten projections are the result of sorting through past and present trends to discern what we might expect in the nineties in the field of evaluating faculty members for promotion and tenure.

1. *State-level influences will continue to emphasize quality and evaluation.* Talking about the resistance to change in secondary education, Theodore Sizer said: "The system is set up to protect itself in many ways. And there's no pressure for change, no serious pressure. There's the rhetoric of the governors. But when you get down to P.S. 200, nobody wants to change it" (Olson, 1987, p. 22). Sizer's observation is relevant to the problems of change in postsecondary education as well. There have, however, been distinct movements at the state level affecting program assessment. For example, a study by R. I. Miller and Robert Barak (1986, p. 42) of undergraduate academic program reviews at the state level found that

twenty-nine of the states (fifty plus the District of Columbia) already had policies and procedures for conducting undergraduate program reviews. Another five states were making plans, and seven states were at the discussion stage. In other words, the state-level activity in this important area of evaluation has been considerable and largely unnoticed.

In his analysis of state-level assessment developments, Peter Ewell (1987, p. 24) writes that "the most notable development of the past twelve months has been the seizure of the 'high ground' of assessment by external agencies and authorities, mostly by state governments—either through direct legislation or indirectly through the action of a statewide governing or coordinating board." A few state legislatures have considered bills that would mandate systems of faculty evaluation, but these efforts have met with uniform resistance from college officials. Continued effective resistance is desirable, not because postsecondary institutions oppose systems of faculty evaluation but because they are better left to individual institutions or groups of institutions, where the systems can be adapted appropriately. State-level activity in assessment has mushroomed since about 1985, and while these initiatives have not yet affected evaluating faculty for promotion and tenure, the situation requires careful monitoring. External vigilance is the price of institutional autonomy in these matters.

2. *Departmental, college, and university priorities are likely to have greater influence on promotion and tenure decision making.* George Geis (1984, p. 107) writes that "evaluation of faculty . . . should be viewed in the larger perspective of the evaluation of the purposes of institutions of higher education." The priority of the institution's vitality when compared with the individual's interests is currently a controlling reality for many colleges and universities that have severe fiscal problems. With continued fiscal prudence likely to be necessary in the decade ahead, the probable increase of this perspective should not be surprising. In one sense it may be unfair because it can penalize a faculty member for being in the wrong discipline at the wrong time; yet institutional health may depend on making selective cuts in human and material resources.

3. *Financial exigency will continue, and perhaps increase,*

in some classifications of postsecondary institutions. The smaller liberal arts colleges are likely to be the most affected; community colleges, heretofore virtually immune to cutbacks, will become affected to some extent, considering the enrollment drop in two consecutive years (1983-1985)—the first such drop in their history.

Tenure will not provide full assurance that a faculty member will not lose his or her position as colleges and universities become more selective in their cuts. The CUPA study quoted in Chapter Six estimated that about 1,290 tenured faculty members were terminated between 1972 and 1977. A 1983 Pennsylvania State University study disclosed that in the U.S. between 1978 and 1983, 4,000 faculty members were terminated in four-year colleges because of financial difficulties. Of the 4,000, 1,200 were tenured (Scully, 1983).

4. *More sophisticated, computerized faculty evaluation systems can be expected.* This should come as no surprise in view of the considerable advances that have been made in computer hardware and software. Aleamoni (1984, pp. 78-79) writes: "I feel that faculty evaluation will be a very comprehensive, well-defined system by the year 2000, with explicit criteria and guidelines for evaluation decisions. These systems will be predominantly computer based, with explicit recommendations for improvement provided along with time lines to achieve improvement." The rate of development of computerized systems may not be as rapid as Aleamoni predicts, but the trend in this direction is unmistakable.

Any evaluation system, however, is only a means to formative and summative evaluation; one should not become enamored of the system itself. To be successful, it needs to be cost-effective and provide some formative assistance; its outputs should be simple enough to be readily understood by faculty members and others; there should be people on campus competent to maintain and tinker with it; and it should be seen as genuinely facilitating fair promotion and tenure decisions.

5. *Individualized and flexible systems will become more prevalent.* Some current evaluation systems (see Appendix B) allow individual faculty members to choose the criteria for

their evaluation from a data bank of possible questions. Other systems, such as the one developed by this writer, allow each faculty member, in concert with the departmental chairperson, to determine his or her professional workload and the weights of the chosen criteria, within constraints imposed by the needs of the department and the directions and nature of the college or university.

Menges (1984, p. 114) notes that "most present evaluation systems, because they are the result of compromise, are inherently conservative." He sees in the future increased flexibility in evaluation systems. Aleamoni (1984, p. 79) predicts that "every new faculty member will be able to construct a contract indicating how much time and effort will be devoted to teaching, research, and service and what criteria will be used to judge his or her effectiveness in each of those areas." While few will reject Aleamoni's vision, the achievement of it may be another matter.

Another element of flexibility allows individual faculty members to choose each year from among available professional activities for their individual workloads. Chapter Eight discusses this approach to individualization. This type of flexibility can be expected to increase in the future, especially among community colleges.

6. *Academic personnel decisions will be more rigorously examined.* External forces, such as the increasing state-level emphasis on quality and greater attention to evaluation, will provide some impetus for increasing rigor. Senior collegiate administrators will also press for higher academic quality as well as lower tenure rates in overtenured faculties. The increasing difficulty of obtaining tenure is documented by Bowen and Schuster (1986, p. 148): "A sizable majority of the respondents (73 percent) thought that tenure had become more elusive, fewer than one percent thought tenure was now easier to obtain, and the remaining 22 percent saw no change. Interestingly, this perception of increased difficulty applied across all types of institutions, ranging from 84 percent of the respondents at the research universities to 50 percent at the community colleges."

Care should be taken, however, that increased rigor does

not make younger professors so nervous about their academic future that their innovation and freshness are stifled and their demeanor becomes anxious. Increased rigor may also deter talented young people from taking their chances in academe.

7. *The predicted shortage of talented young professors may cause some relaxing of academic rigor, as in the 1960s.* This trend is the opposite of the previous one, but contradictory trends are nothing new in higher education.

The retirement of professors hired in the sixties, decreases in those who accept early retirement, and the difficulty of attracting outstanding young men and women into the academic profession are very likely to cause a professional shortage by the middle nineties. Bowen and Schuster (1986, p. 268) write that major problems in recruitment and retention of academic faculty may make it very difficult to fill adequately the 400,000 to 500,000 faculty openings expected in the next twenty-five years. "Three congeries of problems today press hard upon the professoriate and affect also those who contemplate academic careers: inadequate compensation, a deteriorating work environment, and an inhospitable labor market. . . . We have concluded that the professoriate is imperiled."

These impending shortages bring into play the classic rule of supply and demand. We may see a relaxing of promotion and tenure standards—in public institutions, to keep student-teacher ratios tuned to state funding formulas; in private colleges, to keep the ratios competitive. Of course, no institution of higher education would ever admit to lowering its standards.

8. *Greater attention will be given to faculty development (growth).* We are likely to see a resurgence in interest in faculty development in the decade ahead, fueled primarily by three factors. First, decreased professional mobility will make it more difficult for faculty members to meet their diverse needs by changing jobs; more institutional approaches to professional improvement will be needed.

Second, younger faculty members will see development and growth activities as assets in their upcoming promotion and tenure trials. Faculty members who have been unsuccessful in their promotion and tenure applications will also regard these activities as assets in their reapplications. Eble and McKeachie

(1985, p. 221) conclude that "younger faculty members feel severe time pressures." Bowen and Schuster (1986, p. 48) quote an unpublished 1980 study by Helen Astin on career satisfaction that found that 50 percent of professors, but only 35 percent of assistant professors, were very satisfied with their careers; 11 percent of professors and 21 percent of assistant professors were marginally satisfied. On the basis of their 1984 interviews, Bowen and Schuster (1986, p. 47) conclude that "an additional half-decade of financial stringency likely has reduced the proportion of faculty who would claim to be 'very satisfied' with their careers." These data refer in particular to the lower academic ranks, where faculty development and growth programs are much needed and increasingly sought.

Third, Eble and McKeachie (1985, p. 3) write that "the modal age of tenured faculty by the year 2000 is estimated to be between fifty-six and sixty-five"; Chait and Ford (1982) found the modal age range in 1981 to be between thirty-six and forty-five. The older faculty will challenge administrators to find ways of energizing their professional performance. Faculty improvement programs may be useful, although it may be difficult to persuade senior faculty members to take advantage of them.

9. *Posttenure evaluation will become more evident.* The National Commission on Higher Education Issues (1982, p. 10) identified posttenure evaluation as one of the most pressing issues facing higher education in the next decade. In its summary report, the commission recommended that "campus academic administrators working closely with appropriate faculty committees should develop a system of post-tenure evaluation"; the commission also warned that "nothing will undermine the tenure system more completely than its being regarded as a system to protect faculty members from evaluation."

The 1986 congressional and presidential decision (H.R. 4154) to outlaw mandatory retirement restrictions on the professoriate by the year 1994 will place posttenure evaluation in a position of greater importance. Two excellent ASHE-ERIC reports on this subject are Licata (1986) and Mortimer and Associates (1985).

10. *Planning will become more important.* Planning ef-

fectively for the future requires candid and hard analyses of the present. Senior academic administrators need a high tolerance for ambiguity, yet there are times when difficult decisions must be made, and it is usually the art rather than the science of administration that comes to the fore on these occasions. Patricia Plante's book *The Art of Decision Making* (1987) is relevant. A number of pitfalls in planning related to academic personnel systems can be mentioned:

A. *Poorly defined goals and objectives can significantly impede planning.* If an institution does not know where it is going, then any plan will do. Statements of goals and objectives may be flawed in a number of ways:

- Unit goals are not related to the overall goals and objectives of the institution.
- Goals and objectives are not closely related to the major tasks to be accomplished.
- They are too low to be challenging or too utopian to be achieved.
- They focus on activities rather than on outputs.
- They are too wordy and full of "academic garbage," or they address unimportant matters.
- They are written more to impress than to guide.

B. *Inadequate attention to the processes of change can be fatal.* Higher education is beginning another cycle of interest in the processes of change. A previous cycle was sparked by the Kennedy-Johnson era in the 1960s, when much publishing, research, and conversation took place about how change occurs. Current interest in strategies for effective change is motivated not by growth but by steadiness or decline in the size of institutions as well as by the problems of the institutions' increasing complexity.

Differences in approaches to change are deeply rooted in academe. At the risk of oversimplification, it can be described as a perceptual problem rooted in differences between academic disciplinarians and administrators. The latter focus more on what is produced, while the former focus more on the processes involved. Both are important, but they are different. Managing academic improvement efforts can raise some genuine problems; these become more apparent when the topic is as complex, important, and sensitive as developing or evaluating an academic promotion and tenure system.

    C. *A "cargo-cult" mentality can cause problems.* Many years ago, the people of the South Sea islands believed that a ship laden with gold and precious gems would someday sail into their harbor and bring a happy ending to all their problems. Some approaches to the problems of higher education similarly look for a simple answer to complex problems. One current example is the tendency of some individuals, both inside and outside academe, to look to the measurement of student outcomes as the answer to evaluating institutional quality. In the mid-1970s, others looked to the use of fiscal indicators as the answer to institutional financial problems.

    The problems facing higher education today are complex and difficult to understand, and every effort must be made to reduce them to manageable proportions. Oversimplification or the use of one approach may result in "solutions" that do not address the real problems.

    D. *Failure to anticipate problems can provide short-term euphoria and long-term extinction.* While ignorance can be a great innovator, failing to foresee weaknesses and problems can be a major impediment to improvement. In order to anticipate problems better, we might consider several reasons that evaluation models and plans fail:

- An obvious reason, but one that we prefer to overlook, is that they are poor plans. Our projects and plans in higher education are rarely acknowledged to have failed. Crop failure analyses are done in agriculture and autopsies are performed in medicine, but in higher education we just write another proposal.
- The model or plan is not vigorously and consistently supported at the top. A study by Davis and Batchelor (1974, pp. 32-36) found that only 7 percent of college presidents got fully involved in the institutional planning process. The

study is several years old, and one would like to think that some improvement has taken place in the intervening years.

• The enterprise is viewed as the preserve of the institutional planners. Institutional researchers and planners are critical, but they function as a means to an end. It is interesting to note what is happening in American industry. The cover story of the September 17, 1984, issue of *Business Week* was titled "New Breed of Strategic Planner." Many major corporations have cut their planning staffs to the bone, and middle management personnel and some line personnel have been given planning know-how and responsibilities.

• Planning is used as a smoke screen. A few administrators have sought to keep people so busy planning and operating that they cannot turn to the real problems (one of which may be the administrator).

• Academic personnel systems do not designate a trouble-shooter. The extensively planned Soviet system includes an individual—the "tolkash"—a procurement specialist who is openly known but officially unrecognized. He or she brings fluidity, creativity, and success to an often awkward planning system. A "tolkash" in our collegiate planning process may be a senior faculty member or someone in the administrative offices or elsewhere who is responsible for contributing fluidity, creativity, procedural adjustments, and evaluations. By leaving the responsibility for adjustments in the planning processes and systems nebulous, we risk significantly weakening their impact.

E. *Failure to follow the KISS Theory can be a pitfall.* In business parlance, "KISS" means: "Keep it simple, stupid." There is another version: "Keep it short and sweet." Plans that become too complicated have less chance of short- or long-term success. Some faculty evaluation systems, for example, have lost credibility and effectiveness owing to the use of computer print-outs that assumed too many computer capabilities and too much patience on the part of faculty members.

F. *Failure to sustain a positive attitude is another danger.* Every college administrator might replace the IBM slogan of

"Think" with "Think Strategically." On this point, King and Cleland (1978, p. v.) note: "The ability to 'think strategically' in comprehensive policy terms is perhaps the least homogeneously distributed personal managerial trait."

With all our present problems and concerns for the future, the United States has developed a system of postsecondary education that dazzles the rest of the world with its size, diversity, innovativeness, and success. There is a puzzlement about our system abroad, however; in spite of its admirable features, some doubts about its quality arise when it is compared with the British system and with aspects of the German system.

Improvements in promotion and tenure decision-making processes, including faculty evaluation, will be an increasingly important aspect of the academic enterprise in the nineties. As postsecondary institutions undertake extensive studies of these areas, they may find that other problems that have been lying dormant will surface, such as inadequate faculty growth opportunities and inadequate definitions of faculty workloads. The heart of the academic enterprise is its people, and the policies and procedures that govern their rewards will have a significant effect on their morale and vitality.

A

Faculty Evaluation
Rating Forms

The following appraisal forms are included in this section:

Advising Résumé for Advisers

Name ——————————— For Academic Year ————

Department ———————— Date ————————————

The advising résumé provides an opportunity for you to describe your activities in this area. Use additional pages if necessary.

1. What were your advising responsibilities? ———————

————————————————————————————

————————————————————————————

————————————————————————————

————————————————————————————

————————————————————————————

————————————————————————————

2. Were there innovative, creative, or special aspects of your advising that you would like to mention? ——————

————————————————————————————

————————————————————————————

————————————————————————————

————————————————————————————

————————————————————————————

————————————————————————————

3. Other comments (any special circumstances or problems that should be considered). ——————————————

————————————————————————————

————————————————————————————

————————————————————————————

————————————————————————————

————————————————————————————

————————————————————————————

Advising Appraisal for Students

Name of adviser _____ Date _____

    This survey is given to learn about how you view your adviser. Please do not sign your name. The space at the end of the survey allows you to use your own words, and extra questions may be added as numbers nine and ten in Section A or as numbers five and six in Section B.

Directions: Please fill in the name of your *faculty adviser* or *counselor* (whoever signs your class schedule) and also the date.

    The appraisal instrument is divided into two sections: (A) Academic Advising and (B) Personal Counseling. Section B is to be used only if you have had personal counseling—if personal counseling is an acknowledged aspect of student advising.

    Each statement describes a basic component of advising and counseling. Rate your adviser on each item, giving the highest scores for exceptional performances and the lowest scores for very poor performances. Place in the blank space before each statement the number that most nearly expresses your view:

Excep-tional			Moder-ately Good			Very Poor	Don't Know
7	6	5	4	3	2	1	X

A.   Academic Advising

_____   1.   Advises in terms of alternatives and encourages me to assume responsibility for decisions.

_____   2.   Has personal interest in assisting me through advising.

_____   3.   Keeps appointments when made in advance.

_____   4.   Keeps up to date in regulations and course offerings.

_____   5.   Maintains accurate files on my progress.

_____   6.   Seeks to plan programs consistent with my stated objectives.

_____   7.   Has advised me effectively in my major areas of study.

_____ 8. Has advised me to take courses that are meaningful to me.

_____ 9.

_____ 10.

B. Personal Counseling (Answer these questions if personal counseling is an acknowledged aspect of student advising.)

_____ 1. Is helpful to me.

_____ 2. Is objective and nonpunitive.

_____ 3. Is willing to use college or community resources when my problems seem to be more than he or she can handle.

_____ 4. Understands my point of view.

_____ 5.

_____ 6.

_____ 7. I am able to start working toward a solution to my problems because of this counseling.

_____ 8. I would wish to return to this counselor for help in the future.

_____ Composite rating.

Classroom Teaching Appraisal by Students

Teacher _____ Course _____
Term _____ Academic Year_____

    Thoughtful student appraisal can help improve teaching effectiveness. This questionnaire is designed for that purpose, and your assistance is appreciated. Please do not sign your name.

    Use the back of this form for any further comments you might want to express; use numbers 10, 11, and 12 for any additional questions that you might like to add.

Directions: Rate your teacher on each item, giving the highest scores for exceptional performances and the lowest scores for very poor performances. Place in the blank space before each statement the rating that most closely expresses your view:

Excep- tional			Moder- ately Good			Very Poor	Don't Know
7	6	5	4	3	2	1	X

_____   1.   How do you rate the agreement between course objectives and lesson assignments?

_____   2.   How do you rate the planning, organization, and use of class periods?

_____   3.   Are the teaching methods and techniques employed by the teacher appropriate and effective?

_____   4.   How do you rate the competence of the instructor in the subject?

_____   5.   How do you rate the interest of the teacher in the subject?

_____   6.   Does the teacher stimulate and challenge you to think and to question?

_____   7.   Does he or she welcome differing points of view?

_____   8.   Does the teacher have a personal interest in helping you in and out of class?

_____   9.   How would you rate the fairness and effectiveness of the grading policies and procedures of the teacher?

_____   10.   _____

—— 11. _____

—— 12. _____

—— 13. Considering all the above items, what is your overall rating of this teacher?

—— 14. How would you rate this teacher in comparison
with all others you have had in the college or university?

Classroom Visitation Appraisal

Teacher _____ Course _____

Term _____ Academic Year_____

Visitor(s) _____ Title_____

The following appraisal form contains 12 questions, many of which are found on the student appraisal of teaching form. In addition, you may want to develop a narrative description of your visit.

Directions: Rate teaching on each item, giving the highest scores for exceptional performances and the lowest scores for very poor performances. Use numbers 13 and 14 for any additional questions.

Excep- tional			Moder- ately Good			Very Poor	Don't Know
7	6	5	4	3	2	1	X

_____ 1. Were the major objectives of the course made clear to you?

_____ 2. How well was the class presentation planned and organized?

_____ 3. Were important ideas clearly explained?

_____ 4. How would you judge the professor's mastery of the course content?

_____ 5. Was class time well used?

_____ 6. Did the professor encourage critical thinking and analysis?

_____ 7. Do you believe the professor encouraged relevant student involvement in the class?

_____ 8. How did the professor react to student viewpoints differing from his or her own?

_____ 9. How would you describe the attitude of students in the class toward the professor?

_____ 10. Do you believe that your visitation was at a time when you were able to judge fairly the nature and tenor of the teaching-learning process?

_____ 11. Considering the previous 10 items, how would you

rate this teacher in comparison to others in the department?

_____ 12. In comparison to others in the institution?

_____ 13.

_____ 14.

_____ Composite rating.

Yes _____ No _____ Did you have a preliminary conference with the teacher before the visitation?

Yes _____ No _____ Did you have a follow-up conference?

Comments after class visitation: _____

_____

Comments after follow-up conference: _____

_____

Faculty Service and Relations Appraisal

Name of teacher _____ Year _____
Appraiser _____ Title _____

Directions: Please write in the blank space the number that describes your judgment of each factor as it relates to an individual's faculty service and relations on the campus. Rate the individual on each item, giving the highest scores for exceptional performances and the lowest scores for very poor performances. Additional questions may be added as items 6 and 7.

Excep-tional			Moder-ately Good			Very Poor	Don't Know
7	6	5	4	3	2	1	X

_____ 1. Acceptance of college assignments. Does the faculty member accept college assignments willingly? Does he volunteer occasionally?

_____ 2. Attitude. Does the faculty member act in the best interests of the department and the college? Does he take a professional attitude toward human relations and personnel problems? Does he have a positive attitude?

_____ 3. Cooperation. To what extent does the faculty member assist colleagues and others with their problems? Is she a good team member?

_____ 4. Performance on college assignments. What is his performance level? How do colleagues perceive his performance?

_____ 5. Professional behavior as it relates to professional activities and the goals and nature of the institution. Does she act responsibly?

_____ 6.

_____ 7.

_____ Composite rating.

Description of specific faculty assignments and services: _____

_____

_____

Comments: _____

_____

_____

Performing and Visual Arts: Self-Appraisal

Teacher _____ Date _____

Title of presentation _____

Place or occasion of presentation _____

Time spent on this project _____

1. Describe the presentation, including a statement of your intention or purpose. _____

2. Discuss briefly any special difficulties that you encountered in producing the work or in making arrangements for its presentation or exhibition. ____

3. Were other faculty members or students included in this production, performance, or exhibition project? If so, who and to what extent? _____

4. How was the work received by the audience or the spectators? _____

5. How was the work received by the critics? _____

6. Do you think the reaction of the audience or spectators and the reaction of the critics were justifiable in terms of your stated intentions for the project?

7. How did you feel about this production or exhibition? _____

Other comments: _____

Performing and Visual Arts: Reviewer's Appraisal

Teacher _____ Date _____

Appraiser _____ Title _____

Directions: In rating each activity, give the highest scores for exceptional performances and the lowest scores for very poor performances. Place in the blank space before each statement the number that most nearly expresses your view. Additional items may be included, and the space at the end of the survey allows a narrative statement.

Excep- tional			Moder- ately Good			Very Poor	Don't Know
7	6	5	4	3	2	1	X

_____ 1. Judgments of colleagues.

_____ 2. Judgments of other professionals.

_____ 3. Self-appraisal (by director of production).

_____ 4. Tenor of newspaper review.

_____ 5. Views of students.

_____ 6.

_____ 7.

_____ Composite rating.

Nature of performance: _____

_____

_____

Additional comments: _____

_____

_____

Professional Growth Appraisal

Name of teacher_____ Year_____
Appraiser _____ Title_____

    Professional growth comprises those activities that assist one in keeping a sense of scholarship, learning, optimism, and forward movement. It relates to teaching, scholarship, and service.

Directions: Please write in the blank space the number that describes your judgment of that factor as it relates to an individual's professional growth. Rate the individual on each item, giving the highest scores for exceptional performances and the lowest scores for very poor performances. Additional questions may be added as items 6 and 7.

Excep-tional			Moder-ately Good			Very Poor	Don't Know
7	6	5	4	3	2	1	X

_____ 1. Attends campus-based programs that are relevant to knowledge or pedagogical advancement (professional renewal).

_____ 2. Attends off-campus programs that can assist in professional renewal.

_____ 3. Keeps up to date in his or her professional field through membership in appropriate organizations and societies.

_____ 4. Seeks personal professional renewal by developing innovative activities in the classroom or laboratory.

_____ 5. Expresses interest in renewal and innovation in informal conversations.

_____ 6.

_____ 7.

_____ Composite rating.

Comments: _____

_____

_____

Professional Service Appraisal

Professor _____ Date _____

Appraiser _____ Title _____

     Professional service includes off-campus activities that are related to one's professional field.

Directions: An individual should be rated on each item that is appropriate for him or her. Give the highest scores for exceptional performances and the lowest scores for very poor performances. Additional questions and comments may be added.

Exceptional			Moderately Good			Very Poor	Don't Know
7	6	5	4	3	2	1	X

_____ 1. Activity in professional associations and societies. (state which ones) _____

_____

_____ 2. Offices in professional associations and societies. (state which ones) _____

_____

_____ 3. Papers or other presentations before professional groups. (state what papers and which groups) _____

_____

_____ 4. Professional service as viewed by colleagues.

_____

_____

_____ 5. Professional service as viewed by the profession.

_____

_____

_____ 6. Professional recognition in terms of awards and honors. (state which ones) _____

_____

_____ 7.

_____ 8.

_____ Composite rating.

Publications Appraisal: Books and Monographs

Professor _____ Date _____

Appraiser _____ Title _____

Directions: Place in the blank space before each appropriate statement the number that most nearly expresses your findings, giving the highest scores for exceptional performances and the lowest scores for very poor performances. Additional questions and comments may be added.

Excep-tional		Moder-ately Good				Very Poor	Don't Know
7	6	5	4	3	2	1	X

List each book (title, publisher, number of pages, date; or list each contract signed and make a progress report if writing is under way): _____

_____

_____

_____ 1. Generally speaking, how does the publisher rank in this particular field?

_____ 2. How do colleagues within the department generally rate the publication?

_____ 3. How do colleagues outside the institution rate the publication?

_____ 4. How does the department chairperson rate the publication?

_____ 5. How has the book been reviewed?

_____ 6. Has the book been cited or quoted?

_____ 7. How does the author rate the book?

_____ 8.

_____ 9.

_____   Composite rating on book (total score/number of items used).

Comments: _____

_____

Publications Appraisal: Chapters in Book

Name _____ Date _____

Appraiser _____ Title _____

Directions: Place in the blank space before each appropriate statement the number that most nearly expresses your findings, giving the highest scores for exceptional performances and the lowest scores for very poor performances. Additional questions and comments may be added.

Exceptional			Moderately Good			Very Poor	Don't Know
7	6	5	4	3	2	1	X

List each chapter in a book:

_____

_____

_____

_____

_____ 1. Generally speaking, how does the publisher rate in this particular field?

_____ 2. How do colleagues within the department rate the chapter?

_____ 3. How do colleagues outside the institution rate the chapter?

_____ 4. How does the department chairperson rate the chapter?

_____ 5. How has the chapter been reviewed?

_____ 6. Has the chapter been cited or quoted?

_____ 7. How does the author rate the chapter?

_____ 8.

_____ 9.

_____ Composite rating on chapter (total score/number of items used).

Comments: _____

_____

_____

_____

Publications Appraisal: Periodical Articles

Name _____ Date _____

Appraiser _____ Title _____

Directions: Place in the blank space before each appropriate statement the number that most nearly expresses your findings, giving the highest scores for exceptional performances and the lowest scores for very poor performances. Additional questions and comments may be added.

Excep-tional			Moder-ately Good			Very Poor	Don't Know
7	6	5	4	3	2	1	X

List each periodical article:

_____

_____

_____

_____

_____ 1. Generally speaking, how does the publisher rate in this particular field?

_____ 2. How do colleagues within the department rate the article?

_____ 3. How do colleagues outside the institution rate the article?

_____ 4. How does the department chairperson rate the article?

_____ 5. How has the article been reviewed?

_____ 6. Has the article been cited or quoted?

_____ 7. How does the author rate the article?

_____ 8.

_____ 9.

_____ Composite rating on article (total score/number of items used).

Comments: _____

_____

_____

_____

_____

Public Service Appraisal

Professor _____ Date _____
Appraiser _____ Title _____

Nature of service: _____
_____
_____

Time involved: Some quantitative appraisal should be made of the professional time spent. The percentage of time given to public service, including consulting, should be calculated as carefully as possible.

100%	90	80	70	60	50	40	30	20	10	0%

Directions: Place in the blank space before each statement the number that most nearly expresses your findings, giving the highest scores for exceptional performances and the lowest scores for very poor performances. Additional questions and comments may be added.

Excep- tional			Moder- ately Good			Very Poor	Don't Know
7	6	5	4	3	2	1	X

_____ 1. Contribution of service: What is the value of the service, judged by those who receive it and by the department chairperson?

_____ 2. Quality of performance: This criterion should be appraised primarily by colleagues and those professionals who can judge the quality of the individual's professional contribution.

_____ 3.

_____ 4.

_____ Composite rating.

Comments: _____
_____
_____

Research Appraisal: Résumé

Professor _____ Date _____

Directions: The person who is undertaking or has completed the research should fill in this form. (Use additional pages wherever necessary.)

1. Nature of research project. _____
    _____

2. Were the goals of the project well defined? _____
    _____

3. Were these goals realistic with respect to time and resources?_____
    _____

4. Which obstacles have been overcome? How was this achieved?_____
    _____

5. Which resources have you found most available and useful? _____
    _____

6. Which resources did you find lacking?_____
    _____

7. Has the college community been receptive to your work?
    _____
    _____

8. Have your colleagues taken an active interest in your research? _____
    _____

9. Has the research changed, modified, or enhanced your theoretical position? _____
    _____

10. If students were involved, what were their reactions toward the project?_____
    _____

11. What are your plans regarding publication?_____
    _____
    _____

Research Appraisal: By Others

Professor _____ Date _____

Appraiser _____ Title _____

Status of research:

    completed _____

    ongoing _____ (when started)_____

Nature of research:

    (brief description or attached outline)

_____

_____

_____

Time involved:

    What proportion of the author's professional time was spent on this project?

_____

100% 90 80 70 60 50 40 30 20 10 0%

Directions: Place in the blank space before each statement the number that most nearly expresses your findings.

Excep-tional			Moder-ately Good			Very Poor	Don't Know
7	6	5	4	3	2	1	X

_____ 1. How do colleagues within the department generally rate the research?

_____ 2. How do colleagues outside the institution rate the research?

_____ 3. How has the report been reviewed?

_____ 4. Has the research been cited or quoted?

_____ 5. How does the author rate the research?

_____ 6.

_____ 7.

_____ Composite rating.

Comments: _____

_____

_____

Self-Appraisal of Teaching

Teacher ———————————— Course ——————————
Term ————————————— Academic Year————

     Thoughtful self-evaluation can help improve teaching effectiveness. This questionnaire is designed for that purpose. You are asked to appraise your own performance in teaching.

     At your option, questions 12 and 13 may be added. Use the back of this form for any written comments you might want to express. These might record any unusual circumstances that relate to the course and to your teaching.

Directions: Rate yourself on each item, giving the highest scores for exceptional performances and the lowest scores for very poor performances. Place in the blank space before each statement the number that most nearly expresses your view.

Exceptional			Moderately Good			Very Poor	Don't Know
7	6	5	4	3	2	1	X

——— 1. Have the major objectives of your course been made clear?

——— 2. How do you rate agreement between course objectives and lesson assignments?

——— 3. Are class presentations well planned and organized?

——— 4. Are important ideas clearly explained?

——— 5. How would you judge your mastery of the course content?

——— 6. Is class time well used?

——— 7. Have you encouraged critical thinking and analysis?

——— 8. Have you encouraged students to seek your help when necessary?

——— 9. Have you encouraged relevant student involvement in the class?

——— 10. How tolerant are you of student viewpoints that differ from your own?

——— 11. Considering the previous 10 items, how would you rate your performance in this course, compared to others in the department who have taught the same course?

_____ 12.

_____ 13.

_____ Composite rating.

Special Incident Appraisal

Date _____

Appraiser _____ Title _____

_____ Individual involved in the special incident

This form is designed to provide a structured record of special incidents, which can be exemplary, negative, or puzzling events.

Description of incident: _____

_____

_____

_____

_____

_____

_____

Analysis and evaluation: _____

_____

_____

_____

_____

_____

_____

Teaching Materials and Procedures Appraisal

Teacher ——————————— Course ———————————
Term ————————————— Academic Year————
Appraiser(s) ——————————— Position ———————————

The following appraisal form contains questions which should be helpful in judging this category. Additional questions may be added. You may also want to add a summary statement in your own words.

Directions: Rate each item, giving the highest scores for exceptional teaching materials and procedures and the lowest scores for very poor performances.

Exceptional			Moderately Good			Very Poor	Don't Know
7	6	5	4	3	2	1	X

——— 1. How would you rate the overall quality of the course outline?

——— 2. Do you believe that the students gain a coherent picture of the course from this outline?

——— 3. Do the grading procedures seem reasonable and fair?

——— 4. Do the course materials include accepted authorities and sources as well as new views and evidence in the field?

——— 5. From what can be gleaned from the course materials and procedures, do you believe that the students have a challenging and meaningful experience in the classroom?

——— 6. On the basis of an examination of course materials and procedures, how would you rate the course preparation and concern for teaching of this individual, compared to other teachers in the department?

——— 7. Compared to others in the institution as a whole?

——— 8.

——— 9.

————— Composite rating.

B

Selected Student Rating Instruments

This appendix of eight proven student rating systems is based on the useful similar appendix that was published in Centra (1979). Centra acknowledged the work of Larry Braskamp of the University of Illinois in collecting the original data.

This appendix updates the rating instruments in Centra's book, omitting systems that have stopped offering their services.

Arizona Course/Instructor Evaluation Questionnaire (CIEQ)
The CIEQ (a result of more than fourteen years of research and experience) was designed to collect student attitudes about a single course and to enable instructors to collect evaluative information about their teaching. The form contains 21 standard items and space for 42 additional diagnostic items that instructors can select from a 373-item catalogue. Interpretive information and normative comparisons (by rank of instructor, course level, department, college, institution, and required or elective status) are made available to each instructor so that he or she may determine the major areas of strength and weakness in the course.

Contact: Lawrence M. Aleamoni, Director
Office of Instructional Research and Development
147 Harvill Bldg., Box 3
University of Arizona
Tucson, Arizona 85721

Specimen Set: The instrument, report describing development,

"Note to the Faculty," user materials, and Optional Item Catalogue are available at no cost.

Availability: Institutions may order the forms from:
Comprehensive Data Evaluation Services, Inc.
6730 N. Camino Padre Isidoro
Tucson, Arizona 85718

When forms are returned for processing, institutions will receive two copies of the computerized report for each class section evaluated along with appropriate interpretive information. Local institutional norms will be provided when enough courses are evaluated. The cost is 40 cents per student questionnaire processed. Arrangements can be made to have an individual institution do its own processing.

Instructional Assessment System (IAS)

The IAS presently consists of six distinct forms, each tailored to provide diagnostic information for one type of course (large lecture, small lecture-discussion, seminar, problem-solving, skill acquisition, and quiz sections). Each form has three sections. Section 1 contains four global evaluative items whose major pupose is normative. Section 2 contains eleven items designed to provide diagnostic information. Section 3 contains seven items designed to provide information to students as well as diagnostic information. Sections 1 and 3 contain items common to all forms.

Contact: Gerald M. Gillmore
Educational Assessment Center
PB-30, University of Washington
Seattle, Washington 98195

Specimen Set: A booklet describing the system and containing sample forms and computer-generated results is available at no cost. Various statistical information is also available at no cost.

Availability: Institutions may purchase IAS forms alone or with processing services. Forms cost 6 cents each. Processing costs 6 cents per sheet scanned plus 1 dollar per class surveyed. All postage must also be paid. The participating institution is responsible for distribution. The rates are the same regardless of the number of classes surveyed.

Instructional Development and Effectiveness Assessment (IDEA) System

IDEA, a student rating system used by over three hundred colleges and universities, has as its criterion of teaching effectiveness students' ratings of progress on course goals selected as important or essential for that specific course. No one model of effective teaching is implied. As well as comparisons with all instructors in the comparison group (there are over 87,000 classes in the data pool), comparisons are made with other courses of similar size in which students report similar levels of motivation. Where students report unsatisfactory progress toward a course goal and also report an instructor's infrequent use of teaching methods that are related to their progress ratings, the computer-prepared report identifies teaching strengths and weaknesses.

Contact: Center for Faculty Evaluation and Development
         Kansas State University
         1623 Anderson Avenue
         Manhattan, Kansas 66502

Specimen Set: A free information brochure is available which includes both the standard and short forms along with sample IDEA reports. Specimen sets and technical reports are available for a fee.

Availability: Institutions must order materials from the center and return them for computer processing. They will receive three copies of an IDEA report for each class. Institutional summaries containing data from all courses in an institution or unit are an optional feature. Written instructional development materials relating to the IDEA reports are also available. A fee schedule is available from the center.

Other Instruments and Systems: Departmental Evaluation of Chairperson Activities for Development (DECAD) uses the ratings of the chairperson and faculty members as a basis for identifying the importance and effectiveness of the department head for various departmental responsibilities and for diagnosing the strengths and weaknesses of the chairperson's administrative behavior. Contact the center for more information about DECAD.

Instructor and Course Evaluation System (ICES)
ICES is a computer-based system in which faculty can select items from a catalogue of over 400 items classified by content (course management, student outcomes, instructor characteristics and style, instructional environment, student preferences, and settings) and by degree of specificity (global, general concept, and specific). Global and general-concept items are normed by rank of instructor and required-elective status; specific (diagnostic) items, recommended for course improvement purposes, are not normed.

Contact: Dale C. Brandenburg, Associate Head
              Measurement & Evaluation
              307 Engineering Hall
              1808 West Green St.
              Urbana, Illinois 61801

Specimen Set: The catalogue, instrument, newsletters describing the rationale and suggested uses of ICES, and faculty user's guide are available at no cost.

Availability: Institutions must order the student questionnaires from the University of Illinois and return them for processing. They will receive two copies of a faculty report for each class section evaluated. Local institutional norms will be available for the three global items and for items selected as part of an institutional core. The distribution and confidentiality of the faculty reports are at the discretion of the local institution. The cost is 27 cents per student questionnaire processed. Catalogues are 30 cents and the remaining newsletters are 10 cents.

Instructor-Designed Questionnaire (IDQ)
The Center for Research on Learning and Teaching (CRLT) Instructor-Designed Questionnaire (IDQ) helps college teachers collect student reactions to courses on individually designed evaluation forms. University of Michigan instructors using this approach to course evaluation first receive a catalogue consisting of 148 items. Each item is a statement about the results of teaching, about a teacher, or about some aspect of a course. The instructor indicates on a requisition form up to 25 items that

are relevant to his or her course. Individually designed questionnaires are then computer-printed. Finally, student responses to these questionnaires are processed by computer.

Contact: James A. Kulik
Center for Research on Learning and Teaching
109 E. Madison Street
Ann Arbor, Michigan 48109

Specimen Set: A specimen set (including catalogue, requisition form, answer sheet, sample questionnaire, and sample report) is available without cost. Also available is a report describing the rationale and use of the system.

Availability: Permission to reprint the item catalogue or parts of the catalogue is given on request. Processing of IDQ forms is currently available only to University of Michigan teachers.

Purdue's Cafeteria System

Purdue's Cafeteria System consists of four FORTRAN computer programs, a 200-page operations manual, a computer-managed catalogue containing 200 diagnostic items, and a norm library. Cafeteria can be installed easily for local operation on virtually any computer with FORTRAN capability. It functions well as a sheet- or card-based system. Cafeteria supports both administrative and instructional improvement processes.

Contact: M. J. Cree
CIS, STEW, G65
Purdue University
W. Lafayette, Indiana 47907

Specimen Set: Available.

Availability: Cafeteria was designed for installation at other institutions as a locally operated service. The system costs $955 and will be shipped, on source decks, within five working days of receipt of a purchase order. Institutions can also contract evaluation services from Purdue's Center for Instructional Services (CIS). CIS provides all materials, and the cost is approximately 22 cents per student evaluation.

Student Instructional Rating System (SIRS)

The Student Instructional Rating System is a means of collecting, analyzing, displaying, and interpreting student reactions to classroom instruction and course content. SIRS is designed to assess student reactions for feedback to instructors to facilitate their improvement and for use by teaching units as one basis for administrative decisions about retention, promotion, salary, and tenure.

Every teaching unit must approve one or more common student rating instruments. Each teaching unit must also develop a policy for the regular and systematic administration of student rating forms and for the use of the data.

All instructors, including graduate assistants, must use unit-approved student instructional rating forms in every section of every class every term.

Contact: LeRoy A. Olson, Professor and Evaluation Consultant
Computer Laboratory/Scoring Office
Michigan State University
East Lansing, Michigan 48824-1042

Specimen Set: The Academic Council's resolution establishing SIRS, a sample form, and a list of SIRS publications are available on request.

Availability: SIRS forms and processing are available through the MSU scoring office.

Student Instructional Report (SIR)

The Student Instructional Report program includes a machine-scorable answer sheet with thirty-nine questions and space for responses to ten additional questions that may be written locally. SIR covers such areas as Instructor-Student Interaction, Tests and Exams, Course Organization and Planning, and Course Difficulty and Workload. Student responses are presented as percentages responding to each alternative to each item, item means, percentile equivalents of the means, and scores of six factors. Comparative data based on national use of SIR are available separately for two-year colleges and for four-year colleges and universities. Comparative data for approximately thirty academic disciplines are included.

Contact: Nancy Beck
Student Instructional Report
Educational Testing Service
Princeton, New Jersey 08541-0001

Specimen Set: A specimen set is available. It includes a sample of the questionnaire, a sample of the output, instructions for administering, an SIR Bulletin (semiannual newsletter), an order form, a list of institutions that have used SIR, and reports on the development and uses of SIR and on reliability and the factor structure ($6). Numerous research reports on utility, validity, and other issues are available as separate publications.

Availability: SIR is available to any institution or instructor wishing to use it. The questionnaire must be purchased from the Educational Testing Service (ETS). Answer sheets are available for ETS scoring and reporting or for local scoring (Digetek [OpScan], IBM 1230, IBM 3881, NCS Transoptic, Scantron). If ETS scoring and reporting are used, ETS will return three copies of a three-page report for each class or section in which SIR is administered. Reports are returned to the institution within three weeks of ETS's receipt of the completed answer sheets. Combined reports are available in combinations designated by the institution (departmental, total institutional, and so on).

Answer sheets ordered at one time:

    First 20,000 (1-20,000) @ 20 cents
    Second 20,000 (20,001-40,000) @ 18 cents
    Third 20,000 (40,001-60,000) @ 15 cents
    Over 60,000 (60,001 +) @ 11 cents

Answer sheets scored at one time:

    First 5,000 (1-5,000) @ 37 cents
    Next 15,000 (5,001-20,000) @ 35 cents
    Next 20,000 (20,001-40,000) @ 30 cents
    Next 20,000 (40,001-60,000) @ 28 cents
    Over 60,000 (60,000 +) @ 23 cents

These are cumulative price reductions for the answer sheets and scoring from one year to the next.

C

Annotated Bibliography
on Promotion, Tenure,
and Performance Appraisal

Alewine, T. C. "Performance Appraisals and Performance Standards." *Personnel Journal*, 1982, *61* (3), 210-214.

A rationale is developed for using performance standards by reviewing the purpose, procedures, and characteristics of an effective performance appraisal and describing how performance standards enhance them. Standards based on the employee's job description are emphasized because they focus the evaluation on job performance, productivity, and objectives related to organization goals. The author concludes by discussing the most common reasons for the failure of performance standard systems.

Altieri, C. "The ADE and Institutional Politics: The Examples of Tenure and Composition." *ADE Bulletin*, 1983, *74*, 24-27.

This article recommends that the Association of Departments of English (ADE) issue a position statement on promotion and tenure, on teaching composition, and on becoming more active politically. The author argues that producing new knowledge is an odd research goal for humanists, unless a caustic twist is given to *new*. Different kinds of institutions need different standards. Faculty can best demonstrate intellectual quality in collegial forums and through innovative teaching. For all types of schools, public service in education should be a basic criterion for tenure and promotion.

American Association of University Professors. "1982 Recommended Institutional Regulations on Academic Freedom and Tenure." *Academe,* 1983, *69* (1), 15a-20a.

Recommendations on academic freedom and tenure include: terms of appointment, probationary appointment, termination and dismissal procedures, governing board action, other sanctions, terminal salary or notice, protection against discrimination, graduate and nonfaculty staff policy, and grievance procedures.

Andrews, J. B., and Daponte, K. J. "Are Professors Fireproof?" *AGB Reports,* 1981, *23* (4), 37-41.

Public sector board members and administrators can help to raise the quality of public higher education by being legally prepared and willing to act when the dismissal of a tenured faculty member is warranted. The authors recommend twelve steps in developing a case for dismissal.

Atelsek, F. J., and Gomberg, I. L. *Tenure Practices at Four-Year Colleges and Universities.* Higher Education Panel Report no. 48. Washington, D.C.: American Council on Education, 1980.

Statistics on tenure practices at 399 four-year colleges and universities are presented. Findings of this study include: the distribution of tenured, tenure-track, and non-tenure-track positions among full-time faculty; tenure decisions during 1978-79 as measured by approval rates, deferred decisions, and early release of tenure-track faculty; the average duration of pretenure probationary periods; and the changes expected in the next five years. Results are expressed for public and private universities and public and private four-year colleges in seven fields: engineering, physical science, life science, social science, mathematical science, humanities, and education.

Baker, K. H., and Morgan, P. I. "Two Goals in Every Performance Appraisal." *Personnel Journal,* 1984, *63* (9), 74-78.

Managers often attempt too much in a single performance appraisal interview by trying to evaluate the employee's past performance as well as plan and counsel for improvement. The
interview is a key element in the total appraisal process and de-
serves more attention than it usually receives. Dividing the interview into two sessions, one for evaluation and the other to develop a strategy for improvement, can improve the results of the
appraisal process. Several characteristics of effective performance appraisal interviews are reviewed with emphasis on the
employee's participation in both evaluation and development.

Baratz, M. S. "Academic Tenure and Its Alternatives." *National
Forum: Phi Kappa Phi Journal,* 1980, *60* (2), 5-8.

The rationale, key attributes, and important criticisms of the
academic tenure system are outlined. The alternatives are to
lengthen the pretenure probationary period, to limit tenure to a
specific length, and to replace tenure with fixed-term, renew-
able contracts. Academic freedom and professional security
must be considered.

Bazerman, M. H., Beekum, R. I., and Schoorman, F. D. "Per-
formance Evaluation in a Dynamic Context: A Laboratory
Study of the Impact of a Prior Commitment to the Ratee."
Journal of Applied Psychology, 1982, *67* (6), 873-876.

The authors conducted experiments involving 298 subjects to
determine whether raters provided with negative performance
data on employees will assess those employees more positively
if they themselves had made the earlier decision to promote
the employees. The subjects in the experimental group made
promotion decisions by analyzing information and selecting one
of three candidates; the control group was told that the decision had been made by another person. Members of both groups
evaluated the promoted individual's performance on the basis
of two years' worth of data. The subjects in the experimental
group consistently appraised the promoted employees more
positively than the subjects in the control group.

Bennett, J. B., and Chater, S. S. "Evaluating the Performance of Tenured Faculty Members." *Educational Record,* 1984, *65* (2), 38-41.

Systematic posttenure evaluation, uniformly and universally applied, preserves the strengths of tenure while allaying public suspicion of tenure and concerns about faculty vigor and accountability. In evaluating the performance of tenured faculty members, it is appropriate to examine accomplishments in teaching, research, and service, the emphasis depending on the institution's mission. The structure in which the evaluation process takes place should be established through collaboration of the administration and faculty. Failure to address increasing public concerns will increase the likelihood of external regulation.

Bergman, J. "Peer Evaluation of University Faculty." *College Student Journal,* 1980, *14* (3), 1-21.

This article analyzes the process of making peer evaluations. The author contends that the factors on which peer evaluation is based are subjective and unconscious. He concludes that until reliable and valid peer rating systems are developed, their use should be supplementary or on an experimental basis.

Bess, J. L. "A New Approach: Tenure for Successful Failures." *Change,* 1982, *14* (2), 7-8.

Institutions should make decisions of academic merit on the basis of academic achievement and decisions of employment on the grounds of economic feasibility. A person could receive tenure but be denied employment for economic reasons. The formalization of a status passage would permit a sensible treatment of talented academic aspirants.

Bouchard, R. A. *Personnel Practices for Small Colleges.* Washington, D.C.: National Association of College and University Business Officers, 1980.

This is a practical guide to personnel administration in higher education, providing materials for the development and maintenance of a sound personnel program, particularly for small colleges. The chapter titled "Training and Development" focuses on the performance appraisal process. It contains sample appraisal forms contributed by a number of colleges and universities. Benefits of performance appraisal are outlined, and the discussion of performance standards emphasizes straightforward communication between supervisor and employee. The appraisal interview is stressed as an important aspect of the training and development effort directed at the needs of employees. The author provides a step-by-step procedure for conducting the appraisal interview and points out a number of pitfalls.

Boyes, W. J., and others. "Publish or Perish: Fact or Fiction?" *Journal of Economic Education*, 1984, *15* (2), 136–141.

The relative importance of teaching and research was the subject of a questionnaire sent to departments of economics throughout the nation. Results indicated that research and teaching are weighted differently in promotion and tenure decisions depending on the type and size of the university or college.

Brubaker, L. "The Assessment Center Method: Developing Employees for Mid-Management Positions." *Journal of the College and University Personnel Association*, 1983, *34* (3), 32–36.

Expected results of the University of California's assessment center method are better performance by participants in their current jobs and greater success in competing for entry-level and middle management positions. The program consists of role-playing exercises similar to those found in most assessment centers. Experience has shown, according to the author, that opportunities for on-the-job development of skills were missed because supervisors of participants did not know how to provide coaching, encouragement, learning opportunities, information, and feedback. This assessment center approach seems to have been effective, and a comprehensive evaluation of the program is under way.

Cadwallader, M. L. "Reflections on Academic Freedom and Tenure." *Liberal Education*, 1983, *69* (1), 1-17.

The author argues that tenure is not essential, as traditionally claimed, to academic freedom, and that in the light of social changes and recent litigation, the modern democracy needs to put into practice a theory of academic freedom independent of tenure.

Cascio, W. F. "Scientific Legal and Operational Imperatives of Workable Performance Appraisal Systems." *Public Personnel Management*, 1982, *11* (4), 367-375.

Workable, effective performance appraisal systems meet both scientific and legal imperatives and operational imperatives. The scientific and legal imperatives assume that the system must be relevant, with a direct relationship between performance standards and organizational goals; it must be sensitive, while separating effective from ineffective workers; and it must be reliable, establishing consistency of judgment through supervisory, peer, subordinate, and self-ratings. The operational imperatives assume that the system must be acceptable—if necessary, participation and support must be generated through education and effort; and it must be practical, not requiring an unreasonable amount of time interfering with routine operations.

Chait, R. P., and Ford, A. T. "Beyond Traditional Tenure—Extended Probationary Periods and Suspension of 'Up-or-Out' Rule." *Change*, 1982, *14* (5), 44-54.

Possible administrative policies for deferring the tenure decision and slowing the addition of tenured faculty are examined, including extended probationary periods, suspension or abolition of the "up-or-out" rule, term contracts, and changes in tenure quotas. Examples of policies in use, strengths and weaknesses of alternatives, and opinions within the profession are discussed.

Cheshire, N., and Hagemeyer, R. H. "Evaluating Job Performance." *Community and Junior College Journal*, 1981, *52* (4), 34-37.

Over a two-year period, the faculty, staff, and administration of Central-Piedmont Community College jointly developed what they believed was a fair, objective, and effective performance evaluation system. The performance of each faculty and staff member is numerically rated on a series of criteria approved by faculty and staff members. The system is intended to encourage better performance by identifying the standards against which performance is measured, recognize superior performers, provide assurance to satisfactory performers, and assist individuals whose performance needs improvement. A Standards Review Committee annually reviews the evaluation factors and criteria to monitor performance levels and prevent the process from becoming static.

College and University Personnel Association. "Tenure and Retrenchment Practices in Higher Education—A Technical Report." *Journal of the College and University Personnel Association*, 1980, *31* (3-4), 18-226.

This is a special issue of the *Journal* reporting the findings of a study of tenure and retrenchment practices in higher education. Over one thousand colleges and universities were surveyed. In tenure policies and practices, areas surveyed and analyzed include the definition of tenure; the policy, procedure, and due process of tenure; the role of governance in the tenuring process; the relation of tenure to funding sources; the relation of faculty ranks to tenure; the relation of tenure to promotion decisions; and tenure policy for part-time faculty and noninstructional staff. In retrenchment policies and practices, areas surveyed and analyzed include the existence of retrenchment policies; the experience with retrenchment from 1974 to 1975 and 1977 to 1978; the retrenchment process; and the effect of retrenchment on affirmative action, employment rights, and benefits.

College and University Personnel Association. "Tenure Policies and Practices: A Summary." *Journal of the College and University Personnel Association*, 1980, *31* (3-4), 18-31.

This summary presents the collected data and the combined findings on tenure for four major Carnegie classifications of institutions. It includes information about the formality of tenure, policies, the notification of tenure eligibility, the locus of tenure, the role of governance in the tenuring process, the relation of tenure to funding sources, the relation of faculty ranks to tenure, and the relation of tenure to promotion decisions.

College and University Personnel Association. "Tenure at Doctorate-Granting Institutions." *Journal of the College and University Personnel Association,* 1980, *31* (3-4), 32-57.

Data on current tenure policies and practices at doctorate-granting institutions are reported and analyzed. Information is provided about the role of governance in the tenuring process, the relation of tenure to funding sources, the relation of faculty ranks to tenure, the relation of tenure to promotion decisions, and tenure eligibility for other than traditional instructional staff.

College and University Personnel Association. "Tenure at Comprehensive Universities and Colleges." *Journal of the College and University Personnel Association,* 1980, *31* (3-4), 58-83.

Data on current tenure policies and practices at comprehensive universities and colleges are reported and analyzed. Information is provided about the role of governance in the tenuring process, the relation of tenure to funding sources, the relation of faculty ranks to tenure, and the relation of tenure to promotion decisions.

College and University Personnel Association. "Tenure at Liberal Arts Colleges." *Journal of the College and University Personnel Association,* 1980, *31* (3-4), 84-108.

Data on current tenure policies and practices at liberal arts colleges are reported and analyzed. Information is provided about the role of governance in the tenuring process, the relation of tenure to funding sources, the relation of faculty ranks to tenure, the relation of tenure to promotion decisions, and tenure eligibility for other than traditional instructional staff.

Daley, D. "Performance Appraisal as a Guide for Training and Development: A Research Note." *Public Personnel Management,* 1983, *12* (1), 159-166.

This study attempted to determine whether and how the state of Iowa's performance evaluation system could be used as a basis for employee training and development plans. A sample of performance appraisals submitted by supervisors was reviewed to assess the use of the system. The emphasis was on whether the appraisals contained enough information to develop educational and training plans, regardless of whether the plans were actually used. The appraisal-by-objectives system under consideration met the test of a multipurpose personnel activity because it contained information on both the strengths and the weaknesses of the employees appraised. Therefore, this performance appraisal system did provide data that could be used as the basis for education and training plans.

Davidson, J. F. "Tenure, Governance, and Standards in the Academic Community." *Liberal Education,* 1982, *68* (1), 35-42.

The author argues that if academic standards—central to the justification for tenure—are maintained in colleges and universities in the future, it probably will be because of tenure. The role of individual faculty members in the maintenance of the academic community is discussed.

Davis, B. L., and Mount, M. K. "Design and Use of a Performance Appraisal Feedback System." *Personnel Administrator,* 1984, *29* (3), 91-97.

Participants in this study were sales managers randomly assigned to either the feedback group (n = 24) or the control group (n = 23). The study found that providing feedback to managers may have important benefits for the organization, managers, and employees. It was also found that feedback significantly reduced the presence of leniency error in the managers' ratings. The results of the satisfaction survey indicated that managers responded favorably to feedback and considered it when completing the performance appraisal. They also indicated that feedback can make ratings more comparable; with increased comparability, employees' satisfaction can be enhanced. It is emphasized that this approach should not be substituted for a formal performance appraisal training program.

DeMarco, J. J., and Nigro, L. G. "Using Employee Attitudes and Perceptions to Monitor Supervisory Implementation of C.S.R.A. Performance Appraisal Systems." *Public Personnel Management,* 1983, *12* (1), 43-51.

This study measured the implementation of revisions in performance appraisal systems generated by the Civil Service Reform Act (C.S.R.A.). Questionnaires were sent to four Navy research and development laboratories in an attempt to assess the degree to which perceptions of supervisory behavior regarding performance appraisals were associated with attitudes toward the workplace in general. Data from a survey conducted before the conversion of the performance appraisal systems were compared with the responses from the data surveyed two years later, after the conversion. The two-year comparison period was found to be too short to allow significant changes in supervisory behavior to occur; confidence in the conclusions was therefore low.

Edwards, M. R. "Productivity Improvement Through Innovations in Performance Appraisal." *Public Personnel Management,* 1983, *12* (1), 13-24.

This article finds a positive relationship between the opinion of employees that an appraisal system is fair and the high productivity of those employees. This relationship was investigated by the author in a study of three organizations: a large public school district, a major international food company, and a large public utility. If employees do not believe the measurement system is fair, they will be less supportive of management or a productivity improvement program.

Edwards, M. R., and Goodstein, L. D. "Experimental Learning Can Improve the Performance Appraisal Process." *Human Resource Management,* 1982, *21* (1), 18-23.

The authors attempted to improve the effectiveness and accuracy of performance ratings by evaluators by providing them with feedback about their assessments. Four different methods were used to improve accuracy: making assessment instruments easier to understand and use; increasing the amount and quality of training for evaluators; requiring that all evaluations be reviewed by the evaluator's immediate superior; and comparing each evaluator's ratings to multiple consensus ratings. The authors concluded that the fourth method alone had a lasting effect on improving rater performance.

Eustace, R. "The Reform of Academic Tenure." *Higher Education Review,* 1983, *16* (1), 65-75.

The purposes of academic tenure practice are examined, and a model of an alternative form of tenure is suggested. This plan calls for two types of appointments. The first is a permanent fellowship that offers security and a life appointment for a scholar without further qualification; the second is a term contract that is designed for promotion and responsibility. The latter offers greater rewards for fixed periods with more specific duties. Beyond a certain age, no duties would be required without contracts. However, eligibility for further contracts would override retirement. This model gives the institution considerable flexibility.

Fisher, C., and Thomas, J. "The Other Face of Performance Appraisal." *Human Resource Management,* 1982, *21* (1), 24-26.

The ways in which managers are affected by conducting performance appraisals and providing feedback are examined, and proposals for countering any negative effects are suggested. The authors maintain that the feedback process can produce some adverse feelings and perceptions for supervisors involved in the process. A major problem for supervisors is their uncertainty about the appropriate procedures for conducting appraisal interviews. Managers' problems with appraisal feedback can be reduced by providing extensive training in the methods and techniques of conducting effective appraisal interviews. Behavior model training, observing properly handled appraisals, and role-playing are suggested as the best approaches to solving these problems.

Fisher, M. R. "Tenure of Employment in the Universities." *Vests*, 1982, *25* (2), 11-14.

Reducing tenure inevitably involves costs to both employer and employee; in particular, it lowers the attractiveness of employment in the institution, thus affecting faculty mobility and goodwill and the institution's academic standing. Long-term implications of tenure reform should be carefully weighed before changes are undertaken.

Fletcher, J. L. "High Performance Patterns: Improving Employee Effectiveness." *Journal of the College and University Personnel Association*, 1982, *33* (1), 1-4.

A significant shortcoming even of good personnel systems that function effectively is the limited knowledge they provide of an individual's characteristics and the conditions that foster the best performance. The usual assessment instruments do not supply these data because people are not fully aware of their own high performance patterns and because most measures classify people into a limited number of categories. High performance patterns are unique to the individual. A conceptually simple process for identifying the best work patterns of employees and some ways of using this information to deliberately improve performance are described.

Flygare, T. J. "The Secret Ballot in Faculty Personnel Decisions: Right or Wrong?" *Phi Delta Kappan*, 1982, *63* (6), 412-413.

Two recent court decisions provide different answers to the question of whether university faculty members have the right to confidentiality when voting on a colleague's promotion or tenure. The controversy over these personnel decisions should lead colleges and universities to consider carefully the appropriateness of secrecy.

Giles, R., and Landauer, C. "Setting Specific Standards for Appraising Creative Staffs." *Personnel Administrator,* 1984, *29* (3), 35-47.

The development and implementation of a performance appraisal system used by a newspaper to evaluate writers, copyeditors, and other members of the news staff are presented. A key objective in developing a new system was to eliminate the subjectivity and lack of consistency inherent in the previous program. The entire system was developed with a great deal of input from employees. In addition to rating performance, the system provides employees with the opportunity to consciously direct their efforts toward short-term improvements and long-term career goals by assigning priorities to performance development suggestions. The performance interview is the key to the system, and significant emphasis is placed on it. After less than one year, the system seemed to be meeting the established objectives.

Hellweg, S., and Churchman, D. A. "The Academic Tenure System: Unplanned Obsolescence in an Era of Retrenchment." *Planning for Higher Education,* 1981, *10,* 16-18.

Changing needs, financial constraints, and accountability issues make the traditional tenure system inflexible and obsolete in an era of retrenchment. A model for the new tenure system is proposed that suggests that tenure, salary, and rank should be independent of one another.

Hobson, C. J., and Gibson, F. W. "Capturing Supervisor Rating Policies: A Way to Improve Performance Appraisal Effectiveness." *Personnel Administrator,* 1984, *29* (3), 59-70.

Three problems in performance appraisal are particularly troublesome. First, supervisors are unable to combine information about several performance dimensions reliably into an overall rating. Second, supervisors are often unaware of the relative importance they attach to the various components of performance in determining an overall evaluation. Third, as a result, subordinates are often unable to describe accurately what their supervisor expects of them or how they are rated. The authors present a *systematic policy capturing procedure* (POLYCAP), used to describe individual decision-making behavior objectively.

Holley, W., and Field, H. S. "Will Your Performance Appraisal System Hold Up in Court?" *Personnel,* 1982, *59* (1), 59-64.

This study reviewed sixty-six court cases dating back to 1976 that involved personnel actions based on performance appraisals. Because appraisal systems are vulnerable to fair employment charges, preventive measures and appropriate defenses are suggested. A set of common factors was produced that had a significant effect in the decisions of all the cases reviewed. In designing and implementing appraisal systems, care should be taken to minimize possible discriminatory factors. Current job analysis and performance rating criteria that are specific, measurable, and job-related must be the basis for the appraisal system. Supervisors and raters must be given written instructions that are clear and specific. Raters must discuss the appraisal with the employee. Finally, supervisors must be effectively educated about these guidelines.

Hruby, N. J. "Is There Life After Tenure?" *AGB Reports,* 1981, *23* (2), 24-27.

A new system instituted by Aquinas College is explained. Each faculty job opening, on a case-by-case basis, is placed on either the tenure track or a rolling contract track; tenure is still possible for newly hired faculty members.

Johnson, J. R. "To Be or Not to Be—Tenured: Statutory Tenure in Illinois." *Community College Frontiers,* 1980, *8* (4), 20-21.

This article describes the new Public Community College Act of Illinois of 1979, which provides statutory tenure for faculty members in community college districts of the state after three consecutive years of satisfactory service. The bill was passed over the veto of Governor James R. Thompson.

Kasten, K. L. "Tenure and Merit Pay as Rewards for Research, Teaching, and Service at a Research University." *Journal of Higher Education*, 1984, *55* (4), 500-515.

The value that faculty at a research university place on research, teaching, and service when making recommendations for tenure and merit pay is examined. Analysis of faculty evaluations of hypothetical candidates and interviews with tenured faculty reveal different links between the three duties and the rewards.

Kaye, B. L. "Performance Appraisal and Career Development: A Shotgun Marriage." *Personnel*, 1984, *61* (2), 57-66.

One way to increase the human resources development potential of performance appraisal and career development is to reinforce the concept that these systems are ongoing processes essential to organizational well-being. This can be done and both processes strengthened by linking them to take advantage of similar concepts and strategies. The information and developmental aspects of career development thus become invaluable to the feedback aspect of performance appraisal, and vice versa. In addition, the honest self-evaluation that is vital to both processes is substantially strengthened.

Kennedy, J. E. "Alternatives to Traditional Tenure." *Journal of Dental Education*, 1984, *48* (9), 506-508.

Dental schools must maintain a collegial environment of academic excellence in which faculty are engaged extensively in scholarly pursuits that improve the quality of instruction, advance the understanding of human biology and pathology, and raise the standard of oral health. Constraints imposed by the tenure system are discussed.

Kreinin, M. E. "Preserving Tenure Commitments in Hard Times." *Academe*, 1982, *68* (2), 37-45.

The involuntary release of about one hundred tenured faculty at Michigan State University in 1981 was avoided through implementation of a plan of financial incentives for early faculty retirement. The plan is explained from the point of view of its author; colleagues' comments are included.

Kurland, J. E. "On Periodic Evaluation of Tenured Faculty: A Discussion at Wingspread." *Academe,* 1983, *69* (6), 24-26.

Recommendations that emerged from a joint conference of the American Council on Education (ACE) and the American Association of University Professors (AAUP) on posttenure evaluation are summarized. The majority agreed that the current procedures for evaluating academic performance of faculty are quite satisfactory; the addition of formal periodic evaluation would bring little benefit and consume unacceptable amounts of money and time, possibly dampening creativity and collegial relationships; and the results of any system of evaluation should not be allowed to be used as grounds for dismissal. Also included is a statement of the Wingspread Conference on Evaluation of Tenured Faculty.

Laurie, J. "Appraisal, Assessment, and HRD." *Personnel Journal,* 1984, *63* (1), 27-28.

The appraisal system, the assessment process, and the human resources development function are all aimed at improving the performance of people in organizations. However, in organizations these factors sometimes operate independently and lose the advantages of collaboration. Appraisal data indicate programs and plans that are focused on the present. Assessment data point to the directions in which people need to grow in order to fulfill their potential. If both are linked directly to human resources development, all three can become more effective.

Lazer, R. I. "Performance Appraisal: What Does the Future Hold?" *Personnel Administrator,* 1980, *25* (7), 69-73.

The historical development of performance appraisal systems is outlined and the main reasons that current systems fail are reviewed. Listed among the characteristics of a good performance appraisal system are job-relatedness, reliability, validity, standardized procedure, and practical administration. The article suggests that the appraisal system will become the link between the organization's overall planning and the individual's planning and development. If the elements of these two functions are properly integrated, they can aid the organization in achieving its objectives while assisting the individual in achieving personal recognition and reward. A model appraisal system is outlined. Correctly implemented, it avoids most of the pitfalls of other programs while meeting the criteria for a good appraisal system.

Lewis, L. S. "Getting Tenure: Change and Continuity." *Academe*, 1980, *66* (4), 373-381.

Tenure appointments appeared to be more difficult to obtain and performance expectations were more stringent in the 1970s than in the 1960s. The two populations examined were reviewed and received tenure appointments during 1967-68 and 1977-78.

Lin, Y., McKeachie, W. J., and Tucker, D. G. "The Use of Student Ratings in Promotion Decisions." *Journal of Higher Education,* 1984, *55* (5), 583-589.

The authors hypothesized that direct quotations from student comments on faculty members' teaching skills would be more persuasive than statistics communicating the same information when the faculty members were considered for promotion or salary increases. Dossiers for hypothetical candidates were prepared that varied significantly only in the evidence of teaching ability (high or moderate) and in the presentation of evidence (using statistical evidence alone or with direct quotations). The dossiers were evaluated by twelve senior faculty members who had served on committees determining faculty promotions. The direct quotations improved the chances of those with excellent teaching ratings and hurt those with only moderate ratings.

Lincoln, Y. S. "The Structure of Promotion and Tenure Decisions in Institutions of Higher Education: A Policy Analysis." *Review of Higher Education,* 1983, *6* (3), 217-231.

Many institutions of higher education do not have clear guidelines and criteria for promotion and tenure. The principles of merit and worth are not clearly differentiated. The author offers some guidelines for devising appropriate criteria for promotion and tenure and advocates that once the criteria have been established, they should be followed and applied consistently.

Loar, M., Mohrman, S., and Stock, J. R. "Development of a Behaviorally-Based Performance Appraisal System." *Personnel Psychology*, 1982, *35*, 75-88.

The four stages in the development of the behaviorally based performance appraisal system used by the Ohio State Highway Patrol are reviewed. The system identifies proficiency levels at specific tasks instead of rating general personality traits such as "diligence" or "initiative." This characteristic is expected to enhance the objectivity of the evaluation process for both appraisal and counseling. Although this system is related to highway patrol tasks, a similar system could be prepared for many types and levels of jobs.

Lovain, T. B. "Grounds for Dismissing Tenured Postsecondary Faculty for Cause." *Journal of College and University Law*, 1983-84, *10* (3), 419-433.

This article focuses on judicial evaluations of substantive grounds for dismissing tenured postsecondary faculty for cause. The most common grounds for dismissal are incompetence, immorality, neglect of duty, and insubordination. Almost all recent challenges by tenured faculty of dismissals for stated cause have been rejected by the courts, despite heightened legal protections of tenure.

McCreight, R. E. "A Five Role System for Motivating Improved Performance." *Personnel Journal*, 1983, *62* (1), 30-34.

The supervisor plays several roles in today's organizations. The most demanding is that of human resources manager, whose principal objective is to manage and motivate improved employee performance. The role of human resources manager can be divided into five subroles: goal setter, trainer, mentor, evaluator, and decision maker. The actions taken by the supervisor during each phase of this system will set the stage for the next evaluation period, and employee performance will contribute to the determination of goals for the next evaluation period.

McKee, P. W. "Tenure by Default: The Non-Formal Acquisition of Academic Tenure." *Journal of College and University Law,* 1980, 7 (1-2), 31-56.

Nontenured faculty's claims to tenure as a property right, by virtue of common-law principles, are examined from historical and litigation perspectives. The common-law analysis proposed is applied to employment relationships in private and public institutions.

McNeece, C. A. "Faculty Publications, Tenure, and Job Satisfaction in Graduate Social Work Programs." *Journal of Education for Social Work,* 1981, *17* (3), 13-19.

Results of a survey of graduate social work faculty show that most publications are produced by a small minority of the faculty, especially tenured faculty, and also by those faculty members in schools with doctoral programs. Sex and job satisfaction show little relationship to publication rates.

Miller, S. "Student Rating Scales for Tenure and Promotion." *Improving College and University Teaching,* 1984, *32* (2), 87-90.

Research on the validity of student rating scales of teacher performance is inconsistent, and the issue of why the scales are used needs examination. Until their criterion validity is raised to correlations of .7 and .8 or construct validity can be established, results should not be used in making tenure decisions.

Moore, K. M. "Introduction: Academic Tenure in the United States." *Journal of the College and University Personnel Association,* 1980, *31,* 1-17.

This article presents a brief history of academic tenure in American higher education. The role of academic tenure as a general concept in the development of the professoriate and in the shaping of major portions of educational policy and practice is discussed. The aspects of legal dimensions, accountability, retrenchment, collective bargaining, and institutional flexibility on tenure practices are explored. The author concludes with a discussion of alternatives to current tenure practices.

Newell, S., and Price, J. H. "Promotion, Merit and Tenure Decisions for College Health Education Faculty." *Health Education*, 1983, *14* (2), 12-15.

The criteria for promotion, tenure, and merit in sixty health education departments are examined. Satisfaction of chairpersons with the established criteria for the various forms of advancement is also explored. This survey indicates that only 48 percent of the respondents had a written policy concerning promotion, tenure, and merit. Furthermore, over half of the department chairpersons were dissatisfied with the policies in these areas.

Newton, R. "Performance Evaluation in Education." *Journal of the College and University Personnel Association*, 1982, *33* (2), 39-43.

The model system presented used performance objectives based on the needs of clients (students) as criteria for performance-based evaluation of faculty. More objective than other systems currently used in education, this system emphasizes visible accomplishments instead of typically vague discretionary judgments or pure objective data. Although every system has evaluative judgments, the specific nature of performance described in this system makes evaluations more independent of administrative judgments than they are in other systems. The system provides the advantages associated with performance-based evaluations. Performance-based evaluation in education has been noted for its misapplication, however; if it is to achieve a place in education, a form must be developed suited to the distinctive needs of the teaching profession.

Olswang, S. G., and Fantel, J. "Tenure and Periodic Performance Review: Compatible Legal and Administrative Principles." *Journal of College and University Law,* 1980, 7 (1-2),
1-30.

The separate concepts of tenure and academic freedom and
their relation to one measure of accountability—systematic reviews of the performance of tenured faculty—are examined. The
authors contend that these reviews can be conducted without
infringing on either academic freedom or the institution of tenure.

Orpen, C. "Tenure and Academic Productivity: Another Look."
Improving College and University Teaching, 1982, *30* (2),
60-62.

Do faculty publish less after they have obtained tenure? The author explores the difference in productivity between tenured
and untenured faculty based on their disciplines, previous de-
grees, and seniority. Cross-sectional and longitudinal analyses
indicate that tenured faculty are no less productive than untenured faculty.

O'Toole, J. "Against Tenure." *National Forum: Phi Kappa Phi
Journal,* 1980, *60* (2), 8-9.

Arguments against the AAUP's position on tenure include tenure's function as a disincentive to productivity in academic careers. Academic freedom is discounted as a reason to use tenure. The cost of using tenure is seen to be too high when there
are alternatives.

Pajer, R. G. "Performance Appraisal: A New Era for Federal
Government Managers." *Personnel Administrator,* 1984, *29*
(3), 81-89.

Performance standards, the most important aspect of the federal performance appraisal process, should focus on measuring
performance instead of personal characteristics and traits. The
Work Results Method (WRM) is an approach to developing stan-

dards that concentrate on each job's products, results, services, and major work activities in the context of organizational goals. WRM functions particularly well when the supervisor and the employee work together to identify performance elements, establish accountability, and develop standards. Providing development and training for managers that centers on job-relatedness, applicability, distinguishability, and communicability has been effective.

Perrucci, R., O'Flaherty, K., and Marshall, H. "Market Conditions, Productivity, and Promotion Among University Faculty." *Research in Higher Education,* 1983, *19,* 431-449.

This study compared the performance levels and promotion experiences of 371 faculty members in buyer's, seller's, and stable markets. Results showed that faculty are most productive and remain in a rank longest before being promoted during a buyer's market. Productivity is greatest for faculty that are untenured and below the rank of full professor. The authors speculate that recent Ph.D. recipients may be better trained and more productive researchers and scholars than those of an earlier period.

Poston, L. "Neither Bane nor Boon: External Reviewing in the Tenure and Promotion Process." *ADE Bulletin,* 1984, *77,* 44-46.

The author comments on the statement and guidelines issued by the Association of Departments of English (ADE) in 1981 and 1983 concerning the position of external reviewers in the tenure and promotion processes. If external reviewers are used, they should be compensated financially. The author's own guidelines for the review process discuss timely notification, payment and working conditions, and legal counsel and anonymity for the reviewer.

Saaty, T. L., and Ramanujam, V. "An Objective Approach to Faculty Promotion and Tenure by the Analytic Hierarchy Process." *Research in Higher Education,* 1983, *18,* 311-331.

Decision making about faculty tenure should be objective and consistent. However, many traditional tenure and promotion decisions are not. An analytical model of a faculty evaluation system that assigns weights to performance factors within a hierarchy is presented. A final composite score is obtained for each faculty member. Based on this score, the tenure and promotion committee makes an objective decision.

Saunders, M. K. "Legal Issues in Terminating Tenured Faculty Members Because of Financial Exigency." *Educational Record*, 1984, *65* (1), 12-17.

This overview of recent court cases concerning dismissal of tenured college faculty for reasons of financial exigency focuses on court definitions of exigency, criteria of just cause for termination, due process requirements, reemployment, compensation for wrongful termination, and legal definitions of good faith. The courts have accepted financial exigency as just cause for faculty layoffs. Due process for terminating tenured faculty members comprises the use of objective criteria in selecting faculty members for termination; the right to a hearing; the right to counsel during the hearing; the right to present witnesses; the provision of evidence in support of the decision to terminate; and the questioning of adverse witnesses.

Shapiro, H. T. "The Privilege and the Responsibility—Some Reflections on the Nature, Function, and Future of Academic Tenure." *Academe*, 1983, *69*, 3a-7a.

The contemporary notion of academic freedom and tenure is inextricably linked to society's attitudes toward progress and to the role of universities and their faculties in it. Tenure confers a special balance of privileges and responsibilities on faculty members. As the role of universities changes, so will this balance. Despite all the negative criticisms of tenure, society's commitment to progress, change, and the role of inquiry is essential both to the future of tenure and to the future of the university. Instead of being abolished, tenure should be strengthened. Periodic evaluation of tenured faculty is a good way to nurture the professional development of faculty; however, it is not a way to strengthen tenure.

Smith, R. J. "Requirements for Faculty Scholarship in Universities and Dental Schools: Implications for Promotion, and the Dual-Track System." *Journal of Dental Education,* 1984, *48* (9), 500-505.

Scholarship may decrease the quality of dental education if gifted and enthusiastic clinical faculty members who do not meet scholarly requirements for tenure or promotion leave full-time teaching for private practice. The loss of outstanding clinical faculty is a consequence of dental schools' affiliation with universities.

Starling, G. "Performance Appraisal in the 'Z' Organization." *Public Personnel Management,* 1982, *11* (4), 343-351.

The author contends that, overall, performance appraisals have not been very effective; the "Z" organization, however, uses concepts and procedures that can contribute to the success of the performance appraisal process. The basic differences between the typical American organization and the "Z" organization are discussed and compared. Some concepts from the Theory "Z" organization that might be applied to American public-sector agencies are presented. Because future legal standards will require performance appraisals to be more job-related, the use of objective standards of performance is important.

Stevens, G. E. "Constitutional Privilege and the College Tenure Committee." *American Business Law Journal,* 1983, *21,* 351-361.

In recent years, rejected tenure applicants have resorted to the courts in growing numbers for redress of their grievances. Citing past court cases, the authors summarize situations considered defamatory and nondefamatory. The constitutional privilege of the tenure committee and department chairpersons to exercise their judgment, and its legal ramifications, are discussed.

Swenson, N. G. "Statutory Tenure: A Response to Erosion of the Tenure System." *Community College Frontier*, 1980, *8* (4), 28-31.

The American Federation of Teachers discusses the escalating attacks on tenure by the administration and governing boards of colleges and universities. AFT's lobbying efforts in Illinois on behalf of a bill to return statutory tenure to community college faculty are outlined. Under the new law, more than five hundred community college teachers in Illinois will be given tenure. The author believes that as the traditional tenure system is eroded by declining enrollments and budgetary problems, more and more faculty will turn to statutory legislation for protection.

Swofford, J. "Part-Time Faculty and Collective Bargaining." *Journal of the College and University Personnel Association*, 1982, *34* (4), 9-12.

In this survey of 317 unionized two-year colleges, four aspects of part-time faculty status were examined: tenure eligibility, salary and fringe benefits, governance participation, and specific working conditions. Results support the conclusion that the situation for part-time faculty at unionized campuses is better now than in the 1970s, especially for those who are included in the full-time faculty's bargaining unit.

Taylor, R. L., and Zawacki, R. A. "Trends in Performance Appraisal: Guidelines for Managers." *Personnel Administrator*, 1984, *29* (3), 71-80.

This 1981 study replicates a 1976 study in which the authors sought to determine what types of performance appraisals were actually used in industry and requested managers to assess the value of their systems. The study also examines three factors that affect the success of performance appraisals to understand better why organizations use the systems they do. The study indicates that firms using collaborative approaches focus on goals and performance; firms using traditional systems are most concerned with potential. Therefore, organizations concerned with both performance and potential might consider a combination of approaches. The study also identifies a trend toward evaluating managers with traditional performance appraisal systems.

Thorne, G. L. "Student Ratings of Instructors: From Scores to Administrative Decisions." *Journal of Higher Education,* 1980, *51* (2), 207-214.

The use of student classroom rating data in making salary, tenure, and promotion decisions is explored. The data can become an important factor in these decisions, but only after very careful development and negotiation.

Tucker, A., and Mautz, R. B. "Academic Freedom, Tenure, and Incompetence." *Educational Record,* 1982, *63* (2), 22-25.

Tenure, with its blanket protection, is the price paid for the benefits of encouraging faculty to stray from the comfortable path of orthodoxy and to challenge the rationalizations used to maintain it. The violence of the attack on tenure is all out of proportion to the percentage of incompetent teachers. Colleagues have ways of minimizing the damage done by those who do not or will not perform according to minimum expectations. Salary raises, when available, can influence faculty performance. Peer pressure, however, exerts influence in more subtle ways. As a guardian of academic freedom, tenure is too important to the welfare of society to be abolished.

Walden, T. "Higher Education: Attitudes Toward Tenure." *Phi Delta Kappan,* 1980, *62,* 216-217.

This survey of faculty members and administrators at a large eastern university finds among other things that tenure status is a key indicator of attitudes toward tenure and that neither the tenured nor the untenured group believes job security to be as important an aspect of tenure as opponents of tenure tend to assert.

Wells, R. G. "Guidelines for Effective and Defensible Performance Appraisal Systems." *Personnel Journal,* 1982, *61* (10), 776-782.

The author states that no performance evaluation systems, not even those for which extensive validity studies have been conducted, are immune to legal challenge. Wells identifies and discusses guidelines that can help eliminate many of the most common problems in defending an appraisal system. Factors whose presence can make appraisal systems more defensible are communicated performance expectations, understandable performance standards, logical subjective criteria, job-related criteria, similar standards for similar jobs, regular appraisal schedules, formal documentation, communication of purposes, system integrity, adherence to privacy laws, and access to results. A system should also emphasize effective evaluators, ensuring that appraisers are technically knowledgeable and well trained in conducting evaluations.

Winstanley, N. B. "How Accurate Are Performance Appraisals?" *Personnel Administrator,* 1980, *25* (8), 53-58.

The psychometric properties of performance appraisals render them inadequate for administrative use in decisions affecting compensation, choices between individuals for promotion, and selection for participation in development activities. The general considerations of validity and reliability make the practical, legal, and ethical implications of performance appraisals very disturbing. The article suggests that the inaccuracy of performance appraisals will lead to increased complaints and court cases, causing organizations to change their use of appraisals.

Yager, E. "A Critique of Performance Appraisal Systems." *Personnel Journal,* 1981, *60* (2), 129-133.

Performance appraisal, performance review, and performance planning are distinctly different phases of the overall evaluation process. They require different skills and have different goals, and they should be practiced individually. The author defines these three aspects of the overall evaluation process and discusses their applications. Some of the most common pitfalls and deficiencies of performance appraisal and performance review are presented and discussed.

Zirkel, P. A. "Personality as a Fourth Criterion for Tenure." *National Forum: Phi Kappa Phi Journal*, 1985, *65*, 34–36.

In a hypothetical case, a public institution denies tenure to a faculty member who has persistent personality conflicts with colleagues. This case is the context for a discussion of related legal issues and the results of previous court litigation.

References

Abrami, P. C., and others. "Can Feedback from Student Ratings Help to Improve College Teaching?" *Proceedings from the Fifth International Conference on Improving University Teaching.* London, 1979.

Adams, W. "The State of Higher Education: Myths and Realities." *AAUP Bulletin,* 1974, *60,* 119-125.

"After the $119 Million Loss." *Business Week,* Sept. 19, 1983, pp. 54-64.

Aleamoni, L. M. "The Usefulness of Student Evaluations in Improving College Teaching." *Instructional Science,* 1978, *7,* 95-105.

Aleamoni, L. M. "Are There Differences in Perceived Teaching Effectiveness Between Males and Females in Anthropology?" Research Report no. 5. Tucson, Ariz.: Office of Instructional Research and Development, University of Arizona, 1979.

Aleamoni, L. M. "Student Ratings of Instruction." In J. Millman (ed.), *Handbook of Teacher Evaluation.* Newbury Park, Calif.: Sage, 1981.

Aleamoni, L. M. "The Dynamics of Faculty Evaluation." In P. Seldin, *Changing Practices in Faculty Evaluation: A Critical Assessment and Recommendations for Improvement.* San Francisco: Jossey-Bass, 1984.

Aleamoni, L. M., and Hexner, P. Z. "A Review of the Research on Student Evaluation and a Report on the Effect of Different Sets of Instructions on Student Course and Instructor Evaluation." *Instructional Science,* 1980, *9,* 67-84.

219

Aleamoni, L. M., and Yimer, M. "Graduating Senior Ratings Relationship to Colleague Ratings, Student Rating, Research Productivity and Academic Rank in Rating Instructional Effectiveness." Research Report no. 352. Urbana: Measurement and Research Division, Office of Instructional Resources, University of Illinois at Urbana-Champaign, 1974.

Alkin, M. C. "Evaluation Theory Development." *Evaluation Comment,* 1969, *2,* 2-7.

American Academy of Arts and Sciences. Assembly on University Goals and Governance. "A First Report." Cambridge, Mass.: American Academy of Arts and Sciences, 1971.

American Association of University Professors. *AAUP Policy Documents and Reports.* Washington, D.C.: American Association of University Professors, 1977.

American Association of University Professors. Committee on Academic Freedom and Academic Tenure. "General Report of the Committee." *AAUP Bulletin,* 1915, *1,* 41-42.

American Association of University Professors v. *Bloomfield College.* 129 N.J. Super. Ct. 259, 332 A.2d 846 (1974); aff'd. 136 N.J. 442, 346 A.2d 615 (1975).

American Council on Education. *Campus Trends, 1985.* Higher Education Panel Report no. 71. Washington, D.C.: American Council on Education, 1986.

Anderson, R. E. *Finance and Effectiveness: A Study of College Environments.* Princeton, N.J.: Educational Testing Service, 1983.

Andrews, J. B., and Daponte, K. J. "Are Professors Fireproof?" *AGB Reports,* 1981, *23* (2), 25-27.

Anikeeff, A. M. "Factors Affecting Student Evaluation of College Faculty Members." *Journal of Applied Psychology,* 1953, *37,* 458-460.

Astin, A. W. *Achieving Educational Excellence: A Critical Assessment of Priorities and Practices in Higher Education.* San Francisco: Jossey-Bass, 1985.

Astin, H. "Survey of Academic Personnel, 1973 and 1980." In H. R. Bowen and J. H. Schuster, *American Professors: A National Resource Imperiled.* New York: Oxford University Press, 1986.

Atelsek, F. J., and Gomberg, I. L. *Tenure Practices at Four-*

Year Colleges and Universities. Higher Education Panel Report no. 48. Washington, D.C.: American Council on Education, 1980.

Aubrecht, J. D. "Reliability, Validity and Generalizability of Student Ratings of Instruction." Idea Paper no. 6. Manhattan: Center for Faculty Evaluation and Development, Kansas State University, 1981.

Aubrecht, J. D. "Better Faculty Evaluation Systems." In P. Seldin, *Changing Practices in Faculty Evaluation: A Critical Assessment and Recommendations for Improvement.* San Francisco: Jossey-Bass, 1984.

Balch, P. *Faculty Evaluation in Higher Education: A Review of Court Cases and Implications for the 80's.* ERIC-RIE, October, 1980. (ED 187 285)

Baratz, M. S. "Academic Tenure and Its Alternatives." *National Forum: Phi Kappa Phi Journal,* 1980, *60* (2), 5-8.

Barszez v. *Board of Trustees.* 400 F. Supp. 675 (N.D. Ill. 1975).

Beal, P. E., and Noel, L. *What Works in Student Retention.* Iowa City, Iowa, and Boulder, Colo.: American College Testing Program and National Center for Higher Education Management Systems, 1980.

Bejar, I. I., and Doyle, K. O. "The Effect of Prior Expectations on the Structure of Student Ratings of Instruction." *Journal of Educational Measurement,* 1973, *13,* 151-154.

Bendig, A. W. "A Preliminary Study of the Effect of Academic Level, Sex, and Course Variables on Student Rating of Psychology Instructors." *Journal of Psychology,* 1952, *34,* 21-26.

Bennett, J. B., and Chater, S. S. "Evaluating the Performance of Tenured Faculty Members." *Educational Record,* 1984, *65* (2), 38-41.

Benton, S. E. *Rating College Teaching: Criterion Validity Studies of Student Evaluation-of-Instruction Instruments.* AAHE-ERIC Higher Education Research Report no. 1. Washington, D.C.: ERIC Clearinghouse on Higher Education, The George Washington University, 1982.

Bergman, J. "Peer Evaluation of University Faculty." *College Student Journal,* 1980, *14* (3), 1-21.

Berkshire, J., and Highland, R. "Forced-Choice Performance

Rating—A Methodological Study." *Personnel Psychology,* 1953, *6,* 355–378.

Blackburn, R. T., and Clark, M. J. "An Assessment of Faculty Performance. Some Correlates Between Administrator, Colleague, Student, and Self Ratings." *Sociology of Education,* 1975, *48,* 242–256.

Blair, A. H. "Student Evaluation: Using It Appropriately." Unpublished paper, Muskingum Area Technical College, 1983.

Blanchard, K., and Johnson, S. *The One Minute Manager.* New York: Berkley Books, 1982.

Bloom, B. S. (ed.). *Taxonomy of Educational Objectives: The Classification of Educational Goals. Handbook I: Cognitive Domain.* New York: Longmans, Green, 1956.

Board of Regents v. *Roth.* 908 U.S. 564 (1972).

Bok, D. *Beyond the Ivory Tower: Social Responsibilities of the Modern University.* Cambridge, Mass.: Harvard University Press, 1982.

Bouchard, R. A. *Personnel Practices for Small Colleges.* Washington, D.C.: National Association of College and University Business Officers, 1980.

Bourgeois, D. P. "A Study of Faculty Opinion Concerning Selected Factors Related to Excellence in Teaching at the University of Southwestern Louisiana, LA." Lafayette: University of Southwestern Louisiana, 1967.

Bowen, H. R. "Systems Theory, Excellence, and Values: Will They Mix?" Address to the annual meeting of the American Association for Higher Education, Chicago, 1976a.

Bowen, H. R. "Where Numbers Fail." In D. M. Vermilye (ed.), *Individualizing the Systems: Current Issues in Higher Education.* San Francisco: Jossey-Bass, 1976b.

Bowen, H. R. *The State of the Nation and the Agenda for Higher Education.* San Francisco: Jossey-Bass, 1982.

Bowen, H. R., and Schuster, J. H. *American Professors: A National Resource Imperiled.* New York: Oxford University Press, 1986.

Boyer, C. M., and Lewis, D. R. *And on the Seventh Day: Faculty Consulting and Supplemental Income.* ASHE-ERIC

Higher Education Report no. 3. Washington, D.C.: Association for the Study of Higher Education, 1985.

Boyer, E. L., and Hechinger, F. M. *Higher Learning in the Nation's Service.* Washington, D.C.: The Carnegie Foundation for the Advancement of Teaching, 1981.

Bragg, A. K. "The Socialization of Academic Department Heads: Past Patterns and Future Possibilities." Paper presented at annual meeting of the Association for the Study of Higher Education, Washington, D.C., Mar. 4, 1981.

Branton, W. A. "Legal Issues in Higher Education." *Business Officer,* Nov. 1984, pp. 19–21.

Braskamp, L. A., Brandenburg, D. C., and Ory, J. C. *Evaluating Teaching Effectiveness.* Newbury Park, Calif.: Sage, 1984.

Braskamp, L. A., Ory, J. C., and Pieper, D. M. "Student Written Comments: Dimensions of Instructional Quality." *Journal of Educational Psychology,* 1981, *73,* 65–70.

Bresler, J. B. "Teaching Effectiveness and Government Awards." *Science,* 1968, *160,* 164–167.

Browzin v. Catholic University of America. 527 F. 2d 844 (D.C. Cir. 1975).

Brubacher, J. S. *The Courts and Higher Education.* San Francisco: Jossey-Bass, 1971.

Burnett, C. W., and Matthews, W. L. "The Legalistic Culture in American Higher Education." *College and University,* Winter 1982, pp. 197–207.

Byse, C., and Joughin, L. *Tenure in American Higher Education: Plans, Practices, and Laws.* Ithaca, N.Y.: Cornell University Press, 1959.

Caplan, R. D., and others. *Job Demands and Worker Health.* Ann Arbor: Institute for Social Research, University of Michigan, 1980.

Carlson, P. G. "A Comprehensive Program for Evaluation of Teaching." *American Journal of Pharmaceutical Education,* 1975, *39,* 446–448.

Carnegie Council on Policy Studies in Higher Education. *Three Thousand Futures: The Next Twenty Years for Higher Education.* San Francisco: Jossey-Bass, 1980.

Carnegie Council on Policy Studies in Higher Education. *A Classification of Institutions of Higher Education.* (Rev. ed.) Berkeley, Calif.: Carnegie Council on Policy Studies in Higher Education, 1976. Quoted in V. A. Stadtman, *Academic Adaptations.* San Francisco: Jossey-Bass, 1980.

Centra, J. A. "The Effectiveness of Student Feedback in Modifying College Instruction." In J. A. Centra, *The Utility of Student Ratings for Instructional Improvement.* Princeton, N.J.: Educational Testing Service, 1972.

Centra, J. A. "The Student as Godfather? The Impact of Student Ratings on Academia." In A. L. Sockloff (ed.), *Proceedings of the First Invitational Conference on Faculty Effectiveness as Evaluated by Students.* Philadelphia: Measurement and Research Center, Temple University, 1973.

Centra, J. A. *Faculty Development Practices in U.S. Colleges and Universities.* Project Report 76-30. Princeton, N.J.: Educational Testing Service, 1976a.

Centra, J. A. "The Influence of Different Directions on Student Ratings of Instruction." *Journal of Educational Measurement,* 1976b, *13,* 277-282.

Centra, J. A. "How Universities Evaluate Faculty Performance: A Survey of Department Heads." Graduate Records Examination Board Research Report no. 75-5bR. Princeton, N.J.: Educational Testing Service, 1977.

Centra, J. A. *Determining Faculty Effectiveness: Assessing Teaching, Research, and Service for Personnel Decisions and Improvement.* San Francisco: Jossey-Bass, 1979.

Centra, J. A., and Creech, F. R. *The Relationship Between Student, Teacher, and Course Characteristics and Student Ratings of Teacher Effectiveness.* Project Report 76-1. Princeton, N.J.: Educational Testing Service, 1976.

Chait, R. P. "Nine Alternatives to Tenure Quotas." *AGB Reports,* Mar.-Apr. 1976, pp. 38-43.

Chait, R. P., and Ford, A. T. *Beyond Traditional Tenure: A Guide to Sound Policies and Practices.* San Francisco: Jossey-Bass, 1982.

Cheit, E. F. "The Management Systems Challenge: How to Be Academic Though Systematic." Address to annual meeting of the American Council on Education, Washington, D.C., 1973.

Chickering, A. W. "College Advising for the 70's." In J. Katz (ed.), *Services for Students.* New Directions for Higher Education, no. 3. San Francisco: Jossey-Bass, 1973.

Chruden, H. J., and Sherman, A. W. *Personnel Management.* Cincinnati: South-Western, 1976.

Chung v. *Park.* 377 F. Supp. 524 (M.D. Pa. 1974).

Clark v. *Whiting.* 607 F. 2d 634, 640 (4th Cir. 1979).

Cohen, M. D., and March, J. G. *Leadership and Ambiguity.* (2nd ed.) Boston: Harvard Business School Press, 1986.

Cohen, P. A. "Student Ratings of Instruction and Student Achievement: A Meta-Analysis of Multisection Validity Studies." *Review of Educational Research,* 1980a, *72,* 468-475.

Cohen, P. A. "Effectiveness of Student-Rating Feedback for Improving College Instruction." *Research in Higher Education,* 1980b, *13,* 321-341.

Cohen, P. A., and McKeachie, W. J. "The Role of Colleagues in the Evaluation of College Teaching." *Improving College and University Teaching,* 1980, *28* (4), 147-154.

Cole, J. R., and Cole, S. *Social Stratification in Science.* Chicago: University of Chicago Press, 1973.

Cole, S., and Cole, J. R. "Scientific Output and Recognition: A Study in the Operation of the Reward System in Science." *American Sociological Review,* 1967, *37* (3), 377-399.

College and University Personnel Association. "Tenure and Retrenchment Practices in Higher Education—A Technical Report." *Journal of the College and University Personnel Association,* 1980a, *31* (3-4), 18-226.

College and University Personnel Association. "Tenure Policies and Practices: A Summary." *Journal of the College and University Personnel Association,* 1980b, *31* (3-4), 18-31.

College and University Personnel Association. "Tenure at Doctorate-Granting Institutions." *Journal of the College and University Personnel Association,* 1980c, *31* (3-4), 32-57.

College and University Personnel Association. "Tenure at Comprehensive Universities and Colleges." *Journal of the College and University Personnel Association,* 1980d, *31* (3-4), 58-83.

College and University Personnel Association. "Tenure at Liberal Arts Colleges." *Journal of the College and University Personnel Association,* 1980e, *31* (3-4), 84-108.

College and University Personnel Association. "Tenure at Two-Year Colleges and Institutes." *Journal of the College and University Personnel Association*, 1980f, *31* (3-4), 109-135.

Commission on Academic Tenure in Higher Education. *Faculty Tenure.* San Francisco: Jossey-Bass, 1973.

Costin, L., and Associates. "Student Ratings of College Teaching: Reliability, Validity, and Usefulness." *Review of Educational Research*, 1971, *41*, 511-535.

Creswell, J. W. *Faculty Research Performance: Lessons from the Sciences and the Social Sciences.* ASHE-ERIC Higher Education Report no. 4. Washington, D.C.: Association for the Study of Higher Education, 1985.

Cross, K. P. *Adults as Learners: Increasing Participation and Facilitating Learning.* San Francisco: Jossey-Bass, 1981.

Davis, J. S., and Batchelor, S. A. *The Effective College and University Board: A Report for a National Survey of Trustees and Presidents.* Research Triangle Park, N.C.: Research and Evaluation, 1974.

Dawson, J. A., and Caulley, D. M. "The Group Interview as an Evaluation Technique in Higher Education." *Educational Evaluation and Policy Analysis*, 1981, *3*, 61-66.

DeVane, W. C. "The Role of the Dean of the College." In A. J. Dibden (ed.), *The Academic Deanship in American Colleges and Universities.* Carbondale: Southern Illinois University Press, 1968.

Dowell, D. A., and Neal, J. A. "A Selective Review of the Validity of Student Ratings of Teaching." *Journal of Higher Education*, 1982, *53* (1), 51-62.

Downie, N. W. "Student Evaluation of Faculty." *Journal of Higher Education*, 1952, *23*, 495-503.

Doyle, K. O., and Crichton, L. I. "Student, Peer, and Self-Evaluation of College Instruction." *Journal of Educational Psychology*, 1978, *70* (5), 815-826.

Dressel, P. L. "Faculty Development, Appraisal, and Reward." Unpublished paper, Michigan State University, n.d.

Dressel, P. L. "A Review of the Tenure Policies of Thirty-One Major Universities." *Educational Record*, 1963, *44*, 248-253.

Drucker, A. J., and Remmers, H. H. "Do Alumni and Students Differ in Their Attitudes Toward Instructors?" In H. H. Remmers (ed.), *Studies in Higher Education: Studies in College and University Staff Evaluation.* Lafayette, Ind: Division of Educational Reference, Purdue University, 1950.

DuCette, J., and Kenney, J. "Do Grading Standards Affect Student Evaluations of Teaching? Some New Evidence on an Old Question." *Journal of Educational Psychology,* 1982, *74,* 308-314.

Duerr, C. A. "Annotation: Reinstatement as a Remedy in Cases Involving Termination of Tenured Faculty." *Journal of College and University Law,* 1981, *7,* 57-67.

Eble, K. E. *The Aims of College Teaching.* San Francisco: Jossey-Bass, 1983.

Eble, K. E. "New Directions in Faculty Evaluation." In P. Seldin, *Changing Practices in Faculty Evaluation: A Critical Assessment and Recommendations for Improvement.* San Francisco: Jossey-Bass, 1984.

Eble, K. E., and McKeachie, W. J. *Improving Undergraduate Education Through Faculty Development: An Analysis of Effective Programs and Practices.* San Francisco: Jossey-Bass, 1985.

"Editorial." *NCHEMS Newsletter,* 1984, *87,* 8.

Elman, S. E., and Smock, S. M. *Professional Service and Faculty Rewards.* Washington, D.C.: National Association of State Universities and Land-Grant Colleges, 1985.

Enthovan, A. "Measures of the Outputs of Higher Education: Some Practical Suggestions for Their Development and Use." In G. B. Lawrence and Associates (eds.), *Outputs of Higher Education: Their Identification, Measurement, and Evaluation.* Boulder, Colo: Western Interstate Commission for Higher Education, 1970.

Equal Educational Opportunity Act of 1972. Pub. L. No. 92-96, 86 Stat. 103. (Codified at 42 U.S.C. sec. 2000(e) (1982).)

Everly, J. C., and Aleamoni, L. M. "The Rise and Fall of the Advisor . . . Students Attempt to Evaluate Their Instructors." *Journal of the National Association of Colleges and Teachers of Agriculture,* 1972, *16* (2), 43-45.

Ewell, P. T. "Assessment: Where Are We?" *Change,* 1987, *19,* 23-28.

Feasley, C. E. *Program Evaluation.* AAHE-ERIC Higher Education Research Report no. 2. Washington, D.C.: American Association for Higher Education, 1980.

Feldman, K. A. "Grades and College Students' Evaluations of Their Courses and Teachers." *Research in Higher Education,* 1976a, *4,* 69-111.

Feldman, K. A. "The Superior College Teacher from the Students' View." *Research in Higher Education,* 1976b, *5,* 243-288.

Feldman, K. A. "Course Characteristics and College Students' Ratings of Their Teachers: What We Know and What We Don't." *Research in Higher Education,* 1978, *9,* 199-242.

Feldman, K. A. "Class Size and College Students' Evaluations of Teachers and Courses." *Research in Higher Education,* 1984, *21* (1), 45-116.

Figuli, D. Unpublished lecture notes, n.d.

Finkelstein, M. J. *The American Academic Profession: A Synthesis of Social Scientific Inquiry Since World War II.* Columbus: Ohio State University Press, 1984.

Finkelstein, M. J. "Life on the 'Effectively Terminal' Tenure Track." *Academe,* 1986, *72* (1), 32-36.

Flygare, T. J. "Federal Courts Refuse to Promote Vernon Clark to Full Professor." *Phi Delta Kappan,* 1980, *61* (7), 486-487.

Flygare, T. J. *"Board of Trustees of Keene State College* v. *Sweeney:* Implications for the Future of Peer Review in Faculty Personnel Decisions." *Journal of College and University Law,* 1981, 7 (1), 100-110.

Flynn, E. A., and Associates. "The Part-Time Problem: Four Voices." *Academe,* 1986, *72* (1), 12-18.

Forbes, Sept. 15, 1968, pp. 51-52.

Fortunato, R. T., and Waddell, D. G. *Personnel Administration in Higher Education: Handbook of Faculty and Staff Personnel Practices.* San Francisco: Jossey-Bass, 1981.

Fowler, E., and McKenzie, G. P. "Instructor Evaluation Based on Student Perceptions of Achievement." *College Student Journal,* 1975, *9,* 217-223.

Franklin and Marshall College v. *Equal Employment Opportunity Commission.* 775 F. 2d 110 (1985) U.S. (1986).

French-Lazovik, G., and Gibson, C. L. "Effects of Verbally

Labeled Anchor Points on the Distributional Parameters of Rating Measures." *Applied Psychological Measurement,* 1984, *8* (1), 49-57.

Frey, P. W. "Student Ratings of Teaching: Validity of Several Rating Factors." *Science,* 1973, *182,* 83-85.

Fries, M. S. "Extended Probation at Research Universities." *Academe,* 1986, *72* (1), 37-40.

Fuller, J. W. (ed.). *Issues in Faculty Personnel Policies.* New Directions for Higher Education, no. 41. San Francisco: Jossey-Bass, 1983.

Fulton, O., and Trow, M. "Research Activity in American Higher Education." *Sociology of Education,* 1974, *47,* 29-73.

Gardner, D. E. "Five Evaluation Frameworks: Implications for Decision Making in Higher Education." *Journal of Higher Education,* 1977, *48,* 571-593.

Gardner, J. W. *Excellence: Can We Be Equal and Excellent Too?* New York: Harper & Row, 1961.

Garrett v. *Matthews.* 474 F. Supp. 594 (N.D. Ala. 1979), aff'd. 625 F. 2d 658 (5th Cir. 1980).

Geis, G. L. "The Context of Evaluation." In P. Seldin, *Changing Practices in Faculty Evaluation: A Critical Assessment and Recommendations for Improvement.* San Francisco: Jossey-Bass, 1984.

Gessner, P. K. "Evaluation of Instruction." *Science,* 1973, *180,* 566-569.

Getzels, J. W., and Guba, E. G. "Role Conflict and Effectiveness: An Empirical Study." *American Sociological Review,* 1954, *19,* 164-175.

Gilford, D. M. "Statistical Snapshot of Adult Continuing Education." *Journal of Higher Education,* 1975, *46,* 409-426.

Gilley, J. W., Fulmer, K. A., and Reithlingshoefer, S. J. *Searching for Academic Excellence.* New York: American Council on Education/Macmillan, 1986.

Gleason, M. "Getting a Perspective on Student Evaluation." *AAHE Bulletin,* 1986, *38* (6), 10-13.

Greenwood, G. E., and Ramagli, H. J. "Alternatives to Student Ratings of College Teaching." *Journal of Higher Education,* 1980, *51,* 672-684.

Gronlund, N. E. *Measurement and Evaluation in Teaching.* New York: Macmillan, 1981.

Guskin, A. E. "How Administrators Facilitate Quality Teaching." In A. E. Guskin (ed.), *The Administrator's Role in Effective Teaching.* New Directions for Teaching and Learning, no. 5. San Francisco: Jossey-Bass, 1981.

Gustad, J. W. *Policies and Practices in Faculty Evaluation.* Washington, D.C.: Committee on College Teaching, American Council on Education, 1961.

Gustad, J. W. "Evaluation of Teaching Performance: Issues and Possibilities." In C. B. T. Lee (ed.), *Improving College Teaching.* Washington, D.C.: American Council on Education, 1967.

Guthrie, E. R. *The Evaluation of Teaching: A Progress Report.* Seattle: University of Washington, 1954.

Halstead, J. S. "A Model for Research on Ratings of Courses and Instructors." *Proceedings of the 78th Annual Convention of the American Psychological Association,* 1970, *5,* 625-626.

Harper, C. L., and Davidson, C. "Faculty Public Service: Concepts and Issues." *Mobius* (by University of California Press), 1983, *1* (3), 5.

Hayes, R. H., and Abernathy, W. J. "Managing Our Way to Decline." *Harvard Business Review,* 1980, *58* (4), 67-77.

Hefferlin, J. B. *Dynamics of Academic Reform.* San Francisco: Jossey-Bass, 1969.

Heilman, J. D., and Armentrout, W. D. "The Rating of College Teachers on Ten Traits by Their Students." *Journal of Educational Psychology,* 1936, *27,* 197-216.

Heinzelman, K. "The English Lecturers at Austin: Our New M.I.A.'s." *Academe,* 1986, *72* (1), 25-31.

Heller, S. "Supreme Court Refuses to Review Ruling that College Must Disclose Tenure Papers." *Chronicle of Higher Education,* June 11, 1986, pp. 43-44.

Heron, A. "The Effects of Real-Life Motivation on Questionnaire Response." *Journal of Applied Psychology,* 1956, *40,* 65-68.

Highet, G. *The Art of Teaching.* New York: Knopf, 1950.

Hill, J. E. "On a Roll: Term Contracts at Curry College." *Educational Record,* 1985, *66,* 52-56.

Hobbs, W. C. (ed.). *Understanding Academic Law.* New Directions for Institutional Advancement, no. 16. San Francisco: Jossey-Bass, 1982.

Hodgkinson, H. L. "The Changing Face of Tomorrow's Student." *Change, 17* (3), May-June 1985.

Holmes, D. S. "Effects of Grades and Disconfirmed Grade Expectancies on Students' Evaluations of Their Instructor." *Journal of Educational Psychology,* 1972, *63,* 130–133.

In Re: Dinnan. 661 F. 2d 426 (5th Cir. 1981), cert. denied sub nom. *Dinnan* v. *Blaubergs,* 457 U.S. 1106 (1982).

Isaacson, R. L., McKeachie, W. J., and Milholland, J. E. "Correlation of Teacher Personality Variables and Student Ratings." *Journal of Educational Psychology,* 1963, *54* (2), 110–117.

Jacobson, R. L. "Low Pay and Declining Working Conditions Seen Threatening Colleges' Teacher Supply." *Chronicle of Higher Education,* Mar. 27, 1985, p. 21.

Jaschik, S. "Community Colleges Are Changing Their Roles to Meet Demands for New Types of Job Training." *Chronicle of Higher Education,* Apr. 2, 1986a, 13–16.

Jaschik, S. "Universities' High-Technology Pacts with Industry Are Marred By Politics, Poor Planning, and Hype." *Chronicle of Higher Education,* Mar. 12, 1986b, 15–17.

Jaschik, S. "University-Industry-Government Projects: Promising Too Much Too Soon?" *Chronicle of Higher Education,* Jan. 1, 1986c, *1,* 12–13.

Jauch, L. R., and Glueck, W. F. "Evaluation of University Professors' Research Performance." *Management Science,* 1975, *22* (1), 66–75.

Johnson v. *Board of Regents.* 377 F. Supp. 277, 240 (W.D. Wisc. 1974; aff'd. 510 F. 2d 975 (7th Cir. 1975)).

Jolson, M. A. "Criteria for Promotion and Tenure: A Faculty View." *Academy of Management Journal,* 1974, *17,* 149–154.

Joughin, L. (ed.). *Academic Freedom and Tenure.* Madison: University of Wisconsin Press, 1967.

Kanter, R. M. *The Change Masters.* New York: Simon & Schuster, 1983.

Kaplin, W. A. *The Law of Higher Education: A Comprehensive Guide to Legal Implications of Administrative Decision Making.* (2nd ed.) San Francisco: Jossey-Bass, 1985.

Kasten, K. L. "Tenure and Merit Pay as Rewards for Research, Teaching, and Service at a Research University." *Journal of Higher Education,* 1984, *55* (4), 500-514.

Keller, G. *Academic Strategy: The Management Revolution in American Higher Education.* Baltimore, Md.: Johns Hopkins University Press, 1983.

Kennedy, W. R. "The Relationship of Selected Student Characteristics to Components of Teacher/Course Evaluations Among Freshmen English Students at Kent State University." Paper presented at annual meeting of the American Education Research Association, Chicago, 1972.

Keyishian v. Board of Regents. 385 U.S. 589, 603, 17 L. Bd 2d 629, 760, 875. Ct. 675 (1967).

King, R. W., and Cleland, D. I. *Strategic Planning and Policy.* New York: Van Nostrand Reinhold, 1978.

Koeppler, H. "Frederick Barbarossa and the Schools of Bologna: Some Remarks on the 'Authentica Habita.' " *English Historical Review,* 1939, *54,* 606-607.

Kurland, J. E. "On Periodic Evaluation of Tenured Faculty: A Discussion at Wingspread." *Academe,* 1983, *69* (6), 1-14.

Lam, T. C. M., and Klockars, A. J. "Anchor Point Effects on the Equivalence of Questionnaire Items." *Journal of Educational Measurement,* 1982, *19* (4), 317-322.

Lee, B. A. "Federal Court Involvement in Academic Personnel Decisions: Impact on Peer Review." *Journal of Higher Education,* 1985, *56,* 38-54.

Lehman v. Board of Trustees of Whitman College. 89 Wash. 2d 874, 576 P. 2d 397 (1978).

Leslie, L. L., and Miller, H. F., Jr. *Higher Education and the Steady State.* ERIC/Higher Education Research Report no. 4. Washington, D.C.: American Association for Higher Education, 1974.

Lewis, E. C. "An Investigation of Student-Teacher Interaction as a Determiner of Effective Teaching." *Journal of Educational Research,* 1964, *57,* 360-363.

Lewis, L. S. *Scaling the Ivory Tower.* Baltimore, Md.: Johns Hopkins University Press, 1975.

Lewis, L. S. "Getting Tenure: Change and Continuity." *Academe,* 1980, *66* (4), 373-381.

Licata, C. M. *Post-Tenure Faculty Evaluation: Threat or Opportunity?* ASHE-ERIC Higher Education Report no. 1. Washington, D.C.: Association for the Study of Higher Education, 1986.

Lincoln, Y. S. "The Structure of Promotion and Tenure Decisions in Institutions of Higher Education: A Policy Analysis." *Review of Higher Education,* 1983, *6* (3), 217-231.

Linowitz, S. M. (chairperson). *Campus Tensions: Analysis and Recommendations.* Report of the Special Committee on Campus Tensions. Washington, D.C.: American Council on Education, 1970.

Linsky, A. S., and Straus, M. A. "Student Evaluations, Research Productivity, and Eminence of College Faculty." *Journal of Higher Education,* 1975, *46,* 89-102.

Lippmann, W. "The University and the Human Condition." In *Whose Goals for American Higher Education?* Washington, D.C.: American Council on Education, 1967.

Long, D. "The University as Commons: A View from Administration." In W. B. Martin (ed.), *Redefining Service, Research, and Teaching.* New Directions for Higher Education, no. 18. San Francisco: Jossey-Bass, 1977.

Lovain, T. B. "Grounds for Dismissing Tenured Postsecondary Faculty for Cause." *Journal of College and University Law,* 1983-84, *10* (3), 419-433.

Lowman, J. *Mastering the Techniques of Teaching.* San Francisco: Jossey-Bass, 1984.

Luecke, D. S. "An Alternative to Quotas: A Model for Controlling Tenure Proportions." *Journal of Higher Education,* 1974, *45* (4), 273-284.

Lumpert v. *University of Dubuque.* 255 N.W.2d 168 (Iowa Ct. App. 1977, aff'd 2-5768 unpub. opinion 4-14-77).

Lynn v. *Regents of the University of California.* 656 F.2d 1337 (9th Cir. 1981).

McCarthy, J., Ladimer, I., and Sirefman, J. P. *Managing Faculty Disputes: A Guide to Issues, Procedures, and Practices.* San Francisco: Jossey-Bass, 1984.

McDaniel, E. D., and Feldhusen, J. F. "Relationship Between Faculty Ratings and Indexes of Service and Scholarship." *Proceedings of the 78th Annual Convention of the American Psychological Association,* 1970, *5,* 619-620.

McDonell Douglas Corp. v. *Green.* 411 U.S. 792 (1973).

McGreal, T. L. *Successful Teacher Evaluation.* Alexandria, Va.: Association for Supervision and Curriculum Development, 1983.

McGuire, C. "A Proposed Model for the Evaluation of Teaching." In *The Evaluation of Teaching.* Pi Lambda Theta Report. Washington, D.C.: Pi Lambda Theta, 1967.

McKeachie, W. J. "Appraising Teaching Effectiveness." In W. J. McKeachie (ed.), *The Appraisal of Teaching in Large Universities.* Ann Arbor: University of Michigan Extension Service, 1959.

McKeachie, W. J. "Research on College Teaching." Memo to the Faculty. Ann Arbor, Mich.: Center for Research on Learning and Teaching, 1971.

McKeachie, W. J. *Teaching Tips: A Guidebook for the Beginning College Teacher.* (8th ed.) Lexington, Mass.: Heath, 1986.

McKeachie, W. J., and others. "Student Ratings of Teacher Effectiveness: Validity Studies." *American Educational Research Journal,* 1971, *8,* 435-445.

McKeachie, W. J., and others. "A Small Study Assessing Teacher Effectiveness: Does Learning Last?" *Contemporary Educational Psychology,* 1979, *3,* 352-357.

Main, J. "The Battle for Quality Begins." *Fortune,* Dec. 29, 1980, pp. 28-33.

Mannan, G., and Traicoff, E. M. "Evaluation of an Ideal University Teacher." *Improving College and University Teaching,* 1976, *24,* 98-101.

Marques, T. E., Lane, D. M., and Dorfman, P. W. "Toward the Development of a System for Instructional Evaluation: Is There Consensus Regarding What Constitutes Effective Teaching?" *Journal of Educational Psychology,* 1979, *71,* 840-849.

Marsh, H. W., and Overall, J. U. "The Relative Influence of Course Level, Course Type, and Instructor on Students' Evaluations of College Teaching." *American Education Research Journal,* 1981, *18* (1), 103-112.

Marsh, H. W., Overall, J. U., and Kesler, S. P. "Validity of Student Evaluations of Instructional Effectiveness: A Comparison of Faculty Self-Evaluations and Evaluations by Their Students." *Journal of Educational Psychology,* 1979, *71* (2), 149–160.

Marsh, H. W., and Associates. "The Validity of Students' Evaluations of Instructional Effectiveness: A Comparison of Faculty Self-Evaluations and Evaluations by Their Students." Paper presented at annual meeting of the Association of Institutional Research, San Diego, May 1978.

Maryland State Board for Higher Education. "Trends in the Characteristics of Faculty at Maryland Public Institutions of Higher Education." Postsecondary Education Research Reports. Annapolis: Maryland State Board for Higher Education, 1982.

Mayberry v. *Dees.* 663 F. 2d 502 (4th Cir. 1981).

Mehrotra, C. M. N. (ed.). *Teaching and Aging.* New Directions for Teaching and Learning, no. 19. San Francisco: Jossey-Bass, 1984.

Meier, R. A., and Feldhausen, J. F. "Another Look at Dr. Fox: Effect of Stated Purposes of Evaluation, Lecturer Expressiveness, and Density of Lecture Content." *Journal of Educational Psychology,* 1979, *71,* 339–345.

Menges, R. J. "The New Reporters: Students Rate Instruction." In C. R. Pace (ed.), *Evaluating Learning and Teaching.* New Directions in Higher Education, no. 4. San Francisco: Jossey-Bass, 1973.

Menges, R. J. "Evaluation in the Service of Faculty." In P. Seldin, *Changing Practices in Faculty Evaluation: A Critical Assessment and Recommendations for Improvement.* San Francisco: Jossey-Bass, 1984.

Menges, R. J. "Colleagues as Catalysts for Change in Teaching." Paper presented at annual meeting of the American Educational Research Association, San Francisco, Apr. 1986.

Menges, R. J., and Binko, K. T. "Effects of Student Evaluation Feedback: A Meta-Analysis of Higher Education Research." Paper presented at annual meeting of the American Educational Research Association, San Francisco, Apr. 1986.

Metzger, W. P. "Academic Tenure in America: A Historical Essay." In W. R. Keast (chairperson), *Faculty Tenure: A Report and Recommendations by the Commission on Academic Tenure in Higher Education.* San Francisco: Jossey-Bass, 1973.

Miller, R. I. "The Academic Dean." Washington, D.C.: Institute for College and University Administrators, 1971.

Miller, R. I. *Evaluating Faculty Performance.* San Francisco: Jossey-Bass, 1972.

Miller, R. I. *Developing Programs for Faculty Evaluation: A Sourcebook for Higher Education.* San Francisco: Jossey-Bass, 1974.

Miller, R. I. *The Assessment of College Performance: A Handbook of Techniques and Measures for Institutional Self-Evaluation.* San Francisco: Jossey-Bass, 1979.

Miller, R. I., and Barak, R. J. "Rating Undergraduate Program Review at the State Level." *Educational Record,* 1986, *67,* 42-46.

Millman, J. (ed.). *Handbook of Teacher Evaluation.* Newbury Park, Calif.: Sage, 1981.

Morris, V. C. *Deaning: Middle Management in Academe.* Urbana: University of Illinois Press, 1981.

Mortimer, K. P., and Associates. *Flexibility in Academic Staffing: Effective Policies and Practices.* ASHE-ERIC Higher Education Report no. 1. Washington, D.C.: Association for the Study of Higher Education, 1985.

Murphy, K. R., and others. "Effects of the Purpose of Rating on Accuracy in Observing Teacher Behavior and Evaluating Teaching Performance." *Journal of Educational Psychology,* 1984, *1,* 45-54.

Murray, H. G. "Use of Student Instructional Ratings in Administrative Personnel Decisions at the University of Western Ontario." *Resources in Education,* Apr. 1983. (ED 223 162)

Naftulin, D. H., Ware, J. E., and Donnelly, F. A. "The Doctor Fox Lecture: A Paradigm of Educational Seduction." *Journal of Medical Education,* 1973, *48,* 630-635.

Naisbitt, J. *Metatrends: Ten New Directions Transforming Our Lives.* New York: Warner Books, 1982.

National Association of College and University Attorneys. "Delivery of Legal Services to Higher Education Institutions: A Survey." Washington, D.C.: National Association of College and University Attorneys, 1984.

National Center for Higher Education Management Systems (NCHEMS). "Decline: Separating Facts from Fallacies." *NCHEMS Newsletter*, 1984, *87*, 8.

National Commission on Excellence in Education. *A Nation at Risk: The Imperative for Educational Reform.* Washington, D.C.: U.S. Government Printing Office, 1983.

National Commission on Higher Education Issues. *To Strengthen Quality in Higher Education.* Washington, D.C.: American Council on Education, 1982.

National Education Association. *Higher Education Faculty: Characteristics and Opinions.* Washington, D.C.: National Education Association, 1979.

Needham, D. "Improving Faculty Evaluation and Reward Systems." *Journal of Economic Education*, 1982, *13* (1), 6-18.

"New Breed of Strategic Planner." *Business Week*, Sept. 17, 1984, pp. 62-68.

New York University Law Review Study. "Dismissing Tenured Faculty: A Proposed Standard." *New York University Law Review*, 1979, *54* (4), 827-850.

Newell, S., and Price, J. H. "Promotion, Merit, and Tenure Decisions for College Health Education Faculty." *Health Education*, 1983, *14* (2), 12-15.

Newman, F. *Higher Education and the American Resurgence.* Princeton, N.J.: The Carnegie Foundation for the Advancement of Teaching, 1985.

Ognibene, P. J. "Is Civil Service Strangling the Government?" *Saturday Review*, Nov. 11, 1978.

O'Keefe, M. O. "What Ever Happened to the Crash of '80, '81, '82, '83, '84, '85?" *Change*, 1985, *17* (3), 37-41.

Olson, L. " 'Less Is More,' Coalition Rethinking the Basic sign of Schools." *Education Week*, Feb. 18, 1987, pp. 1+.

Olswang, S. G., and Fantel, J. "Tenure and Periodic Performance Review: Compatible Legal and Administrative Principles." *Journal of College and University Law*, 1980, *7* (1-2), 1-30.

Oran, D. *Oran's Dictionary of the Law.* St. Paul, Minn.: West, 1983.

Orpen, C. "Tenure and Academic Productivity: Another Look." *Improving College and University Teaching,* 1982, *30* (2), 60-62.

Ory, J. C., Brandenburg, L. A., and Pieper, D. M. "Selection of Course Evaluation Items by High and Low Rated Faculty of Varying Academic Rank." *Research in Higher Education,* 1980, *12* (3), 245-253.

Ory, J. C., and Braskamp, L. A. "Faculty Perceptions of the Quality and Usefulness of Three Types of Evaluative Information." *Research in Higher Education,* 1981, *15,* 271-282.

Ory, J. C., Braskamp, L. A., and Pieper, D. M. "The Congruency of Student Evaluative Information Collected by Three Methods." *Educational Psychology,* 1980, *72,* 181-185.

O'Toole, J. "Against Tenure." *National Forum: Phi Kappa Phi Journal,* 1980, *60* (2), 8-9.

Owens, T. R., and Hiscox, M. D. "Alternate Models for Adversary Evaluation: Variations on a Theme." Paper presented at the annual meeting of the American Educational Research Association, 1977.

Palmer, S. E. "Measure Outlawing Forced Retirement at Age 70 to Include Professors in 1994." *Chronicle of Higher Education,* Oct. 29, 1986, pp. 1, 17.

Partin, R. L. "A Case Study: Evaluating Faculty at Bowling Green State University." *Change,* 1984, *16* (3), 31-53.

Patton, C. V., and Marver, J. D. "Paid Consulting by American Academics." *Educational Record,* 1979, *60,* 175-184.

Peltason, J. W. Foreword. In A. Tucker, *Chairing the Academic Department.* Washington, D.C.: American Council on Education, 1981.

Perkins v. *Todd.* 436 F. Supp. 1101 (N.D. Ill. 1977).

Perry v. *Sindermann.* 408 U.S. 593 (1972).

Peters, T. J., and Austin, N. *A Passion for Excellence.* New York: Random House, 1985.

Peters, T. J., and Waterman, R. H., Jr. *In Search of Excellence: Lessons from America's Best-Run Companies.* New York: Harper & Row, 1982.

Peterson, D. "Legal and Ethical Issues of Teacher Evaluation: A Research Based Approach." *Educational Research Quarterly*, 1983, *7* (4), 6-16.

Pettigrew, H. W., and Howard, L. B. "The Probationary Professor and the Constitution: A Suggested Model Hearing Code for Contract Nonrenewal Cases." *California Western Law Review*, 1971, *8*, 1-74.

Plante, P. R. *The Art of Decision Making*. New York: American Council on Education/Macmillan, 1987.

Pollak, J. S. "The Erosion of Tenure in the California State University." *Academe*, 1986, *72* (1), 19-24.

Popham, J. *Education Evaluation*. Englewood Cliffs, N.J.: Prentice-Hall, 1975.

Poston, L. "Neither Bane nor Boon: External Reviewing in the Tenure and Promotion Process." *ADE Bulletin*, 1984, *77*, 44-46.

Ratner, L. A. "Creating Shared Values Through Dialogue: The Role of the Chief Academic Officer." In A. E. Guskin (ed.), *The Administrator's Role in Effective Teaching*. New Directions for Teaching and Learning, no. 5. San Francisco: Jossey-Bass, 1981.

Reskin, B. "Scientific Productivity and the Reward Structure of Science." *American Sociological Review*, 1977, *42*, 491-504.

Revised Report of the Ad Hoc University Committee on Appointments, Renewal and Tenure. Nashville: Vanderbilt University, Mar. 29, 1985.

Rhodes, D. M., and Riegle, R. P. "Conceptions of Teaching and Teaching Effectiveness in Higher Education." *Review of Higher Education*, 1981, *5* (1), 15-24.

Roach, J. H. L. "The Academic Department Chairperson: Functions and Responsibilities." *Educational Record*, 1976, *57*, 13-23.

Rodin, M., and Rodin, B. "Student Evaluations of Teachers." *Science*, 1972, *177*, 1164-1166.

Rotem, A., and Glasman, N. S. "On the Effectiveness of Students' Evaluative Feedback to University Instructors." *Review of Educational Research*, 1979, *49*, 497-511.

Ryans, D. G. "Teacher Behavior Can Be Evaluated." In *The*

Evaluation of Teaching. Pi Lambda Theta Report. Washington, D.C.: Pi Lambda Theta, 1967.

Saaty, T. L., and Ramanujam, V. "An Objective Approach to Faculty Promotion and Tenure by the Analytic Hierarchy Process." *Research in Higher Education,* 1983, *18,* 311-331.

Salzberg, H. F., and Schiller, B. "A Decade of Student Evaluations." *College Student Journal,* 1982, *16,* 84-88.

Saunders, M. K. "Legal Issues in Terminating Tenured Faculty Members Because of Financial Exigency." *Educational Record,* 1984, *65* (1), 12-17.

Schultz, C. B. "Some Limits to the Validity and Usefulness of Student Ratings of Teachers: An Argument for Caution." In *The Evaluation of Higher Educational Systems.* Newcastle-upon-Tyne, Eng.: Third International Conference on Improving University Teaching, 1977.

Scranton, W. (chairperson). *Report of the President's Commission on Campus Unrest.* Washington, D.C.: U.S. Government Printing Office, 1970.

Scriven, M. "Value vs. Merit." *Evaluation News,* 1978, *8,* 1.

Scriven, M. *Evaluation Thesaurus.* (3rd ed.) Reyes, Calif.: Edgepress, 1981.

Scully, M. G. "4,000 Faculty Members Laid Off in 5 Years in 4-Year Institutions, Survey Shows." *Chronicle of Higher Education,* Oct. 26, 1983, p. 16.

Scully, M. G. "Endowment Chief Assails State of the Humanities on College Campuses." *Chronicle of Higher Education,* Nov. 28, 1984, p. 1.

Seldin, P. *Changing Practices in Faculty Evaluation: A Critical Assessment and Recommendations for Improvement.* San Francisco: Jossey-Bass, 1984.

Sharon, A. "Eliminating Bias from Student Ratings of College Instructors." *Journal of Applied Psychology,* 1970, *54,* 278-281.

Sharon, A., and Bartlett, C. "Effect of Instructional Conditions in Producing Leniency in Two Types of Rating Scales." *Personnel Psychology,* 1969, *22,* 251-263.

Sloviter, D. K. "Faculty in Federal Court. Decreasing Receptivity?" *Academe,* 1982, *68* (5), 19-23.

Smock, H. R. "The Practice of Evaluation as a Purposeful Activity." Paper presented at the annual meeting of the American Educational Research Association, 1975.

Smock, H. R., and others. "A Plan for the Comprehensive Evaluation of College Teaching." *Journal of Higher Education,* 1973, *44,* 577-586.

Snow, C. P. *The Two Cultures and the Scientific Revolution.* New York: Cambridge University Press, 1959.

Solmon, L. G., Bisconti, A. S., and Ochsner, N. L. *College as a Training Ground for Jobs.* New York: Praeger, 1977.

Sommer, R. "Twenty Years of Teaching Evaluations: One Instructor's Experience." *Teaching of Psychology,* 1981, *8,* 223-226.

Southern Regional Education Board. *Faculty Evaluation for Improved Learning.* Atlanta, Ga.: Southern Regional Education Board, 1977.

Special Committee on Education and the Law of the Association of the Bar of the City of New York. "Due Process in Decisions Relating to Tenure in Higher Education." *Journal of College and University Law,* 1984, *11,* 323-344.

Spencer, R. E. *The Illinois Course Evaluation Questionnaire: Manual of Interpretation.* Research Report no. 270. Champaign: Office of Instructional Resources, University of Illinois, 1968. (Mimeographed.)

Stark, B. J., and Miller, T. R. "Selected Personnel Practices Relating to Research and Publication Among Management Faculty." *Academy of Management Journal,* 1976, *19,* 502-505.

Stasny v. *Board of Trustees of Central Washington University.* 32 Wash. App. 239, 647 P. 2d 496 (1982).

"Statement on Teaching Evaluation." *AAUP Bulletin,* 1975, *61,* 200-202.

Stevens, J. J., and Aleamoni, L. M. "The Use of Evaluative Feedback for Instructional Improvement: A Longitudinal Perspective." *Instructional Science,* 1985, *13,* 285-304.

Study Group on the Conditions of Excellence in American Higher Education. *Involvement in Learning: Realizing the Potential of American Higher Education.* Washington, D.C.: U.S. Government Printing Office, 1984.

Stufflebeam, D., and Associates. *Educational Evaluation and Decision Making.* Itasca, Ill.: Peacock, 1971.

Sweezy v. *New Hampshire.* 354 U.S. 234 (1957).

Taliaferro v. *Dykstra.* 434 F. Supp. 705 (1977).

Tennyson, R. D., Boutwell, R. C., and Frey, S. "Student Preferences for Faculty Teaching Styles." *Improving College and University Teaching,* 1978, *26,* 194–197.

Tetenbaum, T. J. "The Role of Student Needs and Teacher Orientations in Student Ratings." *American Educational Research Journal,* 1975, *12,* 417–429.

Thorne, G. L. "Student Ratings of Instructors: From Scores to Administrative Decisions." *Journal of Higher Education,* 1980, *51* (2), 207–214.

Timper v. *Board of Regents of the University of Wisconsin.* 512 F. Supp. 384 (W.D. Wisc. 1981).

Trustees of Keene State College v. *Sweeny.* 569 F. 2d 169 (1st Cir. 1977), vacated and remanded per curiam, 439 U.S. 24 (1978), aff'd 604 F. 2d 106 (1st Cir. 1979), cert. denied 444 U.S. 1045 (1980).

Truxal, J. G. "Learning to Think Like an Engineer." *Change,* 1986, *18* (2), 10–19.

Tucker, A. *Chairing the Academic Department.* Washington, D.C.: American Council on Education, 1981.

Tyler, R. W. *Basic Principles of Curriculum and Instruction.* Chicago: University of Chicago Press, 1950.

Tyler, R. W. "The Evaluation of Teaching." In R. M. Cooper (ed.), *The Two Ends of the Log.* Minneapolis: University of Minnesota Press, 1958.

Walden, T. "Higher Education: Attitudes Toward Tenure." *Phi Delta Kappan,* 1979, *62,* 216–217.

Walker, B. D. "An Investigation of Selected Variables Relative to the Manner in Which a Population of Junior College Students Evaluate Their Teacher." *Dissertation Abstracts,* 1969, *29* (9-B), 3474.

Waltzer, H. *The Job of Academic Chairman.* Occasional Paper. Washington, D.C.: American Council on Education, 1975.

Watkins, B. T. "Typical Chief Academic Officer: He's 50, Earns $61,000, Has Been on the Job 5 Years, and Wants to Be a

President." *Chronicle of Higher Education,* Nov. 27, 1985, p. 21.

Webb, W. B., and Nolan, C. Y. "Student, Supervisor, and Self-Ratings of Instructional Proficiency." *Journal of Educational Psychology,* 1955, *46,* 42-46.

Webster, D. S. "Does Research Productivity Enhance Teaching?" *Educational Record,* 1985, *66,* 60-62.

Weinbach, R. W., and Randolph, J. L. "Peer Review for Tenure and Promotion in Professional Schools." *Improving College and University Teaching,* 1984, *32* (2), 81-86.

Whitman, N., and Weiss, E. *Faculty Evaluation: The Use of Explicit Criteria for Promotion, Retention, and Tenure.* AAHE-ERIC Higher Education Research Report no. 2. Washington, D.C.: ERIC Clearinghouse on Higher Education, The George Washington University, 1982.

Wilhelms, F. T. *Evaluation as Feedback and Guide.* Washington, D.C.: Association for Supervision and Curriculum Development, 1967.

Wilson, L. *The Academic Man.* London: Oxford University Press, 1942.

Wilson, R. C., and Dienst, E. R. *Users Manual.* Teacher Description Questionnaires. Berkeley, Calif.: Center for Research and Development, 1971.

Wood, K., Linsky, A. S., and Straus, M. A. "Class Size and Student Evaluations of Faculty." *Journal of Higher Education,* 1974, *44,* 524-534.

Worzella v. *Board of Regents.* 77 S.D. 447, 449, 93 N.W.2d 411 (1958).

Wuhs, S. K., and Manatt, R. D. "The Pace of *Mandated* Teacher Evaluation Picks Up." *American School Board Journal,* 1983, *170* (5), 28.

Zahornik v. *Cornell.* 729 F. 2d 85, 96 (2d Cir. 1984).

Zirkel, P. A. "Personality as a Fourth Criterion for Tenure." *National Forum: Phi Kappa Phi Journal,* 1985, *65,* 34-36.

Zook, G. F., and Haggerty, M. E. *The Evaluation of Higher Institutions.* Vol. 1: *Principles of Accrediting Higher Institutions.* Chicago: University of Chicago Press, 1936.

Index

245

"The components of the faculty evaluation system," says Richard I. Miller, "constitute the foundation on which credible and effective promotion and tenure systems are built." In this book, Miller provides practical recommendations for implementing an effective faculty evaluation system—and explains why quality promotion and tenure decisions are not possible without one.

He discusses the weaknesses of today's promotion and tenure methods—such as casual approaches and inadequate attention to the decision-making process—and details eight characteristics of effective systems, including policies and procedures that are clearly articulated in writing, compatibility of the system with current institutional goals, and others.